Elections and War

*The Electoral Incentive in the Democratic
Politics of War and Peace*

Elections and War

The Electoral Incentive in the Democratic Politics of War and Peace

KURT TAYLOR GAUBATZ

STANFORD UNIVERSITY PRESS

STANFORD, CALIFORNIA

Stanford University Press
Stanford, California

© 1999 by the Board of Trustees of the Leland Stanford Junior University

Printed in the United States of America
CIP data appear at the end of the book

For Kathy

Acknowledgments

There are many to whom I have come to owe very much in the process of writing this book. My most substantial debts are to the academic advisors who helped guide the dissertation that formed the core of this book: Alexander George, Bruce Bueno de Mesquita, Stephen Krasner, and Richard Brody. It would be hard to imagine a more intellectually powerful set of advisors. Much of what is good in this dissertation is a reflection of the extraordinary scholarly insight of this group. This is true in the narrow sense of their useful guidance in the dissertation process and in seminars before that. It is even truer in the cumulative impact that their scholarly work has had on my own approach to the substantive and methodological dimensions of the study of international relations. In many ways, this project represents an attempt to come to terms with both the commonalities and the important differences in their approaches to international relations.

There are a number of other colleagues at Stanford who have also made important contributions either directly or indirectly to this work. Judy Goldstein, John Ferejohn, and Doug Rivers have been particularly important in this role.

Beyond Stanford, Michael Doyle, Geoff Garrett, Ole Holsti, John Owen, Bruce Russett, and John Zaller have made important contributions to my thinking on this project.

The man who sparked my interest in international relations in general, and in particular on the problems of war and democracy, is Robert Pickus. He remains a mentor and an inspiration for me, as well as a goad to careful thinking, clear argument, and deep respect for the normative elements in the study of international relations.

I would also like to acknowledge the financial support of Stanford University, the MacArthur Foundation, the United States Institute of Peace, and the Hoover Institution, where I had the opportunity to work on this project as the Susan Louise Dyer Peace Fellow during the 1996–97 school year.

For the data that serves as a centerpiece for this work, I am indebted to the collection efforts of the Correlates of War Project and to the ICPSR, which makes the data easily available. Of course, their provision of the data in no way represents an endorsement of the findings reported herein.

My children, Jayne and Andrew, are probably unaware of the importance of their contributions to this work. They have sustained and supported me in many ways. Most important, they have helped me keep perspective. While I have struggled to put together a few thoughts in this small scholarly corner, they have learned to walk, to talk, to laugh, to think, and to love.

Finally, there is Kathy. Her contributions are on every page and in almost every thought. She has been an editor, an advisor, and most of all an advocate for getting this book finished. But more important, she has been friendship, love, and purpose in my life. It is to her that this work is dedicated.

K.T.G.

Contents

List of Figures and Tables

TABLES

Elections and War

The Electoral Incentive in the Democratic Politics of War and Peace

Democratic Politics and International Relations

There are two things that will always be very difficult for a democratic nation: to start a war and to end it.

—Alexis de Tocqueville

When Alexis de Tocqueville made his historic journey to observe American democracy in the 1830s, there were five countries that could be called democratic. By 1976, there were 33 states that could make a reasonable claim to that status. Today, there are so many states that are on the path to democratic status that it is difficult to make anything but the most transitory inventory. As of 1996 the human rights organization Freedom House identified 117 states as formally democratic.[1] It is still too early, however, to be confident that this recent wave of democratization will not be reversed.[2] Many states seem to be standing with one foot in the authoritarian past and one in a democratic future, trying to decide in which direction to go. Nonetheless, this historical development has led many to ask whether the spread of democracy will bring a fundamental change in the nature of international relations. In particular, it has been asked whether the world will be a more peaceful place if this trend should prove durable.

This is a study of the relationship between democratic domestic politics and international relations. I look here both at the impact of democratic politics on international relations and at the impact of international relations on democratic politics. The window I use is the relationship between electoral politics and entry into wars. I chose this focus because elections are a defining characteristic of democratic politics and war is a defining characteristic of international relations. The intersection of these characteristic phenomena should place into clear focus the potential for democratic domestic institutions to have an impact on the international arena.

I argue in these pages that there is a relationship between electoral politics and the conflict behavior of democratic states. Contrary to the hopes of some liberals, democratic publics are not consistently pacific in their approach to international relations. Rather, there is significant variation in the public mood. As elections approach, the belligerent or conciliatory nature of democratic foreign policy increasingly reflects the mood of the mass public. But, even when democratic leaders pander to a belligerent public mood, they also have an incentive to avoid actually getting into a war as an election approaches. What is more, there are important interactions between the electoral politics of democratic states and the behavior of foreign states that reinforce this war avoidance. The observable result of these internal and external dynamics is a cyclical pattern of democratic war entries that follows the electoral calendar.

The proposition that democratic states are distinctive in their international relations is frequently invoked by democratic politicians. The political plaudits for democracy emerge primarily from the liberal tradition. It has been an abiding faith of liberal doctrine that democracies should behave differently in the international arena than do nondemocracies. More specifically, a number of advocates of the liberal paradigm have asserted that democracies should be more pacific than nondemocracies. In the purest version of the liberal faith—what I call here the *populist* view—war is inherently inimical to "the People" and remains a perverse luxury of despots and kings.

Despite the dominance of the liberal faith in Western political life, the possibility that the international behavior of democratic states might be connected to their domestic institutions is a surprisingly controversial proposition. A strong tenet of the "realist" school of international relations has been that the political arrangements of states in the domestic realm should be irrelevant to their basic behavior in the international realm.[3] It is the realist view that as autonomous actors in an anarchic state system all states face similar incentives and inevitable conflicts. Thus, the international behavior of individual states is best explained by considering their position in the distribution of power among states.[4]

Since the 1930s, realism has been the dominant analytical framework for the study of international relations in the academic world. Likely, the cause of this state of affairs is that history has not been kind to the liberal view of democratic pacifism. The empirical reality is that democracies have fought wars with a regularity that is statistically indiscernible from the behavior of nondemocracies.[5]

France has been involved in wars in 40 percent of the years that it has been a democracy, compared to 39 percent of its nondemocratic years. The United States has been involved in some level of international war in 29 of the 170 years between 1815 and 1985 (17 percent). Great Britain has been involved in war in 51 of the 153 years between the Great Reform Act of 1832 and 1985 (33 percent). This does not compare particularly favorably with Russian or Soviet involvement in international wars in 43 of the 170 years between 1815 and 1985 (25 percent).[6]

The likely frequency of war in a more democratic world is not fully addressed by these statistics. In fact, there has been a recent resurgence of interest in the liberal perspective. This renewed interest has been fueled by an empirical observation that poses a serious anomaly for the realist paradigm. In 1972, Dean Babst, writing in an obscure business journal, observed that there has never been a war between two democracies.[7] This fact has provided liberals with a measurable and striking difference in the external behavior of states that appears strongly connected to their internal system of organization. A literature has since emerged that explores this finding more rigorously.[8] Most of this literature has involved statistical work on the relative incidence of war. The tentative conclusion has been that democracies are distinctively pacific in their relations with each other, but that they are just as war-prone in their relations with nondemocratic states.[9]

Although a large literature is now growing around these findings, there is a surprising lack of effective work drawing connections between the internal political processes of democratic states and these outcomes at the international level. Likewise, the literature that focuses on the domestic level in order to assess more directly the process whereby democratic politics affect foreign policy and international relations has primarily addressed the general role of public opinion. There has been little systematic consideration of either the role of elections or the domestic politics of war.

Public Opinion, Elections, and War

Although many historians have attributed wars to domestic influences, most political analysts who have taken a broader look at the domestic/international nexus have stopped short of carrying their analyses all the way to the level of war.[10] Those who write about domestic sources of foreign-policy behavior tend to focus on everyday matters such as tariff policy, foreign aid, and military budgets. They often share the realist belief that war is a phenomenon of such seriousness that it is considerably less susceptible to the pull of domestic forces than other foreign-policy problems. Steven Brams and Marc Kilgour, for example, adopt this perspective in *Game Theory and National Security*.

> In most major confrontations or crises, nation-states can be considered as unitary actors for the purpose of modeling their *international* behavior.
>
> Of course, domestic political games among elites are ubiquitous. However, these almost always pale to insignificance when issues of war and peace come to the fore and a nation-state, its national security imperiled, must act. Its key leaders do act, and usually together, making the unitary-actor assumption a sensible theoretical simplification in matters involving national security.[11]

Likewise, a number of analysts have attempted to tackle the role of public opinion in the formation and conduct of foreign policy,[12] but few have addressed the specific phenomenon of democratic elections.[13] Rosenau, for example, makes no explicit mention of the electoral process in his book that outlines the channels through which public opinion can influence foreign policy.[14] Bernard Cohen, in his 1973 study of public opinion and foreign policy, devotes three pages to the possibility that there might be some electoral accountability in the foreign-policy process, but concludes that "democratic control of foreign policy . . . by means of electoral accountability functions weakly when it even functions at all."[15]

Another limitation of the literature on democratic domestic politics and international conflict is an almost exclusive focus on the United States during the past sixty years. This focus is primarily a result of the very real advantage of the more effective public-opinion polling done in the United States during this period than has been done elsewhere or in other periods. A few analysts have branched out to give some consideration to Britain, although they still have focused on the late twentieth century.[16] Yet there is no a priori reason to assume that either the United States or the past few decades are representative of democratic politics in general.

A broader view of the impact of democratic politics on foreign policy requires consideration of three kinds of theoretical elements that might make the international relations of democratic states distinctive. The first, in the cultural and ideological realm, is the distinctive set of beliefs and conceptual frameworks that order the preferences of actors in the democratic decision-making process. The second element is the decision-making process itself—that is, the institutions that aggregate these preferences into social choices. The third element is the interaction of democratic foreign policy-making with the behavior of other states. Fitting these three elements together requires a broader consideration of the place for domestic, and particularly democratic, politics in contemporary thinking about international relations.

The Theoretical Setting

The principal solution to the problem of finding understanding amidst the historical noise in world affairs is to examine international events through the lens of theory.[17] Theories are abstractions from reality that identify important variables and how they relate to each other. The challenge is to select the right degree of abstraction to explain a particular phenomenon and to identify the circumstances under which a given theory is appropriately applied.

Kenneth Waltz, looking at the international system and the state units that comprise it, has suggested that when the behaviors of states are consistent despite variance in the nature of those states, the appropriate degree of abstraction is at the level of the international system.[18] And indeed, there is a large body of international behavior that remains constant across wide variance in the types of states that make up the international system. It is for this reason that the realist model has been a powerful abstraction for understanding international relations.

In the realist view, the conditions of international anarchy lead to an inflexible system in which states' options are tightly constrained. At a minimum, states must have enough power to maintain their own political and territorial integrity. Beyond this minimum, states strive for the power to enforce their own interests. Because power is a relative rather than an absolute phenomenon, states can never be satisfied with the amount of power they possess. Even small sacrifices of power for other goals can be disastrous in the long run, as differential growth rates work their effects over time.[19] War, then, results from competition for power and from the inevitable conflicts of interest that arise in a world of relative gains.[20]

The realist vision has been a useful model for the study of the state system.[21] It has provided a powerful and parsimonious framework for understanding the systemic nature of international relations. Waltz acknowledges, however, that it is an error to "mistake a theory of international politics for a theory of foreign policy."[22] He warns that "A theory at one level of generality cannot answer questions about matters at a different level of generality."[23] Realism treats states as opaque units interacting in the international system. Understanding the influence of elections on the conflict behavior of democratic states requires a theoretical approach that will allow us to gather information about what is taking place within the domestic realm.

My examination of the effect of elections on international conflict behavior draws on a statist model of the behavior of states. The statist approach is one level of abstraction removed from the pure realist approach. Both are self-consciously state-centric.[24] In the statist approach, however, states have two faces. They interact both with other units in the international system and with their own societies. In this model, the state is seen as an entity with its own interests to advance against both the external pressures of other states and the internal pressures of its own society.[25] As envisioned by Stephen Krasner, for example, the state must defend the national interest against both the competing interests of foreign states, and the pull of particularistic interests within its own society. The ability of a state to protect these interests is a function of its power relative to the power of the external and internal forces of competing interests.[26]

Both the realist and the statist approaches can picture all states as functionally similar units; in this view, all states have similar interests in simultaneously maximizing both their domestic and international power. Much of the power of the realist model, however, comes from collapsing all of the goals that states might have into the single goal of maximizing *international* power.[27] There is a quantum change in complexity in the move from single-dimensional to two-dimensional maximization problems. Theories about the process of balancing the international and domestic realms will require a significantly more rigorous modeling of interests and institutions. Hans Morgenthau outlines the essence of the balancing problem for state leaders:

> Especially when foreign policy is conducted under conditions of democratic control and is inspired by the crusading zeal of a political religion, statesmen are always tempted to sacrifice the requirements of good foreign policy to the applause of the masses. On the other hand, the statesman who would defend the integrity of these requirements against even the slightest contamination

with popular passion would seal his own doom as a political leader and, with it, the doom of his foreign policy, for he would lose the popular support which put and keeps him in power.[28]

Krasner attempts to solve the dimensionality problem with an assumption that the international realm always takes precedence over all other realms. In *Defending the National Interest*, he argues that it is only the overwhelming advantage of hegemony that has allowed central decision makers in the United States to pursue goals that were suboptimal from an international standpoint: "By the end of the Second World War, American central decision makers commanded a set of power resources unprecedented in modern times. These resources allowed them to turn toward projecting America's vision of a properly ordered society into the international system. They were freed from specific strategic and economic concerns."[29]

The limitation of this approach is that even with a clear hierarchy of realms, states must make value trade-offs between the different realms. Even before World War II, American leaders could consider the possibility of trading off a small amount of international power for a large gain in domestic power. America's isolationist policies in the interwar years may have been just such a trade-off. In general, large reserves of international power may decrease its marginal utility and make trade-offs of international power for other goals more likely. But even when international power reserves are low, there may be trade-offs in which the domestic gains are seen as sufficient to warrant some degree of losses in the international realm.

Quincy Wright, in his monumental work, *A Study of War*, opens the chapter "Conditions of Government and War" with the assertion that, in the interest of retaining office, governments may pursue foreign policies they believe are certain to fail.[30] The concern for retaining power in the domestic realm always has the potential to override broader concerns about the national interest. Thucydides presents a particularly potent form of this phenomenon in his discussion of the relative preferences of the Athenian oligarchs who had to make decisions that simultaneously affected the independence of Athens and their own personal and political fortunes:

Their first wish was to have the oligarchy without giving up the empire; failing this to keep their ships and walls and be independent; while, if this also were denied them, sooner than be the first victims of the restored democracy, they were resolved to call in the enemy and make peace, give up their walls

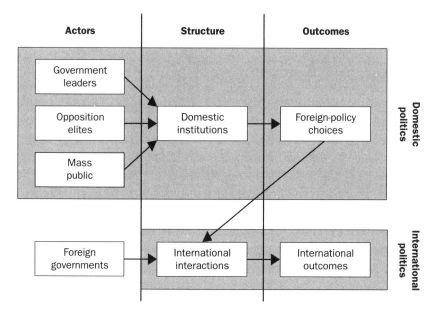

Figure 1. A two-level model of international politics

and ships, and at all costs retain possession of the government, if only their lives were assured to them.[31]

A central issue in this study will be to assess the degree to which state leaders balance these internal and external pressures. Is it adequate, as Brams and Kilgour and many others have asserted, to treat external pressures as overwhelming, and thus to assume that internal pressures are irrelevant? An examination of the intersection of wars and elections is useful for making this assessment because it presents clear examples of both internal and external pressures.

The analysis of election dynamics and war naturally suggests a two-level model that incorporates both domestic and international politics.[32] In Figure 1, I offer a schematic view of the theoretical structure that guides the present analysis. The upper shaded box represents domestic politics, and the lower one represents international politics. At both the domestic and international levels of the model, actors have interests and capabilities. The structure determines how capabilities interact such that interests are aggregated to produce political outcomes.

Domestic Politics

At the domestic level, I have posited three stylized actors: government leaders, opposition elites, and the mass public. This is the minimum number required to consider the role of elections as contests between elites for the vote of the mass public. In contrast, the traditional statist model is underspecified in that it posits a two-actor domestic model consisting of a state and a society. In Krasner's formulation, for example, "the state" is the central governmental institutions that make foreign policy, and society is everything else: Congress, interest groups, the electorate, etc.[33] The specification of three actors recognizes that democratic publics are not an undifferentiated mass of public pressures, but are a mix of pro- and antigovernment elites who have an interactive relationship with the democratic masses.

The interaction of these three actors is governed by domestic institutions that translate the mix of actor preferences into foreign-policy choices. There are many different domestic institutions that govern this process on a day-to-day basis. I focus in this study on electoral institutions as a characteristic element of democratic politics.

The appropriate starting point to systematically consider this two-level model is the review of three traditional perspectives on the nature of mass attitudes toward war in democratic states.

PERSPECTIVES ON MASS ATTITUDES

David Hume, writing of England in the seventeenth century, expressed a concern that popular pressures would lead toward two opposite failings in international relations: undue caution and imprudent vehemence.[34] Similarly, there are two contradictory poles in the common wisdom that can be applied to the effect of elections on war. At the first pole is a traditional Kantian view that "the People," who face the loss of family members in war, will always act as a restraint on the militaristic inclinations of national leaders.

At the other pole are those who worry that popular passions are easily exploited for violent international adventures. Those who espouse this view argue for the insulation of foreign policy from the excessive influence of democratic politics.

Between these two poles is a set of views that see popular preferences as highly changeable. Each of these three perspectives—the public as pacific, the public as belligerent, and the public as changeable—warrants fuller discussion.

The Pacific Public

The belief that the public will always be a restraint on war is well ingrained in the liberal tradition. Kant set out the central logic of this view:

> If, as is necessarily the case under the [republican] constitution, the consent of the citizens is required in order to decide whether there should be war or not, nothing is more natural than that those who would have to decide to undergo all the deprivations of war will very much hesitate to start such an evil game. For the deprivations are many, such as fighting oneself, paying for the cost of war out of one's own possessions, and repairing the devastation which it costs, and to top all the evils there remains a burden of debts which embitters the peace and can never be paid off on account of approaching new wars. By contrast, under a constitution where the subject is not a citizen and which therefore is not republican, it is the easiest thing in the world to start a war.[35]

This perspective was particularly popular following the slaughters of World War I. In the United States, it was embodied in the movement for a "war referendum" process that would require a popular vote for the declaration of war.[36] Alanson Houghton, the American ambassador to England and a staunch advocate of the referendum approach, argued that wars were caused not by peoples but by "little groups of men called governments."[37] One prominent proposal by a retired admiral even suggested that those who voted "yes" in a war referendum involving all women and men older than seventeen years of age should be obligated to enlist for the duration of the war and should be the first assigned to combat duty on the front lines![38] In 1938, Congress debated the Ludlow Amendment, which would have required a popular referendum to declare war. It was defeated only narrowly after intense lobbying from the White House. In Britain, this perspective emerged in the movement spearheaded by the Union of Democratic Control, which merely argued for an increased public role in foreign policy-making.[39]

The Passionate Public

Of course, liberals do not have a monopoly on theories about the relationship between public pressures and war. It has long been a popular endeavor to link war behavior and the legitimization needs of the state. There is no better way to knit together a fractious community than to find some external group that everyone can agree to hate together. Kissinger makes a general argument of this sort about the leaders of newly independent states facing the pressures of economic development and artificial borders.[40] A truly extreme form of this phenomenon is suggested by the recent disclosure that agents of the communist government in Cuba infiltrated Cuban expatriot groups in Florida and encouraged them to launch violent attacks on Cuba.[41] It is not implausible that democratic leaders face a similar temptation to loose the dogs of war when their authority most needs reinforcement. There is a persistent worry that the masses are too easily mollified by foreign adventures and democratic politicians are too quick to pander to these mob instincts.[42] George Kennan captures the gist of this view:

> People are not always more reasonable than governments; . . . public opinion, or what passes for public opinion, is not invariably a moderating force in the jungle of politics. . . . The truth is sometimes a poor competitor in the market place of ideas—complicated, unsatisfying, full of dilemmas, always vulnerable to misinterpretation and abuse. The counsels of impatience and hatred can always be supported by the crudest and cheapest symbols; for the counsels of moderation, the reasons are often intricate rather than emotional, and difficult to explain. And so the chauvinists of all times and places go their appointed way: plucking the easy fruits, reaping the little triumphs of the day at the expense of someone else tomorrow, deluging in noise and filth anyone who gets in their way, dancing their reckless dance on the prospects for human progress, drawing the shadow of a great doubt over the validity of democratic institutions.[43]

Vicarious military adventures are often surprisingly popular in the public imagination. American displays of force abroad are often followed by a surge in public support for the president.[44] Many scholars argue that this surge in popularity following international crises takes place regardless of whether the crisis is resolved successfully or not.[45] Gerald Ford enjoyed an eleven percentage point improvement in his approval rating in June 1975, after the 39 members of the *Mayaguez* crew were rescued at the cost of 38 Marines killed and 50 wounded. Jimmy Carter's approval rating went up four percentage points after the dramatic failure of the Iranian hostage rescue attempt in April 1980.[46]

The potential belligerence of public opinion, as demonstrated by these events, is well accepted in the conventional wisdom. At the same time, however, the basic trust in the pacifism of the masses is also a part of common thinking on this issue. This confusion may be resolved by turning to a third perspective that allows for significant variation in public attitudes.

The Protean Public

Proteus, the Roman god of the sea, was assumed, like the ocean, to be ever-changing in his appearance. A number of analysts have attributed to public sentiments a protean quality of change. For these writers, both the pacific and passionate views of democratic publics are accurate, but at different times. Louis Hartz is perhaps the best known of those who believe that a democratic public can swing between belligerence and isolationism.[47] He argues that the ideal of democracy that is manifested in American political beliefs is messianic in character. When American ideals encounter the inevitable limitations of the external world, the only two possible reactions are withdrawal or an evangelical attempt to convert the world. A similar outcome is predicted by the mood/interest approach of Klingberg and Holmes.[48] They advance a theory in which public moods oscillate around a fairly consistent national interest. Mood cycles result when belligerence becomes excessive relative to the needs of the national interest, and the public then moves toward withdrawal. After a while, isolation exceeds the optimal level for the national interest, and the resultant policy failures swing the pendulum back to belligerence.

Gabriel Almond also offers a mood theory for the role of public opinion in the formation and conduct of foreign policy.[49] But Almond rejects any regular cycling or periodicity to public moods. Instead, he suggests that the nature of public moods is shifting and superficial; therefore it is necessary to recognize that "an overtly interventionist and 'responsible' United States hides a covertly isolationist longing, that an overtly tolerant America is at the same time barely stifling intolerance reactions, that an idealistic America is muttering *sotto voce* cynicisms, that a surface optimism in America conceals a dread of the future."[50]

Several recent scholars have rejected the instability implied by Almond's view. Reviewing American public opinion on foreign-policy issues in the postwar era, Robert Shapiro and Benjamin Page, for example, argue that public opinion has been reasonably stable.[51] In their view, public attitudes are reasonably connected to international events. Changes in public views come about as reasonable responses to changes in the external environment.

The postwar era may be too short to see some of the more dramatic changes in public attitudes. Another perspective on changing public moods is represented in the recent work of John Mueller, who argues that World War I marks a fundamental shift in public attitudes. Mueller believes that before the First World War the public imagination was fascinated by war and largely approved of highly conflictual foreign policies. He argues that after the slaughters of that conflict the public mood changed unmistakably in favor of peace.[52]

I offer a protean view of the public in this book. I show that there is little basis for the naïve views of the public as inherently pacific or inherently bellicose. But where the protean view advanced by the authors mentioned is focused on the masses alone, my model emphasizes the interaction of mass and elite views. This approach accords with the dominant empirical and theoretical work on the nature of mass opinion. This work emphasizes the role of opinion leaders in the creation of coherent public views and the role of institutions in translating those views into political outcomes.

WAR AND DEMOCRATIC ELITES

To understand the nature of public opinion and its role in public policy, it is essential to consider the relationship between mass and elite opinion and the institutions that mediate that relationship. One of the most important research lines in this area is defined by the work of Philip Converse, who argues that most members of the public lack coherent political belief sets.[53] Most political arguments, in this view, take place within that sector of the public that pays sufficient attention to politics to hold coherent sets of beliefs and preferences. Understanding the role of public opinion in political processes requires a distinction between the amorphous and shifting preferences expressed by the mass public and the more cogent and sustained opinions of the small proportion of attentive citizens.

William Riker uses a different logic to arrive at a similar conclusion.[54] Drawing on the social-choice literature, he argues that notions of "direct democracy" are unworkable because it is impossible to sustain coherent majorities.[55] He advances a notion instead of liberal democracy that is based on popular control of officials through elections. In his view, democracy can function only retrospectively. The power of individual voters in a liberal democracy is their power to choose and reject political leaders. The essence of democracy in Riker's view is the competition of elites for popular approval in regular elections. The evaluation of public opinion, therefore, requires consideration of both elite and mass views and of the interaction of these views within the institutional framework of democratic elections.

ELITES AND MASS PUBLICS

Returning to the domestic-politics model that I presented in Figure 1, if each of the three kinds of actors (government, opposition, and public) can be either pro-war or antiwar, there will be eight permutations for the domestic environment.[56] These eight possible combinations are illustrated in Table 1. The four permutations in which the government and the opposition agree require little analysis. Permutation 8, the case of all three actors opposed to war, is probably the most common situation, but is not very interesting.[57] Permutations 2 and 7 both put all elites at odds with the public and thus seem far-fetched. It is unlikely that the public could come to a strong position on a high-profile public policy issue like war without some effective connection to elite opinion.[58] Permutation 1, with government, public, and opposition all pushing for war is both relatively uninteresting, and, as I argue at more length in Chapter 2, unlikely. Prior to shots being fired, there is no case of a democracy going into war with unanimous elite support.

One of the traditional concerns about democratic foreign policy has been that there will always be elites who see some profit in appeals to nationalistic or militaristic sentiments. I argue in this book that just as there have always been demagogues who, in Kennan's words, "danc[e] their reckless dance on the prospects of human progress,"[59] during the past two centuries there always have been politically legitimate antiwar elites. This brings us to the four middle permutations (shaded) in Table 1. These cases, in which there is disagreement between government leaders and some politically legitimate opposition, require further elucidation. One way to break these down for analysis would be to consider them symmetrical and focus on the public's tendency to support the government or the opposition. In this view, permutations 3 and 6 would be analyzed together as cases in which government leaders have public support for their stand against a minority opposition view. In permutations 4 and 5, the government would be pushing an unpopular policy against the resistance of

TABLE 1

Permutations of Domestic Attitudes Toward War

	Government leaders	Opposition elites	Mass public
1	For	For	For
2	For	For	Against
3	For	Against	For
4	For	Against	Against
5	Against	For	For
6	Against	For	Against
7	Against	Against	For
8	Against	Against	Against

both the public and the opposition. But such a symmetry is misleading in this area because of inherent differences in the nature of pro-war and antiwar policies. It is necessary to move beyond the analysis of institutions and look at the interaction of institutions and ideas. There is an asymmetry between the roles of antiwar and pro-war ideas in democratic electoral politics.[60]

The asymmetry between pro-war and antiwar views comes about because support for a policy of belligerence is not necessarily support for a policy of war. Support for belligerence, both among elites and the mass public, has usually emerged from a belief in deterrence. War, even for the most belligerent elites, has often represented a policy *failure* rather than a policy success.

On occasion, the general public has seemed enthusiastic about war per se. In most of these cases, this enthusiasm has run with a perception, or a *misperception*, that the anticipated conflict would be somewhat of a lark for the forces of democracy.[61] When elites accurately assess the potential costs of a conflict to be high, there is a high risk for an exploiter of pro-war enthusiasm that an opponent could correct the public's expectation of a quick and easy victory. In the longer run, those who might pander to public enthusiasm for a war that subsequently proves much costlier than the public anticipated may pay a very high domestic price. Certainly this was the experience of those who pushed for conflicts such as the Crimean War, the Boer War, World War I, and the Vietnam War.[62]

By definition, democracy allows a variety of views to be heard: political conflict is a constant in democratic states. I argue, however, that elections can create a particularly open political space for diverse views to be aired and, especially when they come from politically legitimate actors, to receive attention. Politicians search for new ideas and issues with which to distinguish themselves; election times offer politically legitimate actors the opportunity to express their views to an unusually attentive public. Tocqueville suggests the general effect: "Long before the appointed day arrives, the election becomes the greatest, and one might say the only, affair occupying men's minds. At this time factions redouble their ardor; then every forced passion that imagination can create in a happy and peaceful country spreads excitement in broad daylight."[63]

Going to war in an electoral environment that offers a forum for antiwar actors is particularly dangerous because of the high need for policy legitimacy and political unity for such an expensive undertaking. War makes great demands on a society, which must be motivated not only to back the conflict financially but also to sacrifice lives and livelihoods. Those who expect war to be a box-lunch picnic soon learn its costs as notification of the dead and wounded begin to trickle back into the community.

There is, furthermore, a multiplier effect for the costs of disunity, since the greater the disunity in a society, the more difficult it will be to marshal the resources that are required to successfully wage war. As the United States learned in Vietnam, there can be a spiral of illegitimacy. If a high degree of policy legitimacy is not achieved, the necessary societal resources will not be forthcoming and the war effort will be impeded.[64] If an impeded war effort degrades performance in the field, the legitimacy of the policy will be further undermined at home.

The need for policy legitimacy further highlights the asymmetry of war and nonwar as policies. Protest as they may, pro-war demagogues will find it difficult to overcome the requirement for social unity for going to war. Not going to war, on the other hand, is a policy that requires relatively little social backing for its implementation. In this regard, antiwar actors have an inherently easier job.

Even when war has been immensely popular in the democratic states, it has required effective justification. "Warmongering" has always been an epithet, and candidates who stray too far into belligerence face the danger of being painted with this damning brush. If politicians go too far in puffing up the justifications for war, there is a serious danger that politically legitimate anti-war voices will be able to shift public sympathies simply by pointing to objective realities.[65]

Politicians particularly cannot afford to be seen as calling for war in order to reap personal electoral benefits. It has long been argued that the most useful model for predicting the behavior of democratic politicians is to conceive of them as single-minded reelection maximizers.[66] There is, however, a limitation on this model that is rarely discussed: politicians cannot afford to be *seen* as single-minded reelection maximizers. This constraint produces an equilibrium wherein politicians seek reelection as vigorously as they think they can get away with. In general, it is apparent that they can get away with quite a bit. But when it comes to policies of war and peace, there is significantly less room to maneuver. Franklin Roosevelt, for example, was concerned that in September 1939, only days after the German attack on Poland and still a year before the 1940 election, polls showed a "strong feeling that the President is playing the European war as an end to be elected for a Third Term."[67] Government leaders who enter wars during an electoral season will always be highly vulnerable to accusations of being motivated by electoral concerns rather than by the national interest.

Thus, wars are very risky political events. Democratic politicians are aware of the potentially disastrous effect of a costly war on a political career or an entire political party.[68] Even a clear victory in a costly war cannot ensure a leader's political success. Winston Churchill and the fate of the Conservative Party in the 1945 election in Britain is the most prominent example. In the United States, the Democratic Party suffered significant setbacks immediately after both the World Wars. Expensive wars in which victory is ambiguous are, unsurprisingly, even more costly in political terms for the wartime leader or party.[69] The Democratic Party after the Korean War, Johnson in Vietnam, Aberdeen in the Crimea, and the Conservatives after the Boer War all bear witness to the cost of a miscalculation in this area.

In the electoral period, foreign-policy leaders have incentives to choose policies that are closer to the desires of the voters. While in some opinion environments this will lead them to pursue more belligerent foreign policies, the constant presence of antiwar elites and the universal opprobrium attached to warmongering will make them wary of foreign policies that they believe will actually lead to war. Although there does seem to be some potential for high political gain from the rally effect, there is also the potential for considerable political loss if things should go poorly or popular passions should shift. Politicians may be attracted to a belligerent policy line when the public is in a belligerent mood; but it is unlikely that many politicians have the stomach for the kinds of risks that would be involved in actually going to war to enhance their electoral prospects.[70]

None of this is to say that democratic political leaders will never choose policies that they expect to lead to war in the electoral period. Sometimes the diplomatic and political costs of avoiding war outweigh all of the political risks. Some political leaders are extraordinarily risk acceptant or are desperate enough about a deteriorating domestic situation to gamble with the "iron dice" of war.[71] But as elections draw near they become increasingly wary of such policy choices.

International Politics

The identification of the foreign-policy choices of democratic states is not sufficient for explaining outcomes at the international level. Making the connection between domestic electoral politics and international outcomes requires consideration of both the internal decision-making process of the state and the interaction of those decisions with the foreign-policy choices of other states.

The structure of the international system defines the conditions of interaction in international relations. This is not an institutional structure, such as the electoral institutions of domestic politics, but rather a set of organizing principles. The primary organizing principle of the international system is anarchy. International interactions take place within a self-help system in which each state is responsible for its own security and wealth. How a state's foreign-policy choices impinge on its wealth and security is a function of the international outcomes that result from the interaction of the foreign policies of all of the states in the anarchic international environment. The foreign-policy literature tends to gloss over the problems of strategic interaction. But without a consideration of the interaction of state policies at the international level, predictions of international outcomes are likely to be flawed.[72]

The failure to consider strategic interaction is characteristic of both critics and defenders of democratic foreign policies. In their view, there is often a simple connection between foreign policy and international outcomes. Belligerent states fight more wars and conciliatory states enjoy the fruits of peace. A view that does not incorporate strategic interaction is based on the belief that it is possible to infer foreign policies from international outcomes. States that get into fewer wars must be conciliatory, while states that get into more wars must be belligerent. These views are naïve: they ignore the basic scholarship on the causes of war that emphasizes that there is no automatic connection between a belligerent foreign policy and war as an international outcome.

There is no universal theory of war prevention, much less of war timing. Both logic and the empirical record tell us that states sometimes have used threats and the judicious application of military force to avoid war and sometimes have used well designed and carefully timed concessions.[73] One need barely scratch the surface of the international relations literature to find theories and examples that point to belligerence or appeasement as the proximate causes of war.

The traditional liberal view of international relations posits an underlying harmony of interests.[74] War, in this view, occurs primarily because of misunderstandings—the failure to recognize these interests. Belligerent policies contribute to these misunderstandings because they make it harder for other states to see the common interest. Conciliatory policies make these underlying interests more apparent and thus promote peace.

The world is at least sometimes a very dangerous place. Since international interactions can be characterized by genuine conflicts of interest and competition for relative advantage, it is necessary to accept that increased belligerence might well decrease the incidence of war. Likewise, excessive weakness and the inability to deter the aggressive tendencies of others might increase the number of wars. It is necessary to consider the interactions of policies on both sides of a conflict in order to determine whether democratic electoral incentives lead to more war or more peace. Otherwise, there is no direct connection from an international outcome of peace or war, back to a domestic pattern of conciliation or belligerence, nor from a distinctive pattern of foreign-policy behavior to war or peace.

An approach that combines international and domestic politics also allows for the possibility of direct connections between the two realms. In particular, the transparency of democratic electoral politics allows other states to observe the interests and incentives that are influencing foreign-policy choices. As I argue in Chapter 5, this has several important results for the impact of democratic foreign-policy choices in the international system. In particular, the electoral process gives democratic governments an effective commitment mechanism to strengthen their negotiating position and to signal their interests in their international relations.[75]

A Summary of Perspectives

The different viewpoints that I have presented so far can be summarized in five categories. First, in the realist view, international incentives should dominate domestic incentives. Democratic states should behave no differently than any other states, and thus electoral incentives should have no effect on international outcomes.

Those who believe that the attitudes of democratic publics and the institutions of democratic politics make a difference in international relations are divided into patricians and liberals. Patricians have a negative expectation of the effects of democracy on international outcomes. Hans Morgenthau captures the tone of the patrician when he attributes a decline in the moral character of international relations to the rise of nationalism and democracy:

> The moral standards of conduct with which the international aristocracy complied were of necessity of a supranational character. They applied not to all Prussians, Austrians, or Frenchmen, but to all men who by virtue of their birth and education were able to comprehend them and to act in accordance with them. It was in the concept and the rules of natural law that this cosmopolitan society found the source of its precepts of morality. . . . When in the course of the nineteenth century democratic selection and responsibility of government officials replaced government by the aristocracy, the structure of international society and, with it, of international morality underwent a fundamental change.[76]

Liberals, on the other hand, expect the impact of democracy on international relations to be positive.[77] They expect the increased role of public opinion in the foreign-policy process to lead to less war in the international system. The world should be a better place with more democratic states.

Both liberals and patricians can be subdivided into sophisticated and naïve categories. Naïve patricians and liberals both expect the effect of public opinion to be consistent and do not incorporate the effects of strategic interaction in international relations. The naïve liberal or populist views the public as basically pacific and is naïve about the role of strategic interaction. In this view, the increased influence of mass opinion in the electoral period should make democratic states more conciliatory. A conciliatory foreign policy is expected to translate directly into fewer wars.

The naïve patrician view is the obverse of the populist view. Naïve patricians expect democratic influences and the increased role of mass opinion in the electoral period to make states more belligerent. This belligerence translates directly into more aggressive foreign policies and into more wars.

Sophisticated views that incorporate the complexities of international interactions cannot reason directly from foreign-policy outcomes to international outcomes. Sometimes belligerence leads to more war and sometimes appeasement will have the same effect. The sophisticated patrician recognizes this complexity, but believes that democratic electoral politics tend to lead to deviations from the optimal policies that the international system requires. The direction of deviation is contingent on the public mood. For the sophisticated patrician, any domestically induced deviation from the demands of the international system makes the world a more dangerous and violent place. Whether electoral politics make foreign policy more or less belligerent is ambiguous; but unwise foreign policies increase the number of serious international conflicts.

The sophisticated liberal view shares with the patrician and populist views the expectation that democratic electoral politics affect foreign policy and international outcomes. It shares with the sophisticated patrician view a recognition that foreign-policy outcomes are contingent on the mood of the public. It sees the intensity of those swings as moderated, however, by the process of elite interaction. Demagogues on both the right and the left are tempted to pander to popular moods, but will be constrained in the degree of that behavior by the realization that there are countervailing elites who will take advan-

TABLE 2
Summary of Predictions for the Electoral Period

Viewpoint	Causal mechanism	Foreign-policy prediction	View of international environment	International-outcome prediction
Realism	System level incentives dominate domestic incentives	Determined by demands of the international system	Sophisticated	No effect
Naïve patrician	Popular jingoism	Belligerent	Naïve	Increase in wars
Sophisticated patrician	Domestic inducements to deviate from optimal policy	Contingent on mood	Sophisticated	Increase in wars
Naïve liberalism (populism)	Popular pacifism	Conciliatory	Naïve	Decrease in wars
Sophisticated liberalism	Temptations to pander, but limited by elite opposition	Contingent on mood	Sophisticated	Decrease in wars

tage of policy failures. Furthermore, at the international level, the transparency of democratic electoral politics affects the threats made by democratic states: it exposes electoral bluster and allows democratic states to make credible threats when there is broad public support. The interaction of domestic and international politics allows democratic states to deviate from an optimal policy without falling into serious wars.

The empirical focus of this study, especially in the quantitative analysis, is the period leading up to elections in democratic states. With this in mind, I outline each of these views and their predictions for the effect of electoral politics on international relations during the electoral period in Table 2.

The Research

The research approach I use to evaluate these perspectives draws both on individual case studies and on the use of statistical methods to look at a large number of events. The case studies are used in two ways. First, I use three nineteenth-century cases to demonstrate the persistence of antiwar elites even in historical episodes where there was intense public pressure to go to war. The Crimean War, the Spanish-American War, and the Boer War all exemplify the view of the public as a unified mass that is easily roused to support foreign wars. It follows that these are cases where a robust and politically legitimate opposition to war is least expected. These cases represent a hard test for my argument that democratic war choices have always been made in an environment that includes politically legitimate antiwar voices.[78] I then draw on three cases from the interwar period leading up to World War II to demonstrate the effects of strongly pacific public sentiments in an electoral environment. These first six cases demonstrate the changeability of public opinion.

Second, I use the case studies to illustrate the dynamics of electoral politics and international relations. I look at two of the most recent cases—Britain in the Falklands War and the United States in the Gulf War—to demonstrate the importance of transparency and strategic interaction. Across all of the cases, I show the importance of latent antiwar opinion, of the electoral opportunities for that opinion to be expressed, of the role of transparency for foreign actors, and of the ultimate importance of strategic interaction.

For the important task of demonstrating the results of these processes in both foreign policy and international outcomes, I turn to statistical tests that look at the entire set of disputes and wars in which democratic states have been engaged from 1816 until 1976. Case studies and the statistical analysis of aggregate experience thus work together to demonstrate both the process and the outcomes that I argue for in this book.

The Task at Hand

The organization of this study closely follows the model in Figure 1. In each of Chapters 2 through 6, I examine one of the squares in Figure 1. I begin in

Chapter 2 with an examination of the preferences of the democratic domestic actors: governments, publics, and opposition leaders. I use the Crimean, Boer, and Spanish-American Wars to show that the relative preferences of governments and publics do vary across cases. In particular, I show that the naïve hope that mass publics are a consistent brake on the military inclinations of the state is ill founded. I also argue, however, that there has always been a politically legitimate opposition voice that rejects the public or governmental arguments for war.

In Chapter 3, I turn to domestic institutions and examine the interaction of democratic actors within democratic electoral institutions. Focusing on the relationship between mass and elite, I discuss the particular impact elections can have on policy and the importance of electoral timing for those policy effects. I argue that elections open a political space that increases the influence of the antiwar views that are identified in Chapter 2. In Chapter 3, I look at three cases with antiwar publics and show how foreign-policy choices are moderated by the pull of domestic politics in the electoral environment.

In Chapter 4, I address empirically the foreign-policy choices of democratic states in electoral periods. I argue that contrary to both the naïve populist and patrician views, there is no *consistent* effect of electoral politics on the relative belligerence of democratic foreign policy. There is some clear evidence, however, for the more sophisticated views that changing public moods can be observed in the conjunction of elections and the international behavior of democratic states.

In Chapters 5 and 6, I turn to the level of international politics. I argue in Chapter 5 that democratic electoral politics can directly affect the policies of opponent states. This interaction effect, I suggest, is primarily manifested in an increased ability of democratic states to make credible commitments as elections approach. The domestic environment discussed in Chapters 2, 3, and 4 suggests a desire by democratic leaders to avoid entering wars as elections approach. The increased ability to make commitments at the international level explains how this foreign-policy choice might be translated into an international outcome.

In Chapter 6, I turn to international outcomes and to an empirical test of the relationship between elections and wars. Looking at the universe of democratic electoral and war experience in the past two centuries, I show that there is indeed a robust relationship between the timing of war entries and the timing of democratic elections. In particular, democratic states are less likely to get into serious wars as elections approach, and more likely to get into serious wars in the period just after an election.

Chapter 7 is the conclusion. I offer there a summary of the argument and point to some of the broader implications of this work. I conclude with a consideration of the implications of the relationship between domestic electoral politics and international conflict for our assessment of the quality of democratic foreign-policy formation. Making such assessments is, of course, a very old enterprise. It began as early as Thucydides, who, although often identified as a patriarch of the realist approach to international relations, was also clearly interested in the connection between domestic politics and international relations and in the contrast between democratic and nondemocratic decision making.[79] A central episode in Thucydides' history of the Peloponnesian War is the story of the Athenian decision to attack Sicily. This story follows closely the progression of the model in Figure 1. It retains its relevance to this day and will serve as a useful frame through which to view the effects of electoral incentives in the modern democratic politics of war and peace.

Attitudes Toward War in Democratic States

We should also remember that we are but now enjoying some respite from a great pestilence and from war, to the no small benefit of our estates and persons, and that it is right to employ these at home on our own behalf.

—*Nicias, trying to dissuade the Athenian Assembly from an expedition to attack Syracuse*

Be convinced then that we shall augment our power at home by this adventure abroad, and let us make the expedition, and so humble the pride of the Peloponnesians by sailing off to Sicily, and letting them see how little we care for the peace that we are now enjoying; and at the same time we shall either become masters, as we very easily may, of the whole of Hellas, . . . or in any case ruin the Syracusans, to the no small advantage of ourselves and our allies.

—*Alcibiades exhorting the Athenian Assembly to attack Syracuse*

In his history of the Peloponnesian War, Thucydides describes the Athenian debates about an expedition to conquer Sicily in 415 BCE. As he tells the story, the principal conflict was between the great Athenian general Nicias, who was widely viewed as responsible for the Spartan-Athenian peace treaty of 421 BCE, and the young general Alcibiades, who had opposed that treaty and taken over leadership of the expansionist faction.[1] Alcibiades was a classic demagogue.[2] He was the scion of a politically prominent Athenian family, and after the death of his father, Pericles himself became Alcibiades' guardian. In 420 BCE Alcibiades had been elected a general at very close to the minimum age of thirty. He was wealthy enough to have entered seven chariots at the Olympic games of 416 BCE—an unheard of feat for a private citizen—taking the first, second, and fourth places. His good looks were sufficiently notable to have garnered comment from Plato, Plutarch, and Xenophon. But most important, he was a brilliant orator who was able to inspire in the Athenian Assembly a considerable enthusiasm for foreign conquests.[3]

Almost two and a half millennia have passed since the Athenians debated the Sicilian expedition. Much has changed since then, but there remains a vigorous debate concerning the tendency of democratic publics to become enthusiastic about foreign military adventures.

In this chapter, I make two arguments about democratic attitudes toward war. First, I show that the ability of democratic publics to become enthusiastic about war has carried to the modern era. Contrary to the populist logic, democratic publics have not been consistently pacific in their perspective on war. Voices like that of Alcibiades have continued to find a receptive audience. Second, I argue that there also remain important and respected voices like that of Nicias that attempt to discourage such enthusiasm. Even when democratic publics were enthusiastic about war, the elite-level debate has consistently involved a politically legitimate antiwar voice.

My approach in this chapter is to look at three prominent cases in which there was considerable public pressure for war: Britain in the Crimean War and the Boer War, and the United States in the Spanish-American War. Even a cursory review of these cases shows that faith in the *inherent* pacifism of the masses is misguided. Kennan and Lippmann are clearly right that, as with the Athenians dreaming of the conquest of Sicily, democratic publics can be moved to passionate support for wars in faraway lands, even when there is little apparent threat to the national interest.[4] It follows, then, that each of these cases represents a critical failure for the Kantian belief that individuals in a liberal state will be reluctant to bear the costs of a war.[5]

The Crimean War, the Boer War, and the Spanish-American War show that there is little basis for the populist view of democratic mass publics as inherently more pacific than their governments. But as I argued in Chapter 1, it is necessary to consider both elite and mass views and the interaction of these views within the framework of democratic institutions when evaluating democratic publics. It is not my goal to argue that democratic elites are somehow inherently pacific even if mass publics are not. History quickly shows that to be as much or even more a folly than the proposition that democratic masses are unremittingly peace-loving. Indeed, the traditional concern about demagogues is that there will always be elites who could see some profit to be gained from an appeal to nationalistic or militaristic sentiments. My immediate goal is to argue that just as there have always been demagogues who pushed for war, in the past two centuries there have been politically legitimate antiwar elites.

To make the argument that democratic mass publics have not *always* been pacific in their international outlook, I need only to show that they have sometimes been strongly in favor of wars that seem to have little connection to the national interest. My current task is more ambitious. I have neither the space nor the resources necessary to offer a complete review of all relevant cases in order to demonstrate that there has always been a politically legitimate antiwar voice in the democracies. An alternative strategy is to examine a few cases in which the historical consensus has been that there was considerable democratic enthusiasm for war. These are the cases in which it should be least likely to find influential elite antiwar voices. It is in these cases that Lippmann's logic of silence is most likely to apply: "There are always correct people in democratic states, but they are forced to keep silent."[6] If there is a role for such voices in these extreme cases, then it would be a reasonable presumption that such voices have been operative in the other cases where, a priori, they are more expected.

The first step, then, is to show the existence of antiwar voices in a few of these "least likely" cases. My goal is to show that in such cases there has not been prewar unanimity among political, financial, and intellectual elites. Three important points about this task need to be clarified before I begin.

First, my interest is in politically legitimate elites, and not in the fringe groups whose dissenting voices were unlikely to play much of a role. Otherwise, I would need only to show that Quakers and Mennonites have been around since the beginning of the nineteenth century to establish the persistence of an antiwar voice over the past two centuries. It is unquestionably an important characteristic of democracy that these minorities have been more or less free to contribute their pacifist beliefs to the mix of public views on war. My task is to show that antiwar sentiments have been expressed by at least some important and politically legitimate elites.

The second point of clarification is to emphasize that I am not referring to antiwar views in the contemporary sense of pacifists and others who oppose *all* war in principle, but to the existence of strong opposition to a specific war under consideration. Usually, the most politically legitimate critique of involvement in foreign conflicts stems from alternative ideas about the utility of force in a specific situation rather than from principled opposition to all use of force.

For example, the conservative Republicans who formed the core of the original opposition to American involvement in Korea did not argue that the war
was immoral or imperialistic, but rather expressed disagreement about whether
vital American interests were truly threatened.[7]

Finally, it is important to note that I am referring only to the period before
the outbreak of war. Once force is engaged and young soldiers begin dying,
there is unquestionably a rally period in which criticism of the war is highly
muted. Kingsley Martin describes this phenomenon in his study of public
opinion and the Crimean War: "Under normal conditions there are many
public opinions competing and changing under constant readjustment. But
on one occasion there is only one public opinion. When war is declared the
minority opinion is so small that it may be neglected. The popular picture of
the world is set and vivid. There is an unanimous response."[8] Martin over-
states the case. Still, I argue that until war breaks out, there has consistently
been a vigorous and politically legitimate antiwar opposition.

The Public and the Crimean War

In the middle of the nineteenth century, the Russian Czar Nicholas I asserted
exclusive jurisdiction to protect Orthodox Christians in Ottoman territories.
Because the Orthodox Christians made up about a third of their population,
the Ottomans were less than enthusiastic about this infringement on their sovereignty.[9] When Russian forces occupied the Ottoman tributary territories of
Moldavia and Wallachia, the Ottomans responded with a declaration of war.
Eventually, Austria, Prussia, England, and France all lined up to aid the Turks
against the Russians.

To follow the domestic political dynamics of this case, I begin with the
challenges to the traditional party alignments in mid-nineteenth-century British politics. In the wake of the Corn Law debates, the Conservative Party was
divided between protectionists and free-traders. The Liberals were divided between traditional Whigs and the Radicals. In 1852, Lord Derby led a minority
protectionist conservative government that limped through to the end of the
parliamentary session and then was mercifully dissolved.

The elections of July 1852 did little to clarify the situation. It took until the
end of the year to work out a coalition government that would be led by the

free-trade conservatives under Lord Aberdeen, but that would include the Lib-eral Whigs led by Lord Russell and Lord Palmerston.[10] In late December a government was finally formed with Aberdeen as prime minister, Russell as foreign secretary, and Palmerston as home secretary. The complete cabinet was made up of seven Peelites (free-trade conservatives), five Whigs, and Palmer-ston, despite the fact that the Whigs and Radicals held 270 seats in the House of Commons, while the Peelites held but 30. The government, therefore, was a precarious one with internal divisions that were nearly as significant as the di-vision between the government and the opposition. It was not a government that was well positioned to deal with the most dangerous international crisis Britain would face between 1815 and 1914.[11]

In 1852, the French, after sending a warship to cruise off Constantinople, had entered into an agreement with Turkey that gave France the right to pro-tect Roman Catholic monks in Palestine. The Austrians likewise succeeded in gaining concessions after the Montenegro crisis in January 1853. This led to Czar Nicholas's demand for the right to protect not only Orthodox monks in Palestine, but also Orthodox Christians throughout the Turkish Empire. This request was of a different order of magnitude. The Russian demands threat-ened the very integrity of Turkey, and thus were perceived as a challenge to the balance of power in Europe.

On May 5, 1853, the Russians presented the Turks with a draft convention that amounted to an ultimatum that Turkey surrender to Russia a standing right to intervene anywhere in the Ottoman Empire. The sultan refused to ac-cept the broad implications of the convention, and as a result, in July 1853, the czar sent troops into the Turkish principalities of Moldavia and Wallachia, with the intention of occupying the principalities until the sultan accepted the expansion of Russian rights throughout the Ottoman Empire.[12]

The relationship between Britain and Russia was made difficult by both ideological and geopolitical concerns. Ideologically, the autocratic government of Russia seemed to embody the spirit of reaction and a willingness to inter-vene against liberalism wherever it might arise. At the same time, Russia was viewed as a rival for imperial control in Asia. The more aggressive British im-perialists believed that the Russian ambitions in Turkey were a prelude to de-signs on northern India.[13]

There was no scientific public-opinion polling in Victorian England. But in-dicators of British enthusiasm to enter the Crimean War are not hard to find. A large majority of British newspapers expressed strongly interventionist views.[14] The czar was regularly excoriated as the great oppressor of Europe, while the sultan—surely as traditional a despot as the czar—was depicted as the great defender of liberalism.[15] Religious leaders and lay enthusiasts were convinced that there was great religious meaning in a battle against the perfidious (though Christian) czar. War was anticipated as a fight of good against evil and as an opportunity for national redemption and moral rebuilding.[16] By mid-1853, public opinion had become vociferous on the Eastern Question. By early June, Conservative papers like the *Press* and the *Morning Herald* were calling for the impeachment of Aberdeen and Clarendon for their "pro-Russian" positions.[17]

The government was well aware of the disjunction between their actions and the desires of the public. In June 1853, the cabinet reluctantly decided to send a fleet to the Dardanelles as a message to the czar. Lord Clarendon, who had replaced Russell as foreign secretary, suggested the official view of public feeling on this issue in a letter to Prime Minister Aberdeen: "I recommend this as the least measure that will satisfy public opinion."[18]

Although the public was becoming quite worked up by the Eastern Question, these concerns were not being translated into parliamentary debate. In the parliamentary session that ran from February through August 1853, only 3 percent of the debate concerned foreign affairs (excluding discussion of reforms of the governing system for India).[19] The real discussion was taking place within the cabinet.

Aberdeen was strongly opposed to a more aggressive policy line toward Russia, but he was not in a position to make policy unilaterally. Although he planned to retire, there were other politicians who were thinking about public opinion and their own futures.[20] Chief among these were Lord Russell, who expected to take over as prime minister when Aberdeen stepped down, and Palmerston.[21]

Early in the crisis, Palmerston's expectation had been that the correct degree of threat would lead to a solution without escalation to the unpleasantness of war. Palmerston's view of Russian intentions in the Crimea echoes contemporary cold-war logic: "The policy and practice of the Russian government has always been to push forward its encroachments as fast and as far as the apathy or want of firmness of other Governments would allow it to go, but always to stop and retire when it was met with decided resistance, and then to wait for the next favourable opportunity to make another spring on its intended victim."[22]

Kingsley Martin suggests that Palmerston was a risk taker who would play on popular passions, but who understood the danger of going too far:

> Palmerston . . . knew that the public would at first be delighted if war broke out with Russia. Not that he wanted war. He had his own method of satisfying the public. He liked to steer "the ship of State in a high wind, on a rough sea, with every stitch of canvas on her that she could carry," and then, at the last moment, to avoid the final collision by a dexterous turn of the wheel which left his colleagues gasping and the country satisfied.[23]

Palmerston, who accused Aberdeen of pursuing a policy of "peace at any price," worked vigorously to move the government toward a more aggressive policy. He argued that the weak British position had misled the Russians into believing they could dictate terms to Britain and France.[24] Despite the fragility of the coalition government, Palmerston was unable to exert sufficient influence over the other cabinet members. Through at least August of 1853, the majority of the cabinet backed Aberdeen's more cautious line. The assessment of Kingsley Martin, writing in 1924, was that Aberdeen's cabinet was "as pacific as any that has ever held office in England."[25]

At the end of July, a compromise had been worked out in Vienna resulting in the Vienna Note, which spelled out a general Turkish willingness to recognize the czar's interests in Turkish Christians along the same lines as the earlier Treaties of Kainardji and Adrianople. The Note also specified that the Orthodox Church should receive the same treatment as other Christians in Turkey. The Russians accepted the Vienna Note as settlement of the dispute. Thus, when the 1853 parliamentary session closed on August 20, 1853, it looked as if the situation in the Near East was under control, despite the continuing virulence of English public opinion. The 1853 parliamentary session was considered a triumph for the Aberdeen coalition, especially in contrast to the ineffectiveness of the previous minority government. Lord Aberdeen's prestige was at its highest level.[26] But, on that same day, the sultan summarily rejected the Note.

The turning point for the government came in late September 1853, when the foreign secretary, Lord Clarendon, switched from his support of Aberdeen to the side of the hawks, Palmerston, Russell, and Lansdowne. The immediate occasion for Clarendon's switch was the leak of an internal Russian interpretation of the Vienna Note that seemed to allow Russia a greater right of military intervention and which would have justified the Turkish rejection of the Note.[27] Several commentators have also attributed his switch to the increasing heat of public outcry over the situation in Turkey.[28]

The newspapers had continued to push for a stronger British stance toward Russia, despite the Vienna Note. The pressure became more intense after the release of the Russian interpretation of the Note. The *Daily News* asked whether Aberdeen was a "willing dupe" or "merely stupid."[29] Even the Peelite *Morning Chronicle* abandoned the government position, and Aberdeen had to write a letter asking why the party's newspaper should be launching personal attacks on its own prime minister.[30]

The important exception to this popular enthusiasm was the *Times*, the dominant newspaper in Victorian English politics. Before the real heat of public opinion on the Eastern Question began to be strongly felt, Clarendon, the foreign minister, characterized the role of the *Times*, observing that "it is a well-known fact that *The Times* forms or guides or reflects—no matter which—the public opinion of England."[31] But even John Thaddeus Delane, the editor of the *Times* and a personal friend of Aberdeen, had trouble keeping his paper in line.[32] In September 1853, he threatened to fire his correspondent in Constantinople for being overly sympathetic to the Turkish point of view. He wrote his Constantinople stringer:

> You seem to imagine that England can desire nothing better than to sacrifice all its greatest interests and its most cherished objects to support barbarism against civilization, the Moslem against the Christian, slavery against liberty, to exchange peace for war—all to oblige the Turk. . . . I trust, therefore, that in the future you will have the modesty to forbear from offhand censures of English policy, to devote your whole attention to collecting and truly describing the facts, and, if you must give opinions, to take care that they are not Turkish but English.[33]

Like the government itself, the *Times* suffered considerable invective for its lack of enthusiasm for the sultan. Karl Marx said of England's leading paper: "The *Times* . . . is printed in the English Language. But that is the only thing English about it. It is, where Russia is concerned, Russian all over."[34] The most virulent attacks came from David Urquhart in the *Morning Advertiser*. Urquhart once described the *Times*'s work on the Eastern Question in these inelegant, though biblical, terms: "The Russian organ of Printing House Square yesterday returned to its vomit."[35] Nonetheless, the *Times* maintained its anti-war position until mid-December.[36]

The traditional liberal argument holds that more democracy is needed to put a brake on the militaristic tendencies of government leaders. In the year leading up to British involvement in the Crimean War, however, this argument was turned on its head. Advocates of British entry into the Crimean conflict argued that more democracy was needed to override the timid and isolationist tendencies of government leaders and to allow the interventionist impulses of the populace to be more directly translated into British foreign policy.[37] In the autumn and winter of 1853, mass meetings denouncing the czar and calling for intervention were held all over the country. Kingsley Martin describes one popular meeting in the fall of 1853: "At this meeting the Government was charged with refusing information, with continuing negotiations, and attempting to deceive English people into the idea that peace was possible. In fact, declared the principal speaker amid great enthusiasm, the people of England had too little share in the management of foreign affairs."[38]

The Turkish crisis escalated on October 4, 1853, when the Turks declared war on Russia. Clarendon, while now favoring a more belligerent line toward Russia, was still far from the public enthusiasm for conflict. He expressed his frustration both with the Turks and public opinion:

> The public seems to think that there is nothing to do but to declare war against Russia, just when she is yielding the point in dispute, and back the Turk, just when he acts contrary to our advice; and thus, without any guarantee on our part obliging us so to act, and without any English or European interest at stake, if the question of the Note be adjusted, as I think it would be, or rather would have been if the Turks could have been kept quiet. I believe they expect to take Petersburg before Christmas![39]

Domestic politics was clearly driving British policies. Aberdeen still favored a more conciliatory line toward Russia, but was clearly concerned about the fragility of his coalition.[40] Clarendon, who by this time was counted as one of the war hawks, as much as admitted that the cabinet's actions were now driven by the need to satisfy public opinion. In a private letter summarizing government actions he wrote: "With reference to public feeling in England, we could not well do less. . . . I see little chance of averting war, which, even in a sacred cause, is a horrible calamity; but for such a cause as two sets of Barbarians quarrelling over a form of words, it is not only shocking but incredible."[41]

In November, the Turks sent a small squadron of warships to the harbor at Sinope on the Turkish coast of the Black Sea. On November 30, the Russians responded with an attack that destroyed the entire Turkish squadron with a great loss of life. News of the attack at Sinope—which at the hands of the press became "the massacre of Sinope"—further inflamed British public opinion. All of the papers, including the *Times*, now joined in criticizing the government's policy as too weak toward Russia.

Popular dissatisfaction with the government's conciliatory policies extended to touch the royal family. Despite the editorial ranting of the *Morning Herald*, which argued against more negotiations with Russia with a warning that "for any Englishman to betray the cause of Turkey is to betray the Queen,"[42] the queen and especially the prince consort were outspoken opponents of excessive support for Turkey. Prince Albert's position led to a crisis for British royalty when several papers accused him of being a foreign influence over British policy.[43] The *Morning Advertiser* took the most extreme line, summing up its view of the prince's influence this way: "There is a power sitting at the Privy Council board of England, not less fatal in its action because unseen. That power is believed to be the interpreter of Russian wishes and the abettor of Russian purposes."[44]

The government agreed to send the British Fleet, along with the French, into the Black Sea and to insist that the Russians keep their fleet in harbor at Sebastapol, in order to prevent a repeat of the Sinope attack. Aberdeen, however, continued to resist the pressures for war. In February 1854, Aberdeen delivered an important speech insisting that peace was a critical goal in the Near East, and that his policies had not been too pacific. Speaking to the war enthusiasm in England, he argued that it is "the duty of the Government as much as possible to resist such feelings, however natural and generous they may be—to direct them in the course of prudence and policy."[45] He referred to Alcibiades and ancient Athens in expressing a desire not to be swayed by public opinion: "In a case of this kind, I dread popular support. . . . On some occasion, when the Athenian Assembly vehemently applauded Alcibiades, the latter asked if he had said anything particularly foolish!"[46]

By March 1854, the majority of the cabinet had come to accept the inevitability of war, and issued an official declaration. The government's declaration was still reluctant.[47] No such reluctance was apparent in the popular press. The newspapers were widely, and appropriately, blamed for much of the war enthusiasm preceding entry into the Crimean War. By March of 1854, when war was declared, the newspapers were unanimous in their call for war or their acceptance that war was inevitable. The Opposition Conservatives were also strongly in favor of war. Disraeli, speaking in Parliament in late February, accused the government of being too soft on the Russians.[48] When war was declared, Lord Derby, the leader of the Conservative opposition, also supported the war and blamed the government for misleading the Russians into thinking England would not respond with force.[49] Again, however, the strongest criticisms came from within the governing party, rather than from the opposition. Most of these criticisms excoriated the government for its failure to send military aid to the Turks sooner.

A few Radical Liberals continued to decry the drift to war. The most prominent of these were Earl Grey in the House of Lords, and Richard Cobden and John Bright in the House of Commons. Cobden, speaking respectively of Russia, Austria, and Turkey, criticized the Crimean War as "a war in which we have a despot for an enemy, a despot for an ally, and a despot for a client."[50] Bright described the Ottoman Empire as "one of the most immoral and filthy despotisms over one of the fairest portions of the earth."[51] Both Cobden and Bright lost considerable support with their unpopular positions. Bright, who had received a majority of votes in every ward except one of his Manchester district in 1852, was burned in effigy by angry Manchester crowds after the war had started.[52] Although their views were unpopular, they continued to garner respect in Parliament and remained legitimate actors on the political stage.[53]

At its outbreak, the Crimean War was unambiguously and immensely popular. However, the difficulties encountered in carrying out the war soon led to a reversal of popular support. Charles Greville, the chief clerk of the Privy Council, had recognized this danger. On the day war was declared, he mused in his diary that the public was ignorant of Russia's power and that before long they "will be as heartily sick of it [the war] as they are now hot upon it."[54]

The danger of shifting opinion after the war started was reflected in the *Times*, which ran a devastating exposé of military corruption and incompetence. Just as the newspapers had played a critical role in fostering public enthusiasm for the war, they also played a critical role in decreasing support for the war and in turning out the Aberdeen government. Although the more militant Palmerston was the immediate beneficiary of this turn of events, in the longer run the Crimean War and the policies that led to it were discredited.[55] It is sobering to contrast the difficulty the United States has had coming to grips with justifications for the Vietnam War and the readiness of British elites to reject the motivations that led to the Crimean War. Within five years after the end of the war, the *Times* was ready to offer this assessment of the struggle in which 22,000 British soldiers were killed:

> We must frankly own that we feel somewhat more free to act like men and Christians than we could five years ago. That ill-starred war, those half-million of British, French, and Russian men left in the Crimea, those two hundred millions of money wasted in the worst of all ways, have discharged to the last iota all the debt of Christian Europe to Turkey. Never was so great an effort made for so worthless an object. It is with no small reluctance that we admit a gigantic effort and an infinite sacrifice to have been made in vain.[56]

In hindsight, it is difficult to see any threat to British national interest in the situation that developed in the Crimea. The historical consensus has largely agreed with the *Times* that the Crimean War was useless and unnecessary.[57] The British could certainly have achieved as much with negotiation, and in the long run the war failed to decrease Russian power.[58] At the time, Disraeli stretched considerably the traditional just-war criteria to label the Crimean conflict "a just but unnecessary war."[59]

The Crimean War is an extreme case of public sentiment in favor of war. By the time the war broke out, there was no organized party or political group that opposed it. Even the Peace Society had taken up the call for war.[60] The historical record suggests that the relative preferences of the masses and the government were the reverse of that predicted by the populist model. Public opinion clearly did not play a role in slowing down or discouraging war. Rather, the government was consistently more pacific than the populace.[61]

Although the fragility of the coalition government was a constant concern of Aberdeen and led to certain policy outcomes, electoral dynamics were not an immediate concern in the Crimean case. Britain declared war on March 27, 1854, in the middle of an electoral cycle that lasted from August 3, 1852, until April 20, 1857. Had an electoral contest been imminent, the Aberdeen government might have felt even more constrained by public opinion and might have been sorely tempted to enter the Crimean fray even earlier than it did.

Despite the extremity of this case on the public side, it is also clear that there were legitimate political actors who were opposed to a belligerent foreign-policy line and who were desperate to keep the country out of war. While the popular majority favored a belligerent line, and even military intervention, a politically legitimate minority viewpoint was present within the collection of elite approaches to the imbroglio in the Near East.

The Public and the Spanish-American War

The vulnerability of democratic publics to pro-war passions is also demonstrated by the American experience in the Spanish-American War. Toward the end of the nineteenth century, the Spanish efforts to maintain control of their Cuban colony were becoming violent in the face of a mounting internal resistance movement. The American public was distressed by the reported abuses of the Spanish imperial forces. As in the Crimean case, public emotions were exacerbated by virulent journalism that offered a steady flow of atrocity stories. Although Spanish rule in Cuba became increasingly violent and inhumane, a number of American newspapers competed to publish wildly inflated accounts of Spanish brutality. Even a cursory survey of the extreme newspaper accounts of Spanish rape, pillage, and murder—many of which emanated directly from the offices of the Cuban liberation forces in Key West, Florida—makes one marvel that public opinion did not force U.S. intervention even earlier.[62]

Many newspapers were unrestrained in their call for war with Spain. Long before the explosion of the *Maine* in Havana Harbor in February 1898, the *Chicago Tribune* was urging the United States to send its fleet to Havana "to sink every Spanish vessel on the coast." In March 1895, the *New York Sun* editorialized in favor of a military solution to the Cuban issue:

> It is evident that the Spanish government whose arrogance and brutality provoke its Cuban subjects to rebellion, requires a sharp and stinging lesson at the hands of the United States. . . . The American flag has been insulted and the lives and property of American citizens have been placed in jeopardy. The next vessel ought to be pursued and blown out of the water. Let it [the State Department] bring Spain to her knees or punish her by the destruction of her navy and the loss of Cuba.[63]

Yellow journalism is not the whole story of public reactions to the prospect of a war with Spain. Unlike the Crimean case, there were a number of newspapers that took a more measured approach to the Cuban issue—although atrocity stories managed to bleed into almost all of the papers. Despite these early calls for war, the Cuban issue did not play a major role in the 1896 election. William McKinley and William Jennings Bryan adopted similar approaches to the issue—platitudinous sympathy for the Cuban insurgents, but no commitment of America's resources to that conflict.[64] Most interventionists favored McKinley, but only because they felt certain that Bryan was not going to take decisive action in Cuba. Bryan had two strikes against him in this regard. First, he was on the record as a strong anti-imperialist. Second, he was the Democratic candidate, and the incumbent Democratic president, Grover Cleveland, had steered the party toward a strongly anti-interventionist line. Nonetheless, McKinley refused to pander to the interventionist constituency. The electoral period was dominated by the debate over the relative merits of the gold standard vs. bimetalism. The Cuban issue was frequently in the headlines, but was not a part of the campaign news.

By 1898, the efforts of Hearst and Pulitzer—the publishers of the most important yellow journals—were rewarded with increasing public demands for a more forceful response to reported Spanish outrages. After the explosion of the battleship *Maine* in Havana harbor in February 1898, and the subsequent report attributing the blast to sabotage, the public demands reached a fever pitch. McKinley remained relatively measured in his views on the Cuban issue, but it is clear that he felt constrained by public demands for action.[65] House Speaker Thomas Reed, a Republican and a supporter of McKinley's desire to avoid war, was asked why he did not dissuade his congressional colleagues from their mounting pressure on McKinley. He responded: "Dissuade them! . . . He might as well ask me to stand out in the middle of a Kansas waste and dissuade a cyclone."[66]

Public reaction to the Spanish-American War raises two points. First, as in the Crimean case, it demonstrates that pressures for international conflict can rise from a democratic public rather than just from government leaders. Second, it illustrates Michael Doyle's argument that democracy itself can provide a focal point for inspiring international conflicts and interventions.[67] The most virulent calls for American intervention in Cuba focused on outrages and purported outrages perpetrated against American citizens; but there was also a strong current of war justification that was based on the inherent democratic rights of the Cuban people. A turning point in public and congressional opinion came when Senator Redfield Proctor of Vermont—a conservative Republican—returned from a trip to Cuba, sponsored by William Randolph Hearst, to give a speech decrying Spanish outrages against the Cubans and outlining the humanitarian rationale for intervention: "To me, the strongest appeal is not the barbarity practiced by Weyler, nor the loss of the *Maine* . . . but the spectacle of a million and a half people, the entire native population of Cuba, struggling for freedom and deliverance from the worst misgovernment of which I ever had knowledge."[68]

Democracy as an idea has the ability not only to legitimate foreign intervention in the abstract, but also to motivate a willingness for self-sacrifice on distant battlefields. This phenomenon is particularly germane to the argument that democracies are pacific because the individuals who make the sacrifices of war participate in the decision to go to war. The experience of the United States in the Spanish-American War should serve as a potent rejoinder to this line of argument. When McKinley sent out a call for 125,000 volunteers for Cuba—twice the number the army had requested—more than a million men sought to enlist.[69] The president was authorized to appoint about a thousand officers but was inundated with some 25,000 applications for military commissions.[70] When William Randolph Hearst volunteered to finance a regiment, in which he would take part as a "man in the ranks," McKinley responded that if he made an exception for Hearst, he would hear complaints from all the states that had been denied their requests to furnish more troops.[71]

Another story of the era illustrates the nature of the war enthusiasm and suggests that these volunteers were not all just adventure-seekers who believed that the Spanish troops would be overawed at the mere appearance of American soldiers. Early in the war, the United States Navy sought to blockade the Spanish fleet of Admiral Cervera in Santiago Bay. To ease the burdens of blockade, Admiral Sampson, the American commander, lit on the idea of bottling up the Spanish fleet by sinking an old coal ship—the 333-foot-long *Merrimac*—athwart the narrow channel leading into Santiago Harbor. The plan required eight sailors to maneuver the unarmed, but explosive-laden, *Merrimac* past the formidable Spanish shore batteries, an uncertain number of remotely detonated mines, and several patrol vessels. At precisely the right point in the channel, the crew was to scuttle the *Merrimac* by detonating torpedoes attached to her hull. The survivors would have a small lifeboat in which to try to escape back out of the bay.

Needless to say, this was considered a dangerous mission. Yet when the American fleet was polled for volunteers, hundreds of seamen responded. It is claimed that all of the 600 crew members of the battleship *Iowa* and all of the officers on the *Iowa* and the *New York* volunteered. On the *Iowa*, the choice was narrowed to two candidates and a coin was flipped. The loser offered the winner $50, but this was refused.[72]

The stories of military recruiting and personal heroism in the Spanish-American War point to a central failing in the utilitarian expectation that individuals in a democracy will consistently vote to save their own lives. People can be motivated to perform apparently selfless acts. Of course, there are stories of heroism and self-disregarding behavior in all political systems. But this only reinforces the central point here that the logic connecting a personal fear of dying or a reluctance to bear the financial costs of war to a dampened war enthusiasm in the general population may be seriously flawed. The force of democracy as a motivating ideology has been frequently demonstrated.[73] This motivation has led democratic publics to be remarkably self-sacrificing when it comes to bearing the costs of war, even though they may appear solely self-serving in domestic battles over the distribution of tax burdens and the like.[74]

As with the Crimean War, the Spanish-American War demonstrates the potential enthusiasm of democratic publics for war. Again, there were political elites who tried to resist the demands of the public and the press. Ultimately, of course, they failed and the United States went to war. The war with Spain was over quickly and remained popular through the 1900 election, although there was some dissatisfaction over the continuing conflict in the Philippines.[75] Once again William Jennings Bryan was the challenger. He campaigned on a strong anti-imperialism platform, warning that "imperialism abroad will lead quickly and inevitably to despotism at home." The significance of the election was noted by the Filipino leadership who offered to help Bryan in the election by announcing that they would immediately stop the insurgency if he were elected. The Democratic party leadership recognized the damage such backdoor negotiating could do to their image and refused a meeting with the Filipinos, though other anti-imperialism activists leaked the news of the offer.[76] Ultimately, the election turned on economic issues, and Bryan could not rouse sufficient popular outrage about imperialism to unseat the popular McKinley who promised "a full dinner pail."

The Public and the Boer War

In 1877, the British annexed the Transvaal—at that time, an independent Boer state. In 1880, the Boers revolted and after several impressive victories over British forces were granted independence over their internal affairs in the 1881 Convention of Pretoria. This ambiguous situation became difficult to sustain after the discovery of large quantities of gold in the southern Transvaal in 1886. In 1885, the Transvaal accounted for just .03 percent of the world's annual gold production. By 1898, the Transvaal mines accounted for a little more than a quarter of the world's gold output.[77] This bounty attracted a flood of foreign miners—the Uitlanders—a majority of whom were British. Their presence greatly exacerbated Boer-British tensions. British demands for both free immigration and political rights for the Uitlanders threatened to swamp Boer control of South Africa. The Boers finally declared war when Britain rejected an ultimatum to remove British troops massed along the border between Natal and the Transvaal.

Great Britain entered the Boer War in October of 1899. It is important to note that the last general election had been four years before in July of 1895, so British politicians were acting in an environment in which an election was expected in the near future. Indeed, the next election was held one year later, in October of 1900. The timing of that election was directly affected by the Boer War. The ruling Tory Party knew that an election had to be held soon, but they waited to ride out a period of military reverses during the first five months of the war, when it became apparent that more than 350,000 men were going to be needed to subdue just 60,000 extremely effective Boer soldiers. For the Conservatives, the hastily called October 1900 election was propitiously timed to follow shortly on the annexation of the Transvaal in September 1900.[78]

Despite the military problems, the Boer War was initially immensely popular with the British public. Some have argued that the apparent popularity of the war is "more a matter of noise than of numbers."[79] But even those who question its popularity admit that it was *perceived* as very popular by both its supporters and opponents.[80] Those who opposed it publicly did so at some risk to their careers and even to their personal safety. A number of those who were labeled "Pro-Boers" were attacked by pro-war mobs.[81] The most colorful of these incidents involved John Burns, a prominent figure in the opposition Liberal Party, who took up a cricket bat to defend his home from a pro-war mob.[82]

There is a retrospective tendency to focus on the more visible instances of the public's enthusiasm for the Boer War, but prior to its start, politically legitimate elites were divided on the prospect of a war in South Africa. Although there was a coterie of Liberal Imperialists who supported an aggressive British policy, the opposition Liberal Party served as the organizational focus of antiwar sentiment. Many opponents of British policy focused on Chamberlain, the colonial secretary, and Milner, the imperial high commissioner in South Africa, as responsible for bringing on the war. Three days before the beginning of the war, the *Economist* suggested this view of the situation:

> We have no desire to be unfair or to blame individuals for errors that appertain to a collective body. But we cannot ignore facts, and the first is that Mr. Chamberlain has conducted the negotiations from London and that Sir Alfred Milner has been supposed to hold the scales even at Capetown, and that, as a result of their joint effort, a problem which, in our judgment, might have been peacefully solved has brought the British Empire to the verge of war.[83]

Although the Liberal Imperialists gained some strength in the Liberal Party as the war progressed, their power at its outset should not be overestimated. In June 1899, four months before the outbreak of the war, E. T. Cook, a Liberal supporter of Milner, wrote to him to warn him of the weakness of his policy position vis-à-vis the Liberals: "I doubt if 20 Liberals would support it [Milner's policy] . . . even a South African Liberal, like Hawksley, is very uneasy and thinks I have gone too far in supporting you."[84]

The Liberal Imperialists had hoped to take advantage of the natural patriotism that accompanied the outbreak of the war to gain power in the opposition Liberal Party.[85] In this they miscalculated. On October 17, six days after the start of the war, during a special parliamentary session, a critical pro-Boer amendment found only fifteen Liberals voting with the Conservative government, while 94 voted against and 42 abstained. The Liberal Party, under the leadership of Henry Campbell-Bannerman, an outspoken critic of Britain's

South Africa policies, remained largely antiwar throughout the conflict. Although the Liberal Imperialists enjoyed some increase in numbers during the war, their actual influence in the Liberal Party declined as the Party polarized on this issue.[86]

Even within the ruling Conservative Party, there was ambiguous enthusiasm for the South African War prior to its outbreak. Some Conservatives shared the belief that Chamberlain and Milner had seriously erred in their approach to the negotiations with the Kruger government in South Africa.[87] Chamberlain himself harbored some reservations about the direction in which things were moving. He had hoped that the correct degree of belligerence would help avoid war in South Africa.[88] In retrospect, it is probably Milner who bears the primary onus for the war enthusiasm. In 1896, Chamberlain—to his later embarrassment—had set out his opposition to a war in South Africa succinctly and forcefully:

> A war in South Africa would be one of the most serious wars that could possibly be waged, and it would be in the nature of a civil war. It would be a long war, a bitter war, and a costly war. It would leave behind it the impress of a strife which I believe generations would hardly be long enough to extinguish. To go to war with President Kruger in order to force upon him the reforms in the internal affairs of his State would be a course of action as immoral as it would be unwise.[89]

Chamberlain did not share Milner's optimism about the imperial loyalties of the Uitlanders. And most reports suggest that Chamberlain objected to Milner's obstructionist approach to the June 1899 Bloemfontaine Conference. At that meeting between Milner and Kruger, the central issues were the procedures for granting the franchise to the Uitlanders and the reservation of some number of seats for the Rand in the Raad.[90] Milner's demand was for a five-year retrospective franchise—that is, a five-year residency requirement that would count the years already spent in the Transvaal—and for seven of the 28 seats in the Raad to be set aside for the gold-mining districts.[91] Midway through the conference, Kruger presented a detailed proposal allowing a seven-year retrospective franchise and five seats in the Raad. Chamberlain indicated to Milner that this proposal was quite adequate: "If Kruger has really given seven year retrospective franchise and five seats . . . I congratulate you on a great victory. . . . No one would dream of fighting over two years in a qualification period. We ought to accept this as a basis for settlement and make the most of it. Kruger, we should assume, has conceded in principle what we asked for, viz. immediate substantial representation."[92]

By this time, however, Milner was already set on war as the best outcome for the British Empire. Contrary to Chamberlain's wishes, he rejected the Bloemfontaine proposals.

In the year leading up to the Boer War, Alfred Milner, the highest ranking British representative in South Africa, told his superior in the Foreign Office, Joseph Chamberlain, that he was "inclined to work up to a crisis."[93] In May of 1899, in a letter to the Earl of Selbourne, he argued that if war came, "we must seem to be forced into it."[94]

Throughout the period leading up to the war, Salisbury, the prime minister, also carried grave reservations about the wisdom of a South African War. Like Chamberlain, he saw the prospect of peace in Kruger's concessions. In commenting on some concessions by Kruger in August 1899, he wrote to Chamberlain with the suggestion that Milner seemed to have been "spoiling for the fight with some glee, and does not like putting his clothes on again."[95] At one point, he described the prospect of conflict over the Transvaal as a war "all for a people whom we despise, and for territory which will bring no profit and no power to England."[96] The week before war broke out, he wrote to Lansdowne concerning Milner's approach: "His view is too heated. . . . But it recks little to think of that now. What he has done cannot be effaced. We have to act upon the moral field prepared for us by him and his jingo supporters."[97]

In the case of the Boer War, the Imperialists were highly constrained in the policies they could propound by a fear of being labeled warmongers, or of appearing too provocative. Even Milner was aware of the importance of not appearing too anxious for war.[98] Colin Matthew describes their predicament: "It was difficult for the Imperialists to organize support in the Commons, for, whereas the Forwards could argue that their organizations were peaceful in intention, any Imperialist organization would be accused of 'warmongering.' Until war actually broke out nothing could be done without the accusation of provocative action."[99]

Until very late in the development of most conflicts, a pro-war policy—as distinct from a pro-belligerence policy—has been an extreme view. The prewar political battles, therefore, have usually been between the forces of belligerence and the forces of conciliation, rather than the forces for and against war.

In retrospect, popular enthusiasm stands as the salient characteristic of public opinion in the Boer War. But when the historical record is examined more carefully, and when attention is focused on the environment of opinion before the war actually began, it becomes clear, as in the Crimean case, that the British political system harbored a greater diversity of views, including a politically legitimate antiwar voice.

Of course, the Crimean War, the Spanish-American War, and the Boer War happened a long time ago. It may be, as Virginia Woolf asserted, that human nature changed fundamentally in 1910. More modestly, it could be that both democratic institutions and democratic preferences have evolved since the mid-nineteenth century. Mueller, for example, argues that before World War I, war was quite popular with democratic publics, but that since 1920 popular opposition to war has been uniform and consistent.[100] Likewise, it would not be hard to argue that democratic institutions were decidedly less "popular" before World War I. Journalism was less professional; populations were less educated; foreign policy was viewed as the preserve of intellectuals and the upper classes. Jeremy Bentham optimistically postulated just such a development of democracy over time, especially with the creation of a nonpartisan press and a more educated population: "Even at the present stage in the career of civilization its [public opinion's] dictates coincide, on most points, with those of the greatest happiness principle; on some however, it still deviates from them; but, as its deviations have all along been less wide, sooner or later they will cease to be discernible: aberration will vanish, coincidence will be complete."[101]

Still, concerns have continued to arise about the vulnerability of democratic masses to the guile of warmongers and demagogues.[102] Certainly the rise of truculent nationalism in Eastern Europe and the former Soviet States, and of militant fundamentalism in the Middle East, suggest that the world is still highly subject to the dangers of popular passions. Even in the West, where there have been changes in the nature of education and the media, the goal of a politically informed and sophisticated mass public remains elusive.[103] And while there have been no recent waves of war enthusiasm before a war, the rally effect remains robust once wars have started. Most recently the Falklands and Persian Gulf Wars generated widespread public support in the United Kingdom and the United States, respectively.

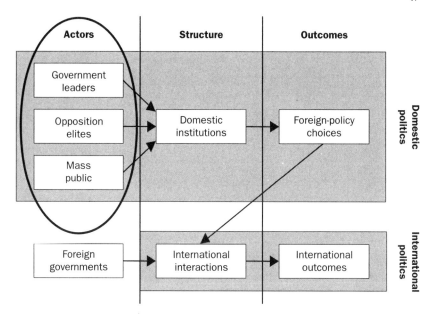

Figure 2. Domestic actors in the two-level model

Conclusion

As indicated in Figure 2, I have focused in this chapter on the actors in the domestic political process. I have suggested three strong cases as evidence for rejecting the view that the masses are inherently pacific. It is not the case that
mass opinion can be the basis for a belief that democratic states face higher domestic costs for getting into wars and will always be reluctant to make war. In
the Crimean, Boer, and Spanish-American Wars, the public clamored for military engagement. Politicians who attempted to resist the tides of public passion did so at considerable risk to their political careers. Obviously, whether
from the domestic political pressure, from some sense of the national interest,
or a combination thereof, in these three cases a sufficient number of political
leaders became convinced that war was the appropriate course of action.

Walter Lippmann worried that democratic publics exercise a sometimes de-
bilitating veto power over the ability of democratic states to act.[104] In this
chapter I have raised the possibility that when it comes to the decision to go
to war in a democratic electoral environment, a strong constraint may also

arise from a relatively small minority of antiwar voices, even in the face of wide public support for war. As Palmerston recognized, public enthusiasm can be induced for foreign wars, but there is a serious danger that it will be very short-lived. The existence of legitimate antiwar views and the electoral institutions that create a space for their dissemination make warmongering a dangerous electoral strategy. In this way, democratic conflict behavior is shaped by the distinctive ideas and institutions that have characterized democratic polities during the past two centuries.

The second point I have developed in this chapter is that understanding the role of public preferences requires consideration of the interaction of mass and elite views. The Crimean, Boer, and Spanish-American Wars are appropriately remembered as cases involving strong public pressure for war. I have argued here that part of the public milieu in these cases was the existence of a politically legitimate antiwar voice. These cases illustrate the existence of this voice where it is least expected.

The mere existence of such a voice is not sufficient to demonstrate that it plays a significant role in shaping the foreign policies that democratic states choose. Nicias was a strong leader in the Athenian Assembly, but Alcibiades' conjuring of the wealth and glory that lay across the Ionian Sea proved more compelling to the Athenians. So too, in these three cases the state did go to war, and did so with widespread popular support. To get from the constellation of elite and mass opinions to the reality of foreign-policy outcomes, it is necessary to consider the institutions that aggregate the various societal preferences into social choices. I turn in the next chapter to a consideration of democratic electoral institutions and the patterns of interaction of different policy views within those institutions.

THREE

Electoral Institutions and the Democratic Politics of War and Peace

By far the warmest advocate of the [Sicilian] expedition was, however, Alcibiades, son of Clinias, who wished to thwart Nicias both as his political opponent and also because of the attack he had made upon him in his speech, and who was, besides, exceedingly ambitious of a command by which he hoped to reduce Sicily and Carthage, and personally to gain in wealth and reputation by means of his successes.

— *Thucydides, describing the motivations for Alcibiades' support of the Sicilian expedition.*

Thucydides presents the demagoguery of Alcibiades as a prime example of the degeneracy of Athenian democracy after the death of Pericles. Ambitious politicians like Alcibiades appealed to the whims and emotions of the masses in order to further their own wealth and power. The common interests of Athens suffered as foreign policy became a weapon in the competition for power within Athens.[1]

As I pointed out in the previous chapter, there are some important parallels in attitudes toward war between the Athenian democracy of the fourth century BCE and the democracies of the past two centuries. Although contemporary politicians may have fewer expectations of gaining personal wealth through plunder, there remain strong domestic temptations for involvement in external conflicts. Alcibiades' appeals to glory and expansion have been echoed in many contemporary conflicts. This suggests a puzzle for our own time: while the incentives to demagoguery are well reflected in the war enthusiasms that have swept democratic nations, there is little evidence of pro-war demagoguery on the electoral stage. In the United States, for example, there has never been a peacetime electoral campaign in which a major candidate actively campaigned on a pro-war platform.[2]

Between 1840 and the outbreak of World War I, there were only two elections in which either party emphasized foreign policy as the central plank in the party platform. In 1844, the Democrats nominated James K. Polk as their presidential candidate and pursued an expansionist platform that called for the annexation of Texas and the occupation of Oregon. The explicit call for marking the border of the United States at 54°40' risked a major confrontation with the British.[3] This is the only example of an explicitly belligerent foreign-policy platform. The only other major foreign-policy plank before World War I came in the 1900 election, when the Democrats denounced the imperialism of the Republicans in the wake of the Spanish-American War. The Republican platform of the same year merely emphasized the prosperity that the Republican McKinley administration had brought to the country. Foreign policy became a more prominent part of party platforms after World War II, but the primary emphasis of these platform planks was on maintaining peace and security. No peacetime party platform plank between 1840 (when the parties began regularly producing platform documents) and today has ever advocated the use of military force abroad.[4]

On the other hand, there have been a number of elections in which opposing candidates competed to assure the public that they were the best candidate for keeping the country out of war. Given the susceptibility of democratic publics to war enthusiasms, the absence of elections in which taking a country into war has been a major issue is highly noteworthy. The question, then, is: Why is it that pro-war politics have not been a regular theme in democratic electoral processes, even though sympathy to such themes seems to infect democratic publics with some regularity?

To address this question, I turn in this chapter to democratic electoral institutions and the interaction of the government, the mass public, and opposition elites in the domestic politics of war and peace. I begin by presenting the logic of electoral influence on major foreign policy decisions. I argue that that influence should be visible in cycles of policy that shadow the cycles of domestic electoral politics. I then turn to a more specific argument about the ways in which different permutations of preferences fit in this institutional setting. I expand on my argument from Chapter 1 that there are important differences between the way pro-war and antiwar ideas work in the electoral process. Even as they pander to isolationist or belligerent public sentiments, democratic leaders have an incentive to avoid war in the electoral period.

I do not, in this study, directly address the sources of public moods. In individual cases, it is possible to hypothesize about the immediate source of widely held public attitudes, such as the revulsion to war that followed World War I, or the war enthusiasm that was generated by yellow journals in the United States during the late 1890s. Likewise, the psychology of public opinion is an important but separable issue that has drawn considerable study in other places but is beyond the scope of this inquiry.

The Impact of Elections

Elections are a defining characteristic of democratic regimes. It is impossible to imagine a viable conception of democracy without elections and the basic rights that make them functional. They are the institutional frame on which all of democratic politics is built. Through elections, politicians are held accountable for the policies that are enacted during their terms in office.[5] When politicians take actions in the international arena, they must do so with an eye both to the substantive effects in that arena and to the domestic political effects. If the effects of a given policy are easily observed, and if voters pay attention to those effects, then the internal and external environments will be connected. Policies that are clearly successful should increase domestic popularity, while clearly unsuccessful policies should decrease a politician's electoral prospects. Foreign conflicts that threaten involvement in war are dramatic events that should have strong domestic effects because of their high visibility and potential for very high costs.[6]

POLICY ACCOUNTABILITY

The connection between policies and outcomes is not always clear. Foreign policy is usually an issue of very low salience to the majority of voters. This can change dramatically in times of international crisis. When war threatens, foreign policy can become the most salient issue for voters to consider.[7] But even in times of crisis, foreign policy can be very difficult for voters to evaluate. The state of the economy and its impact on the financial conditions of individuals are reasonably easy to assess. It is considerably harder to assess the state of international affairs. Despite the high visibility of militarized foreign conflicts, the policy implications of these conflicts are not always clear-cut.

In the first place, many disputes will be resolved with a combination of costs and benefits to both sides. Assessing the net winner and apportioning responsibility in a democratic society can be very difficult. The diffusion of political power in democracy can cause ambiguity when accounting for policy successes and failures. Politicians willingly take credit for successful policies, but failures lead to finger-pointing rather than apologies.

Finally, evaluating the connection between policies and outcomes will be difficult because many policies involve long-term efforts and their results may not be visible for years. Was George Bush responsible for the end of the Cold War, or was he merely reaping the benefits of the more aggressive policies that Ronald Reagan had put in place? Or, was the collapse of the Soviet Union the ultimate fruit of President Carter's emphasis on human rights?

If the connection between policies and outcomes was unambiguous, political leaders could focus on maximizing outcomes with the confidence that this also would maximize their electoral prospects. To the degree that these connections are ambiguous, voters must hold their leaders accountable for policies rather than simply for outcomes. Was the Gulf War a successful policy—Iraqi aggression was rebuffed at a minimal cost in American lives and American dollars; or was it a policy failure—the Bush administration failed to signal its interests in the region to deter Saddam Hussein from his attack on Kuwait? Even where there is a strong consensus about the desirable goals, if the satisfaction of those goals is difficult to assess, debates can occur over which policies are most likely to lead to the desired results.

When leaders' policy preferences are different from the public's, they face competing electoral and international policy incentives. The short-term domestic incentive is to choose the policy preferred by the voters, while the international incentive (and the long-term domestic incentive) is to choose a policy that is expected to lead to the best possible outcome. As a result, the electoral process of accountability will lead to some policy choices that are different than they would have been in the absence of such a process.

The effect elections have depends on how politicians weigh the impact of policies on the national interest and on their electoral prospects. One would hope that no politician would run a significant risk of nuclear war for a modest electoral gain. Likewise, it should not be surprising to find politicians making small compromises on their preferred policies in order to make significant electoral gains.[8]

Elections and Policy Cycles

Electoral accountability leads to changes in policy, but the magnitude of policy change will vary with the expected time until the next election. There is a story that one of President Kennedy's first questions, on being told of the Soviet placement of missiles in Cuba, was to ask if American action could be held off until after the rapidly approaching congressional elections.[9] When elections are imminent, politicians are more likely to compromise on their policy principles in ways that are calculated to improve their electoral prospects. Tocqueville describes the democratic election process in terms of the increased influence of the masses: "The President, for his part, is absorbed in the task of defending himself. He no longer rules in the interest of the state, but in that of his own reelection; he prostrates himself before the majority, and often, instead of resisting their passions as duty requires, he hastens to anticipate their caprices."[10]

More recent analysts have shared Tocqueville's view of the electoral process. Gerald Pomper argues that "The effect of elections is to require government to pay greater attention to unorganized mass groups and comparatively less to elite groups of smaller numbers."[11] Samuel Kernell similarly describes the dynamics of the electoral season: "As election nears, a president will be tempted to husband even what he regards as surplus support. Accordingly, an unpopular president nearing election should come as close to resembling a single-minded popularity maximizer as one will find."[12]

The idea of electoral-policy cycles is controversial for several reasons, including a concern that rational voters should see through short-run political pandering.[13] But there are several good reasons to expect electoral cycles to lead to policy cycles.

In the first place, electoral shortsightedness may not be so unreasonable an assumption.[14] Presidential popularity does track events; negative events early in the term are less likely to have a strong effect on electoral prospects than events that immediately precede an election.[15]

Even with farsighted voters, government leaders who believe that an unpopular policy will bring success in the long run, will have an incentive to pursue that policy early in their term when elections are still far off. This is somewhat less true of parliamentary governments, where policies that are too unpopular may lead to a vote of no-confidence. Still, within some reasonable range, there will be an incentive to take unpopular, but unavoidable actions early in the election cycle rather than later so that they will have more time to yield favorable outcomes. If the policies do not work, politicians can hope that there will be time for the public to forget about them or to move on to another issue. Of course, as I shall show in the case of the Gulf War (Chapter 5), the public may also lose the enthusiasm generated by good outcomes.

This should have a particularly powerful effect on policies that are expected to carry the danger of violent international conflict. Wars that start early in the term are more likely to end before the next election. A politician who is optimistic about the prospects of keeping a war short and winning it will perceive the costs to be less at the beginning of the term, when there is a greater chance that the next election will be held in the afterglow of victory, rather than while casualties mount in the middle of a conflict. Of course, this would not explain behavior if a conflict was expected to be long and drawn out. But few wars are begun with the expectation of several years of protracted fighting.[16]

Electoral-policy cycles may also occur when the exact timing of some politically inexpedient action is flexible, even though the action itself is viewed as ultimately essential. In asking about the possibility of postponing American action in the Cuban missile crisis until after the election, President Kennedy was evaluating the costs of *delaying* action, rather than the costs of action per se. In that case it was decided that the political and diplomatic costs of waiting were too high. In other cases, the calculation might come out the other way, as I will argue later is the case for the decisions Roosevelt made to balance domestic and international demands in the period leading up to American involvement in World War II. The decision to take a politically inexpedient action is dependent on the relative valuation of the effect of that action on the probability of being reelected as compared to the effect of that action on policy goals. There are many situations in which the choice of acting immediately versus postponing action is considerably less critical than the choice of whether or not to take the action at all. In the interest of political expediency, democratic leaders may be willing to absorb some small substantive costs from changing the timing of an action even when they are not willing to bear the costs of abandoning an action altogether.

The willingness to make political trade-offs can work even for the serious issues of war and peace. There are both internal and external pressures for war that operate on democratic states. When these pressures are very high, political leaders may consider war inevitable, and the costs of avoiding it too high. There will be a set of cases, however, in which the costs of changing the *timing* of war entry are manageable, even where the war policy itself would not be compromised for electoral concerns.

ELECTIONS AND THE POLITICAL SPACE FOR ANTIWAR VIEWS

It is during the electoral period that public policy should come the closest to following the most salient preferences of the voters. Foreign policy should look increasingly belligerent if the public is basically belligerent, and increasingly conciliatory when the public is in a largely isolationist mood. Even in the electoral period, however, public opinion is a phenomenon of mass-elite interaction, rather than simply a mass phenomenon. V. O. Key argues in his classic *Public Opinion and American Democracy* that the critical public opinion in an electoral system is not the actual constellations of opinion, but rather the perception of politicians about the opinions that might be mobilized at the time of the next election. The *potential* an opponent has to present an alternative policy line can induce changes in the behavior of the incumbent.[17]

In Table 1, I outline the eight possible permutations of government, opposition, and public attitudes toward war and argued that there would be an asymmetry in the role of pro-war and antiwar ideas in public debate. As I argued in Chapter 1, the electoral environment enhances the potential for antiwar actors to influence policy. Antiwar ideas can be constraining even in an environment with a strongly pro-war public. Politicians have to avoid the "warmonger" label. They have to be especially careful in the election process not to appear to be advocating war for their own political benefit. The exploiters of mass enthusiasm for war also face potentially high political penalties when the true costs of a war are finally assessed. Certainly this was the experience of those who pushed for conflicts such as the Crimean War, the Boer War, World War I, and the Vietnam War.[18]

The nature of the political risks entailed in going to war is evident in the literature on rallies in public opinion related to foreign-policy events. Rallies are short-term events. What is more, this literature highlights the important role that politically legitimate antiwar elites can play in determining the length and strength of such rallies. Looking at the United States since 1945, Brody and Shapiro have shown that the existence of opposition views shortens rally effects.[19] When a crisis first breaks out, the government often has a monopoly on information and interpretation. The rally effect occurs within the environment of this interpretive monopoly. When opposition voices are able to get media time, the rally effect begins to dissipate. Brody and Shapiro looked at a number of lower-level crises. These are events where domestic opposition forces are more likely to be taken by surprise. For example, there was no political force specifically focused on preventing the United States from intervening in Granada in 1982. In high-level crises that have brought a country to the brink of war, it is likely that a politically legitimate antiwar voice will be in place. When an election is imminent, it is more likely that those voices will have access to the media and other political forums. Thus, pro-war political actors must take a country into war with the knowledge that this disunity is just under the surface. Sometimes it takes time to work its effect, but the result can be disastrous for the pro-war party—even if that party enjoys a short-term success.

Wars have both unifying and disunifying effects. When state leaders calculate the respective costs and benefits of going to war, they can include any expected unifying effects on the benefits side, but they must also include any expectation of significant and persistent disunity as a cost. Those who have focused on the rally effect and the legitimating benefits of external conflict have often pointed to the unifying effect of war. But these effects can be limited by conflicts within the society that call into question the legitimacy of the external conflict.[20] Arthur Stein has argued that even for the United States in World War II—a conflict that engendered high domestic support—the net social costs were more disunifying than unifying.[21] Policy legitimacy is particularly important in the process of going to war. A lack of policy legitimacy can weaken the war effort. A spiral of illegitimacy can result as poor performance further weakens legitimacy, which further degrades performance.

Electoral periods can also open up a political space for opposition views because of the important role that new or distinctive ideas can play in the campaign process, even if they have relatively little effect in the subsequent process of governing. In the famous Midlothian campaign of 1880, Gladstone sought to present a foreign policy that would be clearly distinct from the policies of the Disraeli government.[22] In particular, he engaged in tirades against the Austrian monarchy. Once in office, however, he promptly retracted these statements and proved as willing to work with Austria as Disraeli had been.[23] Gladstone also found a useful political target in "Beaconsfieldism"—the use of military force for imperial aggrandizement. But after his election he found himself entangled militarily in Egypt and the Sudan, a victim of the same logic that had committed Disraeli militarily in South Africa and Afghanistan.[24]

The existence of a pro-war public is not sufficient to push politicians into international conflicts on the eve of an election. The political risks of such pandering are simply too high. In Chapter 2, I showed the dynamics of three cases with strong pro-war publics. A fuller sense of the interaction of electoral institutions and ideas about war and peace is gained by looking at the dynamics of some cases in which the public holds antiwar views. I turn now to a discussion of British, Canadian, and American elections at the end of the interwar period. These are helpful cases to consider both because they demonstrate more directly the dynamics of the war/peace issue in electoral campaigns and because they demonstrate the important combination of a strongly antiwar public with a patently threatening international environment.

ELITES, ELECTIONS, AND ANTIWAR PUBLICS IN THE INTERWAR YEARS

The electoral pressures on state behavior in an antiwar environment are relatively straightforward. When the public is in a strongly conciliatory or isolationist mood, then the pressures of popular interests reinforce the electoral incentives to avoid war, and leaders pursue a more conciliatory course of action than they would if they were subject only to the international pressures. In the aftermath of World War I, the Western democracies faced a strongly antiwar opinion environment and behaved in this manner as World War II approached. A. J. P. Taylor writes of the effect of electoral dynamics on the French reaction to the German reoccupation of the Rhineland on March 7, 1936, with a general election scheduled for late April: "With a general election approaching in France, none of the ministers could contemplate general mobilization; only a minority supported the recall of reservists. All thought of action disappeared; diplomacy took its place."[25]

Electoral politics tend to force restraint on democratic leaders when the public mood is generally antiwar. This restraint should not, however, be viewed as pushing leaders to the extremes of pacifism or passivism. Except, perhaps, in the most extreme cases, the democratic process forces a certain degree of prudence. In most public opinion environments, the "peace" candidate cannot afford to be seen as the "peace at any price" candidate, any more than the candidate running on a platform of strength and rearmament can afford to be seen as a warmonger. An incumbent who is pushing a conciliatory international posture will not be able to afford to appear willing to give up vital national interests for electoral gain.

The years leading up to World War II suggest an environment where successful pro-war actors could be expected to come to the fore in electoral politics. After all, there was a very real threat. It should not have been hard to portray Hitler as a leader bent on world domination and the spread of noxious ideas and policies that were inimical to freedom and justice. The final prewar elections in Britain, Canada, and the United States are illustrative of the dynamics of electoral politics in a threatening world when public opinion is overwhelmingly opposed to war.

The seeds of World War II were planted in the final years of World War I. First, there was a punitive peace imposed on Russia by the Germans. The Treaty of Brest-Litovsk in March 1918 transferred some 60 million people from Russian to German rule and let German troops farther into Russia than Hitler's armies would ever extend during World War II. Then the punitive peace imposed on Germany by the victorious allies in the Versailles Treaty stripped Germany of these gains, overseas colonies, shipping, and military forces, as well as taking Alsace-Lorraine and the Polish Corridor. The loss of these latter two areas accounted for only about an eighth of German prewar territory, but some 65 percent of German iron ore and 45 percent of German coal resources. In addition, the "war guilt" clause demanded that Germany pay economically crippling war damages.

In many ways, the "victors" in World War I were only slightly better off than the vanquished. Most important, of course, they had paid similarly high costs in blood and treasure. The British national debt was sixteen times greater in 1920 than it had been in 1910. Throughout the West, the horrific costs of the war led most of the allies to isolationism and strong antiwar attitudes. But Germany had suffered the sting of defeat compounded by the blatantly punitive peace. The combination of economic destruction and moral affront created an environment ripe for the rise of a revanchist nationalism like that peddled by the Nazi Party.

In 1928, the Nazi Party was a small extremist party that attracted only a tiny proportion of the popular vote. Then the ravages of the Depression plunged Germany back into economic despair after the modest stabilization of the late

1920s. By 1932, Adolf Hitler polled 13 million votes, just barely losing the presidency to Field Marshall Paul von Hindenburg. Hindenburg won on the second ballot only because the Communists switched their vote to his side. By the end of the year the conservatives around Hindenburg had convinced him to ally with Hitler, rather than continuing his dependence on the Communists. In January 1933, Hindenburg reluctantly appointed Hitler to the chancellorship of Germany. By the end of the summer of 1933, Germany was a one-party state openly committed to rearmament and unwilling to repay any more of its Versailles debts.

Meanwhile, the collective security system of the League of Nations was challenged in Asia by the Japanese invasion of Manchuria in 1931 and then by the Italian attack on Ethiopia in 1935. In both of these cases the League system was found wanting. Mussolini's move on Ethiopia became part of a chain of events that led to the British general election of 1935.

The British Election of 1935 and World War II

On first blush, the British general election of November 1935 is not particularly interesting. The Labour Party had the bad luck to form its first majority government in 1929 on the eve of the Depression.[26] Blamed for the effects of that worldwide financial collapse, it suffered a crushing defeat in the 1931 election. In 1935 the Labour Party was still in disarray, the economy was notably improving, and no one was surprised that Labour was unable to mount a significant challenge to the government. Nonetheless, the 1935 election is important to look at as the last election before the war, and as the only British election since 1880 to be fought primarily on foreign-policy issues.[27]

To more fully appreciate the character of the 1935 elections, it's necessary to return to the end of World War I and place interwar politics in context. The British economy never really recovered from the First World War. British industry was largely outdated and inefficient compared to the more recently developed industries in the United States, Germany, and Japan. Britain was also more dependent on international commerce than the other powers and found its trade cut to less than half the prewar levels. The British Empire was at its zenith, but there was little willingness to pay for its upkeep. The combination of national poverty with the popular pacifism engendered by World War I led to a dramatic disarmament. The Left cut military spending out of an ideological belief in disarmament and international cooperation. The Right cut military spending to save money. In 1920, British defense spending was 519 million pounds. By 1929, it had dropped to 123 million pounds.[28] In 1928, Winston Churchill, as chancellor of the exchequer, told the navy not to expect a war for twenty years and to make major cuts accordingly.[29]

This complacence was rudely interrupted by the 1931 Japanese attack on Manchuria, which presaged a direct challenge to the safety of the British Empire. That event was followed by the rise of Hitler, whose long-run intentions were still subject to some debate, but whose immediate virulence and hostility were not difficult to discern. A third jolt came in October 1935 with Mussolini's attack on Ethiopia. Although pursuing the policy of appeasement, the Conservative government of Stanley Baldwin began a quiet but determined movement for rearmament predicated on the prescient assumption of a war with Germany in 1939.[30] Defense spending had reached its lowest point in 1932 at 103.3 million pounds. By 1935 it had risen to 137 million pounds.[31] These increases, engineered by then Chancellor of the Exchequer Neville Chamberlain, were made difficult by the competing demands for government spending in the wake of the Depression, by the need to avoid wrecking the economy through the diversion of too much capital and labor to the military, and by the persistent pacifism of the British public, even in the face of these ominous international developments.

As in the other Western democracies, the enormous human and financial costs of World War I left the bulk of the British population profoundly opposed to war and to the use of British force to deal with continental conflicts. In February 1933, a month after Hitler assumed the chancellorship in Germany, the Oxford Union passed its famous resolution that "This House will in no circumstances fight for its King and Country." In 1934, the depth of antiwar feelings were indicated in a national straw poll on foreign policy. In what has been called the "Peace Ballot" of 1934, some 10 million voters favored economic sanctions, while only 6 million favored military sanctions to deal with international aggression.[32]

The election was called shortly after the Italian invasion of Ethiopia in early October. This was almost a year before the next election would have been constitutionally required. Historians are divided as to whether the motivation was Conservative Party opportunism in face of the disarray in the Labour Party with the transition from the pacifist leadership of George Lansbury to that of internationalist Clement Attlee;[33] or the desire of Baldwin to get a mandate from the people for "rearmament in the interest of Britain, world peace, and collective security."[34] Most likely both factors were involved.

The Conservative prime minister, Stanley Baldwin, ran for reelection on the slogan of "all sanctions short of war."[35] As the "Peace Ballot" had demonstrated, this was an attractive position to the majority of voters. The Conservative Party leadership was largely united around this stand—the most dramatic exception being Winston Churchill.

Churchill's was the primary voice for a stronger stand toward Germany throughout the 1930s. Churchill had resigned from the Conservative shadow cabinet in late January 1931, in protest over the granting of dominion status to India.[36] He had fallen further out of the graces of Stanley Baldwin and the Conservative leadership for his strident warnings about the rising Nazis and the weakness of the government response through the early 1930s. Nonetheless, the Conservatives welcomed his offer to help on the hustings in the 1935 campaign.

Churchill used the election campaign to push for British rearmament and for greater use of the League of Nations to challenge aggression. "Arms and the Covenant" was his regular election refrain.[37] It was during the 1935 campaign that he gave his famous speech in Parliament declaring that "Germany is an armed camp" where "[t]he whole population is being trained from childhood up to war."[38] Party whips asked Churchill to tone down his rhetoric and warned him that his chances of a role in the government would be better if he would limit his attacks on the Nazis until after the election.[39]

The international transparency of democratic electoral processes is also evident in this case. Churchill's campaign rhetoric was noted beyond England's borders. Germany officially protested Churchill's attacks on Hitler, calling them "intolerable."[40] During the campaign, Churchill published an article in the *Strand* describing the concentration camps with which Germany was "pock-marked" and showing how Hitler's "ferocious doctrines" were foretold in *Mein Kampf.* Hitler responded with a thinly veiled threat, asking in an official correspondence: "What is to be the fate of the Anglo-German Naval Agreement if the writer of this article is to be the Minister of the British Navy?"[41]

Churchill was out of step with the Conservative's appeasement policy disguised under the slogan of "all measures short of war." The dominant Conservative Party position put the opposition Labour Party in a difficult position. To take a more militant stand would risk alienating their large pacifist base. A softer stand would anger the important internationalist wing of the party. The tension between these approaches had been building since the fall of the Labour government in 1931.

In the 1931 general election disaster, the Labour Party had gone down to stunning defeat, taking only 46 seats compared to the 556 seats collected by the Conservatives and their allies.[42] Most of the Party leadership lost their seats. Parliamentary leadership of the Labour Party fell on three men with dramatically different foreign-policy visions. Sir Stafford Cripps was on the left wing of the Party and viewed the League of Nations as an organization of capitalist states. He preferred that Britain quit the League and build strong relations with the Soviet Union and other socialist states.[43] George Lansbury was a Christian Pacifist of long standing. He opposed any use of force in international relations. Finally, Clement Attlee favored a strong role for the League, with strong sanctions and even international military force to back up its rulings as required.

None of these three men had been part of the Executive Committee of the Parliamentary Labour Party that was swept out of office in 1931. Cripps was a relative newcomer, having only been in the House for a year. Lansbury had the highest visibility of the three, so he was elected as the opposition leader with Attlee as his deputy. Lansbury became very sick, however, and by the end of 1933 Attlee had taken over as acting leader.

At the same time, Attlee's foreign-policy views were stiffening. In 1933, after Hitler gained dictatorial powers in Germany, Attlee gave a speech warning of the grave implications of Nazi ambitions and the importance of taking a hard line toward Germany and Japan. Security, he argued, was an essential preliminary of disarmament.[44] The League, which was at the center of his foreign-policy vision, was of no use without enforcement powers behind it.[45] On occasion, Attlee even found himself making arguments similar to those of Churchill.[46]

A critical Labour Party Conference in October 1933, centered on foreign-policy debate and the question of a united front of all socialists against Fascism. The Labour Party rejected the united front and instead issued a statement on *Democracy versus Dictatorship* that condemned the dictatorial government in Moscow as well as the Nazis in Berlin. At the same time, the Party passed a resolution refusing to support any British war, even a war of self-defense, without the sanction of the League of Nations.[47] Both of these positions reflected the growing influence of Attlee on the Party's foreign policy.

Still, Attlee's position was not yet fully formed. Throughout 1934, as acting leader of the Labour Party, he opposed the government's rearmament plans and argued for a focus on the League of Nations. In a parliamentary debate on disarmament he stressed that it was necessary "to put loyalty to the League above loyalty to your country."[48] But in a private letter to his brother he confided that the Labour Party "has not really made up its mind as to whether it wants to take up an extreme disarmament and isolationist attitude or whether it will take the risks of standing for the enforcement of the decisions of a world organization against individual aggressor states."[49]

Attlee pushed for resolution of this ambiguity at the 1934 Southport Party Conference. He engineered a statement that the Labour Party would strongly "support our Government in all the risks and consequences of fulfilling its duty to take part in collective action against a peace-breaker."[50] At the same time, the Party rejected a move by its left wing to pass a resolution calling for the use of every means possible, including a general strike, to resist any war entered into by the current government.[51]

In 1935, Italian pressure on Ethiopia intensified. Attlee was one of the earliest advocates of vigorous sanctions to support the League position and prevent the Italian attack on Ethiopia. As the principal spokesperson for the Labour Party on defense issues, he supported whatever sanctions were required to make the League effective. The public seemed to be increasingly in favor of strong support for the League and collective security on this issue.[52] In September, the government accepted the idea of economic sanctions to support the League and indicated it would consider collective security if it were truly collective.

The Pacifist and left-wing forces made one more attempt to derail the Labour commitment to an internationalist policy. In late September, the Party convened its annual conference in Brighton. In that forum, Attlee again turned back attempts by the Pacifists to abjure all use of force, and by Cripps and the left wing to pursue a socialist league. A broad internationalist program was approved by an overwhelming majority. Included was a call for more vigorous economic and military sanctions to prevent the imminent Italian attack on Ethiopia.[53] Cripps and Lansbury both resigned from the National Executive Council of the Party.

The attack on Ethiopia came less than twenty-four hours after the Labour Party passed its resolution. The government proved unwilling to consider military sanctions. Instead it responded to the Labour pressure, and the apparent turmoil in Labour leadership, by calling for the election.

As the campaign got underway, Attlee accused the government of coming too slowly to the support of League sanctions and thus failing to stop Mussolini earlier in the year. If the position of the government was "all measures short of war," then Labour's forceful position implied "sanctions even if it means war." Still, the Labour Party's endorsement was for collective security and did not extend to support of the military spending that would be required to make their position a reality.[54] This incongruity gave them a platform from which to warn that the Conservatives would present a threat to peace with their "vast and expensive rearmament programme."[55] But Baldwin responded in a speech at the Peace Society: "I give you my word there will be no great armaments." To the great consternation of Churchill, he downplayed the Nazi threat, asserting that in his experience he had never encountered a government with all the malevolent qualities that people attributed to the Nazis.[56] The Conservatives ran on the slogan, "The Socialist Policy Means War!"[57] In the minds of English voters, Labour was branded the war party.[58]

The Conservatives, who had begun their significant, if quiet, rearmament,[59] won the election by more than 2 million votes. The Conservatives took 388 seats to 154 for Labour. For Labour this was a substantial improvement over their losses in 1931, but still translated into a largely impotent role in parliamentary affairs. Once in office, Anthony Eden, the Conservative foreign minister, defined British policy as "peace at almost any price."[60] Churchill, who had defied the Tory hierarchy in campaigning with speeches about the imminent dangers posed by the Nazis, was pointedly not given a cabinet position.

In 1936, the opposition Labour Party took a strong stand for collective security but still refused to endorse the rearmament program. Finally, in 1937, under Attlee's leadership, Labour's policy on armaments was aligned with the stronger policy on collective security. The Labour Party continued to gain strength in the late 1930s, arguing for a more vigorous policy of collective security, in contrast to Chamberlain's appeasement policies.[61] Vocal Labour support for the Republican side and against the fascists in the Spanish Civil War also helped bolster Labour's image as the more resolute party. No more elections were held until the end of the war, but Labour's policy on rearmament and collective security was the basis for its entering Churchill's coalition government in 1940.[62] Ultimately, Attlee biographer Burridge suggests, it was the Labour Party's strong foreign-policy stand in the 1935 election that put the Party and Clement Attlee on the road to victory in the 1945 election.[63]

The Canadian Election of 1940 and World War II

On the eve of World War II, Prime Minister Mackenzie King of Canada had spent more time in office than any of the other leaders of the Western democracies.[64] He was a highly talented politician who has been called "Canada's greatest Prime Minister."[65] Still it was not at all clear that he had the necessary vision or skills to see Canada through the trials of another great war. King had traveled to Britain for the Imperial Conference of 1937, at which he had strongly asserted Canada's role as a central part of the British Empire. After the conference he went to Germany, where he was favorably impressed with Hitler's rebuilding program, and on meeting Hitler recorded in his private diary his impression that the Nazi leader was "one who truly loves his fellowmen and his country . . . [who had the face of] a calm passive man, deeply and thoughtfully in earnest . . . [and eyes] which indicate keen perception and profound sympathy."[66] King came away from his trip to Germany convinced that war could be averted and that appeasement was the appropriate policy.[67] As with many of King's convictions, this one was conveniently aligned with the overwhelming demands of public opinion in Canada.

War caught King and Canada largely unprepared. When war broke out with the German attack on Poland on the morning of September 1, 1939, King was making preparations for a trip to the Third Reich with a group of Canadian students and politicians at Hitler's invitation. King saw the trip as an opportunity "to practice appeasement at the eleventh hour, and to vindicate it in the eyes of its detractors."[68]

Unlike the British under Chamberlain, Canada had not embarked on a military buildup to parallel the appeasement process. The Canadian military had entered the 1930s in truly woeful condition. It was not until 1929 that the

Canadians officially scrapped "Defense Scheme No. One," which outlined a limited offensive thrust into the United States to counter an American invasion of Canada.[69] From 1931 until 1934, the Canadian military budget was actually reduced each year. In 1935, General A. G. L. McNaughton, chief of the Canadian general staff, issued a report urging a strengthening of the military and predicting war in Europe by 1939. Nonetheless, one of the greatest worries was that Canada was so weak that the United Sates would take over in order to protect its northern border.[70] By the mid-1930s, the Canadian military had no modern anti-aircraft guns, only 25 obsolete warplanes, and a stockpile of just 90 minutes worth of artillery.[71] Despite the grim picture painted by McNaughton, the military budget for 1935 was increased by only 5 percent, and did not return to the level it had been at the beginning of the decade until 1937. By September 1939, Canada's standing army still numbered only 4,500 troops who were largely equipped with World War I vintage equipment. There were not enough steel helmets to outfit even this small force.[72] The Canadian Navy consisted of seven destroyers with fewer than 2,000 sailors.[73]

With the outbreak of war, King's commitment to appeasement proved less important than his commitment to the maintenance of Canada's place in the British Empire. Despite entreaties to continue the appeasement policy from his dead mother and William Gladstone at a séance on the night of the Polish invasion, King dedicated himself to becoming Canada's war leader.[74] Just nine days later Canada joined Britain in the war.

In bringing Canada into World War II in 1939, King had to deal with a public spirit that had been deeply instilled with the isolationism and pacifism of the post–World War I years. As in the United States, the memory of World War I was still fresh, and many had come to see that conflict as a less than noble endeavor. In particular, the division between French- and English-speaking Canadians was exacerbated by the debate over the appropriate response to the European crisis. French-speaking Canadians were particularly opposed to rushing in to help save the British empire. The first challenge to King's war strategy came from Quebec.

Two weeks after Canada's declaration of war, Maurice Duplessis, the premier of Quebec, called for a provincial election on the grounds that Ottawa's war measures had infringed on provincial rights.[75] More specifically, Duplessis wanted to go on the record in Quebec as opposing conscription—an issue that had wrecked havoc in Quebec politics during World War I. King's Liberal

Party deputies campaigned ferociously, regularly calling Duplessis' Union Nationale Party the "Union NAZI-nale."[76] Duplessis miscalculated in thinking that antiwar politics could enhance Quebec's freedom from federal encroachments. In fact, the public worried that Duplessis was trying to sabotage the war effort. The Liberal Party gained an overwhelming victory in the late-October election, winning 70 seats to just fourteen for the Union Nationale. In King's view, the election victory in Quebec had saved the British Empire. But the price of victory would prove to be very high. The Liberal Party campaigned in Quebec with an explicit promise that there would be no conscription in Canada.[77] The sons of Quebec would not be required to go abroad to fight for England.

The second wartime challenge to King came from the province of Ontario. On January 18, 1940, Mitch Hepburn, Ontario's flamboyant premier and a member of King's own Liberal Party, pushed a resolution through the Ontario legislature condemning King for his lack of vigor in prosecuting the war. King's response was to immediately call the national election that was constitutionally required sometime before October 1940. Like Duplessis, Hepburn miscalculated. Canadians saw Hepburn's strategy as disunifying and as an attempt to gain politically from the war.[78] King's calling an election to force the issue was a complete success. The Liberal Party took 184 of the 245 seats in Parliament. Hepburn and his dissident Ontario Liberals were thoroughly discredited, and the government even picked up seats in Quebec. King had overcome two serious political challenges and had received the mandate he desired to direct Canada's war effort. There remained, however, the problem of the no-conscription promise in Quebec.

Despite a similarly isolationist public, King was able to bring Canada into the war more than two years before the United States entered and without the motivation of a direct and dramatic attack on Canada, or for that matter, on any part of the British Empire. The price for this feat and for the victories in the Quebec and national elections was the explicit promise not to use conscripts for overseas duty.[79] This self-limiting commitment raised serious problems for Canadian military planners throughout the early years of the war.

Canada's war planners quickly realized that total war without conscription was an impossibility. Instead of conscription, Parliament on June 21, 1940, passed the National Resources Mobilization Act, which required all Canadians to make themselves and their property available to the government in any way deemed necessary for Canadian defense. This bill created a system of compulsory military service, but was deemed to meet the spirit of the government's promises by limiting this service to home defense. No conscripts would be sent overseas. Not everyone bought the deceit. Camillien Houde, the mayor of Montreal, announced his intention to urge Quebecers not to register for national service. He was arrested for sedition and spent the rest of the war in prison. To King's great relief, the incident did not lead to more generalized troubles in Quebec, although Houde was given a hero's welcome on his release in 1944, was quickly reelected mayor of Montreal, where he held onto power until shortly before his death in 1957.[80]

The conscription of Canadians for service at home was still not enough for the war planners who were dealing with serious manpower shortages. Politically, the ban on overseas conscription was causing serious resentment among English-speaking Canadians who considered the Quebecers slackers. Finally the decision was made to hold a national plebiscite seeking to release the government from its no-conscription promise. The plebiscite was held in April 1942, and was overwhelmingly approved.[81] But even this vote was not sufficient to convince King that sending Canadian conscripts overseas was politically viable. In Canada as a whole, 2.9 million people voted in favor of releasing the government from its commitment, while 1.6 million voted against the release. But in Quebec, the release lost by a vote of 993,663 to 376,188. King resisted increasing pressure from military planners and the pro-conscriptionist members of his cabinet until late 1944.

In September 1944, after Paris had been liberated and Germany was clearly on the way to a complete defeat, a wounded Canadian war hero published an accusation in the Toronto *Globe and Mail* that Canadians were being killed because the shortage of reinforcements meant that insufficiently trained and even wounded soldiers were being put on the front lines.[82] Defense Minister James Ralston went to visit the front lines—a visit that confirmed these charges. On his return, he informed King that he would resign if conscripts were not sent overseas. King accepted his resignation.

In the mid-October 1944, remembering the conscription riots of 1917, King recorded his foreboding about the fallout of conscription for overseas duty in his diary:

> I could not bring myself to being the head of a government which would take
> that course—a course which might . . . lead to spurts of civil war in our own

country. It would be a criminal thing, and would destroy the entire war record, as well as help to dismember the Empire, for I am certain that its after effects would be all in the direction of demand for complete independence, if not annexation with the U.S. Anything to be separated from being in wars because of Britain's connection with them. I want to see the Empire endure. It can only endure by there being complete national unity in Canada.[83]

King's public pronouncements on the issue were not quite as dire, but he was willing to predict that if conscripts were sent overseas "the Liberal Party would be completely destroyed and not only immediately but for an indefinite time to come."[84] King's first move was to replace Ralston with a defense minister who believed that the manpower issue could be resolved without sending conscripts overseas. This ploy failed both because more volunteers simply could not be found, and because of the now intense resentment of the majority English-speaking public who demanded that the well-trained conscripts be sent abroad. There were reports of a veiled threat that a significant number of senior army commanders would resign if the conscripts were not used to reinforce the soldiers in the field.[85] It at last became clear to King that the imminent collapse of his government over the conscription issue was of more immediate concern than the long-term threat of party decline or even civil war. In November 1944, he finally weighed the balance of domestic and international pressures in favor of sending Canadian conscripts overseas. The Liberal Party survived, and there was no civil war, although there was a small-scale revolt by some of the conscripts, who at that time were the best-trained and best-armed military force in Canada.[86]

In 1944, the restriction on conscription was finally overturned, but to the end of the war, there remained a strong sense of political limitations. After the European war ended, King was in favor of a Canadian presence in the Pacific; but, once again in the face of an impending election, he could not send Canadian troops to Southeast Asia.[87] In his view "No government in Canada once the European war was over could send its men to India, Burma and Singapore to fight with any forces and hope to get through a general election successfully."[88]

The case of Canada's entry into World War II shows the potential of electoral politics to make clear the political mandate for international conflict. In both the Quebec election of 1939 and the national election of 1940, King was able to use his considerable political skills to discourage opponents from challenging his policies. Nonetheless, through five years of "total war," a minority of anticonscriptionists were able to hold Canadian war planning hostage with the threat of social disunity and electoral punishment. As I have argued, it is more difficult for pro-war minorities, and even pro-war majorities, to draw on this stratagem to force their program on a reluctant government.

The American Election of 1940 and World War II

A final highly important example of electoral politics in an antiwar public opinion environment is the case of Franklin Delano Roosevelt in the 1940 election. Roosevelt clearly favored a more active U.S. role in the burgeoning world crisis of the late 1930s. As the 1940 election approached, however, he was significantly restrained by the enormous strength of isolationist sentiments in the United States.

In the 1930s, public opinion in the United States was dominated by the isolationists and the noninterventionists, both of whom opposed a forceful response to the growing world crisis. The isolationists simply favored American withdrawal from international responsibilities. From their perspective, the United States had been duped into bailing out the British and the French in World War I, and now both nations were repudiating their substantial war debts to the United States. The noninterventionists were less wary of international involvement, but rejected war as a tool of national policy. The pacifist movement was stronger and better organized in the United States than in any of the other Western democracies. By the early 1930s there were an estimated 12 million members of organized antiwar groups.[89]

Roosevelt, who had been elected in 1932 in the wake of the Depression, was primarily interested in the domestic reforms packaged together in his New Deal program. Many isolationists in the West and Midwest harbored a deep distrust of the Eastern financial establishment and supported broad social changes. Roosevelt was dependent on this part of the isolationist vote to get the New Deal through. The implicit cost of isolationist support was a firm commitment to staying out of international entanglements. As long as Roosevelt's foreign policy followed these lines, many Republican isolationists proved ready to vote for the major elements of the New Deal.[90]

Just as France and Britain were beginning to recognize the need for rearmament in light of the rise of Hitler and Mussolini, the United States was going through a new round of recriminations aimed at the armaments industry. In 1934, the Senate began a formal investigation into the behavior and business practices of the armaments industry. The Senate Munitions Inquiry produced a stream of revelations about the iniquities of the "merchants of death" that fed into isolationist and peace movement ideologies. In 1935, by a vote of 79 to 2, the Senate passed the first of the Neutrality Acts that aimed at keeping the United States out of any future war. The events in Manchuria, Ethiopia, and Spain did little to shake this determination to stay out of international conflicts.

In his 1936 reelection bid, Roosevelt focused his campaign on the isolationist states in the West and Midwest. While Roosevelt and his secretary of state, Cordell Hull, would clearly have preferred a more internationalist approach to the aggression of Japan in China and Italy in Ethiopia, and to the growing revisionism of Hitler in Germany, his public stand during the electoral campaign explicitly denied a role for the United States in these conflicts. Roosevelt's famous speech at Chautauqua, New York, in August 1936, encapsulates his public stand on these issues, and on the issues raised by the Senate Munitions Inquiry: "We shun political commitments which might entangle us in foreign wars . . . if we face the choice of profits or peace, this Nation will answer—this Nation must answer—'we choose peace.'"[91]

The first three years of the second Roosevelt administration, 1937–39, largely lived up to the isolationist expectations raised in the 1936 campaign. American military expenditures rose from $914 million in 1936 to $1,075 million in 1939. This represents an 18 percent increase in three years, compared to a 270 percent increase in Germany, a 286 percent increase in Britain, and a 520 percent increase in France during the same period. Even Canada managed a 100 percent increase in these three years. A rearmament program was finally, although quietly, approved in December 1938, but could not begin to have significant effects until the 1940 budget, when defense spending jumped almost 50 percent to $1,498 million.[92]

Like Mackenzie King in Canada, Roosevelt was an intensely political actor. More so than any previous president, he attempted to keep abreast of public opinion. His room to maneuver in foreign affairs was significantly reduced by several domestic political reversals in 1937 and 1938, including an economic recession, the Supreme Court's rejection of two major New Deal programs, and the negative public reaction to his transparent and unsuccessful attempt to undo that decision by enlarging the Court with his own appointees.

In October 1937, Roosevelt sent up a trial balloon for a more internationalist policy with his "Quarantine Speech," in which he called for an international quarantine against those states that were disturbing the peace. The speech was delivered in Chicago and was quickly picked up by the isolationist press. A campaign of protest convinced Roosevelt of the political dangers in this effort. In a letter to Colonel House shortly after the Chicago speech, he complained that he was "fighting against a psychology of long standing which comes very close to saying 'Peace at any price.'"[93]

Later that same month, Roosevelt gave the head of the American delegation to the Brussels conference the instruction to tell the British that "there is such a thing as public opinion in the United States . . . [we] cannot afford to be made, in popular opinion at home, a tail to the British kite."[94] Concern about the state of public opinion continued to limit Roosevelt's actions even as the war drew closer.

Throughout 1939, public opposition to a war against Germany actually increased from 83 percent before to 94 percent after the invasion of Poland.[95] In the summer of 1939, Roosevelt attempted to get around the neutrality acts by allowing "equal access" to American armaments by all belligerents. The cash-and-carry policy he proposed would clearly favor Britain and France since they could control access across the Atlantic. The Senate defeated the proposal. When Roosevelt called a special session of Congress to take up neutrality reform again after the German attack on Poland in September, Congressional offices received 1 million letters in three days against lifting the arms embargo.[96] Roosevelt's political friends expressed concern that these policies could jeopardize the prospects for the election of a Democrat in the 1940 election.[97]

The quick German victory in Poland and the continuing Japanese encroachments in China and the Pacific began to turn opinions in Congress. Despite a continuing and vigorous campaign by the isolationists, Congress finally agreed to lift the prohibition on arms sales. Public opinion also started to shift at this time, but remained staunchly opposed to any direct military involvement. The public overwhelmingly approved of Roosevelt's foreign-policy moves, and two-thirds of the public favored giving the British and French all the help they wanted, short of sending the army and navy. At the same time, a very large majority wanted the government "to keep us out of war, unless we are attacked, no matter what happens abroad."[98]

In 1940, the European situation went from bad to worse. Denmark and Norway fell in April; the Low Countries succumbed in May, and British soldiers evacuated the continent at Dunkirk; France fell in June. The deteriorating situation in Europe led to Roosevelt's decision to seek an unprecedented third term. New York governor Thomas Dewey looked to be the Republican nominee throughout the beginning of the year. But Dewey was caught by the rapid pace of international developments. He had been a vocal interventionist, but then had adopted a more isolationist line in seeking the nomination. When the Republican nominating convention met in late June 1940, just eight days after the fall of France, an uncertain isolationist was not to be the candidate of the hour. Instead, the Republicans turned to Wendell Willkie, who until recently had been a Democrat, but who had a consistent record as an internationalist. Dewey's convention speech attacked the Democrats as "the War Party," while Willkie pronounced himself in favor of "all possible aid to the Allies without going to war."[99]

Despite the fact that Willkie seemed to share most of his foreign-policy views, and despite evidence that the majority of the public was also willing to support a more active American response, Roosevelt was convinced that such a position was not politically viable.[100] The isolationists were still a powerful force. Indeed, isolationists had succeeded in putting strong antiwar planks in both the Republican and Democratic platforms. The Republican's isolationist plank stated that "The Republican Party is firmly opposed to involving this Nation in foreign war."[101] At the Democratic Party Convention, isolationists led by Burton Wheeler threatened to form a third party unless the platform included a strong antiwar statement. Roosevelt pledged that "We will not send our men to take part in European wars."[102] The Democratic platform stated that "The American people are determined that war, raging in Europe, Asia and Africa, shall not come to America. We will not participate in foreign wars, and we will not send our army, naval or air forces to fight in foreign lands outside of the Americas, except in case of attack."[103]

Given the continued strength of isolationist sentiments in the United States, Roosevelt had to determine the appropriate political line to prevent the Republicans from taking advantage of these sentiments. The very manner in which Roosevelt chose to deal with the war was highly conditioned by his sense of domestic political necessity and the latent threat that Willkie would listen to the many Republicans who were urging him to take a more isolationist line in order to more strongly differentiate himself from the incumbent and break apart the New Deal coalition. When the British urged joint military staff talks in early October 1940, the response was "At the moment conversations should be confined to exchange of information in London, but the position it was thought, might alter in two to three weeks time."[104]

Facing similar pressures, the general direction of Willkie's campaign was toward an increasingly isolationist line. Willkie initially supported the Destroyers for Bases deal in August 1940, but then switched to criticism when pressured by Republican isolationists. As the election drew nearer through October 1940, there was escalation in antiwar rhetoric by both candidates.

All political leaders have to find the appropriate trade-off between their view of the national interest and their electoral prospects. By the summer of 1940, when Germany effectively controlled continental Europe, Roosevelt was convinced that America would eventually be at war with Germany.[105] The fact that Roosevelt was willing to sacrifice some foreign-policy goals for his electoral needs does not mean that he sacrificed everything. For example, against the advice of his political advisors, Roosevelt allowed the Conscription Act to move forward requiring draft registration by all 21- to 36-year-old males on October 16, 1940.[106] On October 29, he allowed the first large-scale call-up, bringing 800,000 more men into the military.

Nonetheless, as the campaign drew to a close he increased his assurances that his policies would not get the United States into the European war. At a campaign meeting in Madison Square Garden at the end of October 1940, he had the audacity to take credit for the neutrality legislation he was working to undermine.[107] In a Boston speech two days later, responding to isolationist criticism of the draft call-up, he promised that no American soldier would have to fight abroad: "And while I am talking to you mothers and fathers, I give you one more assurance. I have said this before, but I shall say it again and again and again: Your boys are not going to be sent into any foreign wars."[108] Under pressure from his advisers, Roosevelt dropped the phrase "except in case of attack" from the end of this statement.[109]

Despite his rising antiwar rhetoric, Roosevelt was continually aided in his campaign by the ominous developments in Europe. In August, the Battle of Britain began and presidential advisor Harold Ickes rejected a Willkie demand for a series of debates, with the assertion that "The President cannot adjourn the Battle of Britain in order to ride circuit with Mr. Willkie."[110] In September, Germany, Italy, and Japan signed the Tri-Partite Agreement. Ickes acknowledged Roosevelt's electoral debt to the turmoil in Europe: "The President's chances [of reelection] seem to be the greater the deeper the danger in which England finds itself."[111]

Apparently Hitler began to recognize this fact. The 1940 election provides several examples of the transparency of democratic processes and the interest that foreign powers can take in them. In October 1940, Hitler attempted to influence American electoral dynamics by urging Mussolini to delay the invasion of Greece until after the American election.[112] Mussolini, perhaps with a jealous eye on Hitler's voracious territorial appetite during the previous six months, rejected Hitler's advice and attacked Greece on October 28, just one week before the election. Roosevelt had already scheduled a major campaign speech at Madison Square Garden for the day the news of the invasion broke. In that audience, he was careful to avoid casting blame on either Italy or Greece, but he did not hesitate in rhythmically castigating the Republicans "Martin, Barton, and Fish" for impeding American preparedness efforts.[113]

Roosevelt and his supporters often seemed to be running against Hitler rather than against Willkie. In his speech accepting the Democratic nomination, vice-presidential candidate Henry Wallace mentioned Roosevelt 28 times, Hitler 23 times, and Willkie not at all.[114] In another speech he asserted that while not every Republican is an appeaser, "You can be sure that every Nazi, every Hitlerite, and every appeaser is a Republican."[115] Herbert Lehman, the Democratic governor of New York, argued in a speech that "nothing that could happen in the United States could give Hitler, Mussolini, Stalin and the Government of Japan more satisfaction than the defeat of the man who typifies to the whole world the kind of free, humane government which dictators despise—Franklin D. Roosevelt."[116]

The *New York Times* called the Lehman speech "reckless" in its implication that "a vote for Mr. Willkie is a vote for Hitler."[117] Unfortunately for Willkie, Hitler seems to have shared this sentiment. Although Hitler was contemptuous of American resolve, the Germans recognized the importance of keeping America aloof from international affairs. For this purpose, the Republicans seemed a better bet than the Democrats. The German embassy in Washington asked for large sums of money to funnel to isolationist causes and to influence the election.[118] The embassy recognized the damage that would be caused if the source of this money were known, so it asked permission to forego the regular accounting procedures. On the other hand, there were some economies to be realized. In a memo of June 19, 1940, the embassy asserted that its "press aide was constantly in touch with cooperative American lawmakers to help them get good publicity." In this way, the memo continues, "German influence is not visible to the outside and, thanks to the privilege of free postage enjoyed by American Congressmen, the cost of this large-scale propaganda can be kept disproportionately low."[119]

It was probably with little enthusiasm that Wendell Willkie read the full-page advertisements on his behalf taken out in newspapers across the country by Hamilton Fish's isolationist groups, but secretly paid for with funds from the German embassy.[120] To add insult to injury, before the campaign was over, Stalin also had embarrassed Willkie by directing American communists to give him their support.[121] Though hardly of the same magnitude, Roosevelt had similar problems in trying not to alienate the large number of voters with isolationist sentiments in light of the overly enthusiastic British support for his re-election effort.[122]

Of course, clumsy and heavy-handed attempts by an adversary state to directly support one candidate or another probably have the opposite of the intended effect. If their real interest was in seeing Willkie elected, Hitler and Stalin would have been better off announcing their enthusiastic support of Roosevelt. The important point is less the success or failure of these attempts at direct influence than their clear indication of the way foreign interests can observe democratic electoral politics and form strong preferences regarding the outcomes of those elections.

Roosevelt defeated Willkie in the 1940 election with 27 million votes to Willkie's 22 million. After the election, Roosevelt was again ready to assert a strong leadership role and to push Congress and the American public to rally behind a more interventionist foreign policy. On December 29, 1940, he gave the famous "fireside chat" in which he called for America to be the "arsenal of democracy." Military spending began to increase even more dramatically. Budget appropriations for the army and navy were four times greater in 1941 than in 1940.[123] A few weeks after the election, Roosevelt authorized the beginning of joint-staff planning that had been put off when the British asked for it a few weeks before the election. The basis of the talks and of American military planning was a secret memorandum drawn up by Admiral Stark, the chief of Naval Operations. That document, called "Plan Dog," assumed hostilities in both Europe and Asia and accepted that the defeat of Germany would require sending a large American army and air force overseas.[124]

There were still significant public constraints on Roosevelt. The lend-lease program was only approved in March 1941, after a very hard fight in Congress. Historian Robert Divine argues that Roosevelt continued to feel constrained by his campaign rhetoric following the election, and that over the next thirteen months he behaved in a less interventionist fashion than he otherwise would have.[125] In April 1941, he refused to approve convoying of merchant ships across the Atlantic because public opinion was not ready for it.[126] He continued to believe that the American public would have to be forced into war: the other side would have to fire the first shot. By the summer of 1941, American naval vessels were escorting merchant ships across the Atlantic and engaging German submarines. Nonetheless, in August the conscription act was renewed by the House of Representatives with only a one-vote margin—203 to 202.

On December 7, 1941, the Japanese attack on Pearl Harbor swept away the final vestiges of isolationism and shattered the myth that the United States could stand on the sidelines while the rest of the world was at war. The direct attack on American soil galvanized public opinion and mobilized the American war effort at a level that could probably not have been sustained with a more gradual drift into war. After the Pearl Harbor attack, the now virtually unquestioned legitimacy of the war showed the strength of the politics of democratic commitment.

Still, the domestic politics of isolationism and pacifism had held off American participation for more than two years after the blitzkrieg attack on Poland. In 1940, the electoral process in this antiwar environment had pushed both Roosevelt and Willkie toward more isolationist policies than they had advocated either before or after the electoral period. The transparent nature of the electoral contest tempted Hitler to get directly involved. The electoral politics of war and peace were much in evidence on the international stage.

Democratic foreign policy in the interwar years, as exemplified by Britain, Canada, and the United States, was risk-averse in the extreme. Hitler, on the other hand, was a highly risk-acceptant actor. As was made clear in the years between the 1935 election and the outbreak of World War II, this risk asymmetry was very costly. The transparent unwillingness of the Western powers to risk war through their choice of actions opposing Hitler and Mussolini gave the Axis powers the freedom to prepare for the war and to set the international agenda between 1931 and 1943.[127]

Conclusion

The preferences of the actors in a democratic state are translated into policy choices through institutional mechanisms. This process is illustrated in Figure 3. Of course, there are a number of different institutions that are important in the formation and conduct of democratic foreign policy. I have focused on the role of electoral institutions as central to democratic politics and highly consequential for foreign policy.

The impact of pro-war and antiwar elites in the electoral process is asymmetric. To look at institutions without a parallel consideration of the ideas that compete within institutional frameworks would lead to an ill-conceived sense of the likely policy outcomes. The policy space is a continuum of degrees of belligerence ranging from capitulation at one extreme to war at the other, but with a number of positions that are belligerent but still short of war occupying the bulk of the spectrum.

As I showed in the cases in Chapter 2, even when war per se seems highly popular with the mass public, the antiwar ideas held by politically legitimate elites have the potential to emerge in the electoral environment. The more an incumbent pushes toward war, the greater will be the danger that an electoral opponent can capture significant ground with an antiwar perspective. Electoral politics create a political space for domestic influences on foreign policy, but the effect of that influence will be consistently toward the avoidance of war even when the public mood is quite belligerent. The existence of politically legitimate antiwar elites and the electoral space for the airing of their views can increase the cost of going to war for the democratic state, even in the face of a mass public caught in the grip of war enthusiasm.

The combination of ideas and institutions in democratic states suggests a regular relationship between elections and conflict behavior. The essence of liberal democracy is not so much mass participation as it is the maintenance of rights that allow for the expression of diverse viewpoints and for the competi-

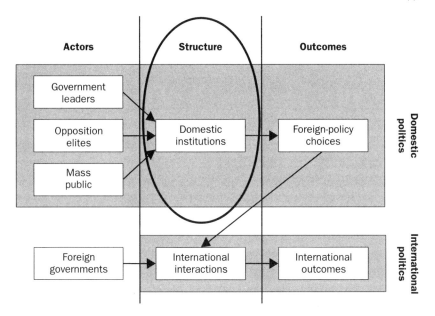

Figure 3. Domestic institutions in the two-level model

tion of those views in electoral contests.[128] In the past two centuries, the liberal democracies that have entered wars have found within their borders politically legitimate actors who were willing to publicly question both the war enthusiasm of the masses and the claims of rational necessity advanced by prowar elites. Sometimes they have expressed these views only at considerable political cost, or even at a risk of personal safety. Nonetheless, democratic institutions, and especially the process of government evaluation institutionalized in electoral procedures, have opened a political space for the expression and dissemination of these views.

Three cases from the period leading up to World War II demonstrate clearly the interaction of electoral politics and public ideas about war and peace. In all three of these cases, despite the presence of highly capable politicians who have wanted to move their societies toward a more belligerent foreign policy, the public has responded slowly and only after international events have become truly dire. These cases also offer a glimpse of the interaction of electoral politics with the interests of other international actors—a dynamic to which I will return in Chapter 5.

To this point I have relied largely on discrete cases to demonstrate the relationship between electoral institutions and the democratic politics of war and peace. It is now time to turn to a more systematic evaluation of the foreign-policy outcomes that emerge from the interaction of ideas and democratic institutions.

FOUR

Electoral Incentives and Foreign-Policy Choices

With this Nicias concluded, thinking that he should either disgust the Athenians by the magnitude of the undertaking, or, if obliged to sail on the expedition, would thus do so in the safest way possible. The Athenians, however, far from having their taste for the voyage taken away by the burdensomeness of the preparations, became more eager for it than ever; and just the contrary took place of what Nicias had thought, as it was held that he had given good advice, and that the expedition would be the safest in the world. All alike fell in love with the enterprise. The older men thought that they would either subdue the places against which they were to sail, or at all events, with so large a force, meet with no disaster; those in the prime of life felt a longing for foreign sights and spectacles, and had no doubt that they should come safe home again; while the idea of the common people and the soldiery was to earn wages at the moment, and make conquests that would supply a never-ending fund of pay for the future. With this enthusiasm of the majority, the few that liked it not feared to appear unpatriotic by holding up their hands against it, and so kept quiet.

—Thucydides' description of the voting in favor of the Sicilian expedition

The respected general Nicias attempted to dissuade the Athenian assembly from launching the campaign against Sicily. He tried to convince the assembly that an attack on Syracuse—the principal city on Sicily—would be a large and costly undertaking. This tack failed miserably. In the end, it was Alcibiades' appeal to glory and plunder that carried the day: The Athenians voted enthusiastically for the Sicilian expedition. The few opponents of the expedition yielded to public pressure and kept quiet for fear of looking unpatriotic. This is a problematic story for the populist view because of what it says about the motivations of demagogues and their ability to move the masses to enthusiasm for foreign adventures.[1]

I have suggested that in the modern era there has been a surprising lack of demagogues similarly exploiting the electoral moment. Part of the difference between ancient Athens and our modern democracies might be found in public attitudes toward the glory of war. But as I suggested in Chapter 2, this is an element that is still found in the rhetoric legitimizing war. The most important distinctions between ancient Athens and our modern democracies is found less in the mix of popular attitudes toward war than in the form of the electoral institutions. Voting in Athens took place in a central location. The balloting was not secret. There was a distinctly martial character to the electoral process, since the most important electoral offices at that time were generalships in the army, which were voted on annually. Most civil offices were simply assigned by lot. Finally, it is important that the decision to go to war was subject to a direct vote. Thus, while generals might find themselves called to account for the quality of their leadership in a war, there were no politicians who would be held directly accountable for a decision to enter a war.[2] Still, as in Athens, modern elections should intensify the effect of popular mood on the foreign-policy behavior of democratic states. Democratic electoral institutions should incline democratic leaders facing elections to choose foreign policies that reflect popular passions.

My argument about elections and war embraces outcomes at both the domestic and international levels. This chapter is devoted primarily to a consideration of domestic outcomes—that is, the foreign-policy choices of democratic states in electoral periods. In particular, I look at the relative belligerence of democratic foreign policy in electoral periods. I do not address war directly in this chapter, because it is an *international* outcome. In Chapter 5, I consider the relationship between democratic electoral politics and the attitudes of other states towards war; and then in Chapter 6, I turn to the international outcomes that result from the interaction of democratic foreign-policy choices with the choices of other states.

There are two basic strategies for empirical assessment of the domestic argument that I have presented here. The first is to look at individual cases and to try to trace the dynamics of electorally influenced decision making through the policy process. The second is to aggregate a large number of cases in an effort to verify statistically the dynamics of electoral behavior. While I have presented a number of individual cases in the previous chapters, here I will argue for the importance of an aggregate empirical test.

Measuring Foreign-Policy Outcomes

It is important at the outset to acknowledge that there are significant problems in testing a theory of foreign-policy choices. At either the case or aggregate level, serious conceptual limitations in our understanding of the nature of foreign-policy outcomes present certain difficulties. There are no objective measures of belligerence and conciliation. It is often difficult to assess the degree of belligerence or conciliation that a given action indicates. Precisely because of the disjunction between foreign-policy behavior and international outcomes, it is difficult to measure foreign-policy outcomes. What one state sees as a great compromise may appear to the other state as evidence of continuing intransigence.

Furthermore, states often choose mixed strategies with both conciliatory and belligerent components. Offers of compromise may go together with threats in any negotiating environment. States frequently want to send the complex message that they are willing to be reasonable and that there are tangible rewards for coming to agreement; but at the same time they want to indicate that there are tangible costs for failing to come to agreement, and that they will not tolerate exploitation.

The belligerence of a given policy is dependent on the international context. An American decision to point ten nuclear missiles at the Netherlands would be viewed as very belligerent. A decision to point ten more missiles at the Soviet Union in the 1980s would have hardly been noticed. Similarly, is the British pre–World War II policy of "all sanctions short of war" a policy of belligerence or of appeasement? The British attempted to craft both rewards and punishments as inducements for better behavior from Hitler. The architects of British policy in this period are now considered great appeasers, but similar policies taken, for example, to try to dissuade the French from withdrawing from NATO in 1968 would have been considered belligerent and inappropriate.

Assessing belligerence is complex and context-dependent. Case studies allow for a more detailed assessment of some of these complexities. In the course of laying out this argument, I have discussed a number of specific historical cases that illuminate the general shape of foreign-policy dynamics and the outcomes that result. However, there are two central problems with relying too heavily on case descriptions as the evidential basis for the kind of phenomena I have been describing here. First, there are limitations in the kind of historical evidence that is available. Second, the fact that the relationship between electoral politics and foreign-policy behavior is probabilistic rather than deterministic makes the use of cases problematic. Both of these issues require some elucidation.

EVIDENTIAL PROBLEMS

What we know of the past can come only through the interpretation of writings and artifacts that are preserved through time. Often, however, there are biases in the selection of what is preserved and what is lost. The interpretation of history requires an understanding of the biases in the way historical materials are created and collected. This problem is most severe in illiberal states that exercise systematic control over the kinds of information that is collected, or even engage in the wholesale falsification of evidence. Liberal regimes offer the historian the advantages of a relatively free flow of information. Nonetheless, liberal states present their own kinds of interpretive complexities. These problems may be particularly acute in dealing with the historical records of wars and elections.

In the first place, elections and wars both have winners; and winners' accounts of events are often motivated by more than just "getting the facts straight." There seems to be a human need to vilify enemies, and the high need for policy legitimacy in democratic states may exacerbate this condition.[3] Those who search for the causes of specific wars may be overly attracted to evidence that suggests black and white phenomena. To assert that wars were fought, and that good people died, for less than noble causes is an unpopular undertaking. To suggest that people have died to fill the prescriptions of campaign spin doctors requires a thoroughly unpalatable cynicism.

Blatant warmongering has never sold very well in the democracies. The normative constraints that work on democratic leaders also act on those who take down the historical record. One example of this kind of bias is provided, again, by the Boer War. In the year leading up to the Boer War, Alfred Milner, the highest-ranking British representative in South Africa, told his superior in the Foreign Office, Joseph Chamberlain, that he was "inclined to work up to a crisis."[4] In May 1899, in a letter to the Earl of Selbourne, he argued that if war came "we must seem to be forced into it."[5] But this passage was suppressed in the official compilation of his papers and was discovered only when access was again gained to the original Milner papers.[6]

Historical assessments of individuals and events are vulnerable to post hoc biases. But contemporaneous descriptions of actions must also be approached with some caution. When political leaders set out the relative advantages or disadvantages of going to war, elections are rarely cited as a factor. But the electoral process is not a mystery. Democratic politicians generally know what sells and what does not. It does not require a great stretch of the imagination to think that political leaders are highly aware of their electoral needs, even if they do not talk about them explicitly. Juicy quotes are not required to argue that electoral motivations are operative.[7]

There is little direct evidence that President Kennedy was motivated by electoral concerns in his response to the Cuban Missile Crisis. Indeed, it is an event that invoked the most fundamental concerns about national interest and even national survival. But the juxtaposition of that crisis and the 1962 Congressional elections allows analysts to jump to the natural conclusion that there was some connection between the two.[8] In this they are helped by the statements of some of Kennedy's close advisors about the domestic political dimensions of the crisis. Robert Kennedy, for example, believed that the voters would not wait for the 1964 presidential election to register their disapproval of a soft reaction to the placement of Soviet offensive weapons in Cuba. He says that his brother also believed that without firm action he would have been impeached.[9]

Another interesting example is provided by former national security advisor Zbigniew Brzezinski in his recollections of the Iranian hostage crisis. Brzezinski notes an observation of Chief of Staff Hamilton Jordan that if President Carter did not act firmly in the hostage crisis, he would not be reelected.[10] Brzezinski also recorded in his personal journal at the time an increasing sense of public pressure to take direct action against Iran.[11] Clearly, as is suggested by these two observations, domestic political concerns pervaded the reaction to the hostage crisis. But just a few pages after these observations, Brzezinski makes the following statement:

> There was never any explicit discussion of the relationship between what we might have to do in Iran and domestic politics; neither the President nor his political advisers ever discussed with me the question of whether one or another of our Iranian options would have a better or worse domestic political effect.[12]

The domestic political implications of the hostage crisis did not require explicit discussion. Indeed, despite Brzezinski's disavowals, one scholar has cited his memoirs as evidence of a strong domestic role in the response to the hostage crisis, stating that "President Carter perceived that using force in some way against Iran would raise his sagging popularity with the American public."[13]

Making explicit connections between the sacrifice of soldiers and impending electoral prospects has always been considered in bad taste, no matter how enthusiastic the public might be for war. It does not seem far-fetched to suppose that these kinds of trade-offs are contemplated implicitly, even if not a word is spoken explicitly. Those rare occasions when such calculations do slip into the historical record are probably just the visible tip of the iceberg of similarly undocumented phenomena.

It is difficult to imagine a leader making a public statement that war is either more or less imperative because of an impending election. All but the most foolish will be highly circumspect in this regard, even in private. As the Brzezinski example suggests, even their staffs are likely to be pretty careful. At the same time, politicians may be overly quick to paint their opponent's actions with the broad brush of electoral motivations. For example, when Senator Sam Nunn expressed reservations about sending additional American troops to Saudi Arabia in the months leading up to the Gulf War, Dick Cheney, the secretary of defense, attributed that reticence to Nunn's early posturing for a possible run for the presidency in 1992, even though there were many others both in and out of the administration who also believed sanctions should be given longer to work.[14] Thus, there may be two opposite contemporaneous descriptions of the relationship between impending elections and impending wars. Regardless of the underlying dynamics of national versus electoral interests, government leaders will downplay the role of electoral incentives, while opposition parties are likely to highlight that role.

This is not to argue that effective historical research is not possible. It is merely to suggest that it will be more difficult in this area than in many others. To reveal the national interest motivations of state leaders for getting involved in a war, there are probably memos, position papers, and the notes of cabinet meetings that cover the relative costs and benefits of getting involved in an international dispute. However, evidence of the connections between electoral motivations and wars will usually be more subtle and tangential. Conclusions are more likely to be based on inference and on imputed motivations, rather than on documentary evidence that lays bare the willingness of national leaders to risk the national interest for their electoral needs.

Evidential problems will make it more difficult to accurately assess the role of electoral pressures in the conflict behavior of democratic states. But even if those assessments seemed very solid, there would be a problem in generalizing from specific cases to the larger phenomenon at work because of the nature of electoral dynamics as a source of pressure on decision makers, rather than an absolute determinate of action. All things being equal, democratic states are less likely to seek out international conflicts when the public is in an isolationist mood and when elections are approaching. This is clearly not an argument that they cannot or never do so. There will be situations where either the domestic or international pressures are perceived as so severe that such a policy course is unavoidable. There will be leaders who do not evaluate the costs and benefits in this way. The dynamic I am describing is probabilistic rather than deterministic.

Since the dynamics of electoral pressures are just that, pressures, rather than absolute determinants, it will be difficult, except in the most extreme cases, to apportion the degree of influence for electoral factors when looking at individual cases. It would be easy to attribute any failures of the theory to countervailing pressures such as major conflicts of interest, irrational leaders, extreme constellations of public opinion, and the like.

An Empirical Test of Foreign-Policy Outcomes

Because of these evidential problems and the problem of drawing inferences from probabilistic phenomena, it will be useful to conduct a larger test of the effects of electoral politics on foreign policy through a consideration of the aggregate experience of a number of democratic states over time. While a consideration of individual cases is useful for understanding the causal dynamics that connect electoral behavior to war, an analysis of aggregate data allows assessment of the strength of democratic electoral pressures on foreign conflicts in an appropriately probabilistic sense. Of course, it may still be difficult to observe the electoral pressures at work because, even though real, they are too often overwhelmed by other pressures that cannot be controlled in the statistical analysis. But to the degree that these dynamics are observed over the noise of the many other significant pressures that work on states, confidence in the significance of electoral effects is increased.

As I suggested at the beginning of this chapter, the assessment of foreign-policy outcomes is a difficult task. The dominant approach to this problem is to look at international outcomes and then make assumptions about the kinds of policies that must have been involved. Wars, the primary subject of this study, are not an appropriate subject for this approach since war is sometimes caused by belligerent foreign policies, but at other times by overly conciliatory policies.[15] It is not reliable to reason backward from the incidence of war to the foreign policies of individual states.

One surrogate measure that comes conceptually closer to foreign-policy choices is looking at a wider range of disputes that involve the threat or use of military force. While, as with war, there is an interactive element to disputes, less serious disputes are more likely to reflect foreign policy. Disputes often arise because of the signals that states are trying to send about their foreign policy.[16] Thus, it makes sense to assume that belligerent states will get into more militarized disputes than conciliatory states. Militarized disputes are also useful because there are distinct differences in my hypotheses about the effect of electoral cycles on disputes in contrast to my hypotheses about the effect of electoral cycles on wars. I have argued that electoral incentives should lead democratic states to avoid wars in the electoral period. I have not, however, made this argument from the traditional populist perspective that democratic decision making should be inherently pacific. Democratic peoples are prone to belligerent foreign policy moods and war enthusiasm. The degree of belligerence in a state's foreign policy should be contingent on these moods.

In Chapter 1, I suggested that traditional views about the nature of public attitudes toward war could be divided between the naïve views that see public influence as either consistently pacific or consistently belligerent, and a set of more sophisticated views that recognize the changeability of public moods. Each of these was contrasted to the realist hypothesis that the behavior of states should be relatively independent of domestic influences. In Table 3, I offer a summary of the predictions of the realist view and of these three different views about public preferences for militarized disputes in the electoral period.

The naïve patricians who view the public as passionate and easily stirred to foreign adventures predict an increase in international disputes as elections draw near and the influence of the public increases. Naïve liberals expect elections to bring fewer disputes as the conciliatory influence of the public is more strongly felt in the electoral period. The more sophisticated views recognize

TABLE 3

Empirical Predictions for Militarized Disputes in the Electoral Period

View of public	Source of behavior	Electoral policy prediction	Disputes prediction
Naïve patrician	Electoral influence of popular jingoism	Belligerent	Increase in disputes
Naïve liberal (populism)	Electoral influence of popular pacifism	Conciliatory	Decrease in disputes
Sophisticated patrician	Electoral reflection of differing moods	Contingent on mood	Contingent on mood
Sophisticated liberal	Electoral reflection of differing moods	Contingent on mood	Contingent on mood
Realism	System-level incentives dominate domestic incentives	Appropriate to international system	No effect

that the public will vary in its mood. The foreign policy response to electoral pressures will be contingent on the public mood: more belligerent when the public is more belligerent and more conciliatory when the public is more conciliatory. Finally, while Waltz has insisted that realism is not a theory of foreign policy, he, and many other realists, have clearly used realism to generate both descriptive and prescriptive statements about foreign-policy behavior.[17] It seems reasonable to assert that the realist prediction would be no electorally induced changes in foreign policy because system-level effects should dominate domestic incentives.

THE DATA

The movement from qualitative conjecture to empirical analysis requires an acceptance of the inevitable imperfections of real world data. Three kinds of data are required for this project, each of which brings its own special problems into the analysis.

The determination of which countries are democratic is a difficult issue.

Philosophers and specialists in comparative politics have spent much time debating the meaning of the term "democracy" and the criteria for its measurement. Rather than introduce some new criteria that would surely ignite a new controversy, I have relied on the coding of liberal states provided by Michael Doyle in his work on democracy and war.[18] While this coding is controversial around the edges, it strikes me as reasonable in the main.[19] For this analysis it is important to maintain a balance between either too restrictive or too loose a definition. Too loose a definition would introduce a danger of confusing the dynamics of popular pressure in highly unstable political settings with the dynamics of constitutionally stable democratic politics. Too restrictive a definition would increase the possibility that the obtained results reflect idiosyncrasies of Western Europe and the United States rather than properties of democracies in general. Although, even with the fairly generous definition allowed by Doyle, stable democracy remains a largely Western phenomenon.

Working from Doyle's list of democracies, I assembled the election data from a number of sources.[20] There are several difficulties associated with even so apparently straightforward a task as this. In the first place, I have had to make judgments about which levels of elections are relevant to the war question. I have tried to use the election cycle for the governmental branch that is most central to foreign policy. This means, of course, the use of national, rather than local level elections. What is more controversial, in systems with a president, I have used elections to that office on the assumption that the president is the central actor in a state's foreign policy.

For data on disputes, I have relied on the Militarized Interstate Dispute Dataset collected by Gochman and Maoz and distributed by the Correlates of War Project and the Inter-University Consortium on Political and Social Research (ICPSR).[21] For each dispute, the starting and ending dates, the participants and the level of intensity for each participant are coded. There are five levels of intensity coded. Level-five disputes are international wars, as coded by Singer and Small.[22] Level-four disputes involve the use of force, but below the threshold of international war. Level-three disputes involve a show of force. Level-two disputes involve the threat of force. Level-one disputes involve "other" uses of force that are not codable in the above categories.

Figure 4 shows the distribution of all democratic disputes per year. Before turning to the analysis of these disputes, there is one more issue that needs to

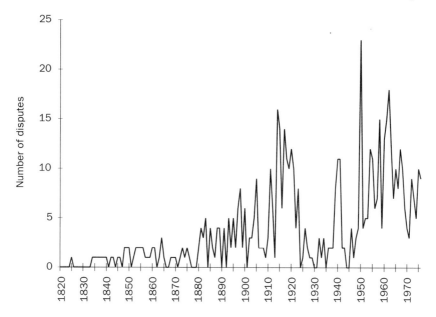

Figure 4. Disputes involving democratic states
SOURCE: Michael Doyle, Correlates of War Project

be addressed. Parliamentary electoral systems do not have fixed election dates. The primary relationship I am interested in here is the effect that elections have on the timing of disputes. If election dates are variable, there may be a concern that the causal relationship runs the other way, that disputes have an effect on the timing of elections. This is actually not such a problem here. In the first place, even if the relationship runs from disputes to elections rather than the other way around, it would not significantly change the dynamics I describe here. The populist view, for example, expects increased public influence to lead to fewer disputes as elections approach. By the same logic, with variable election dates they would expect leaders to avoid elections shortly after disputes. So, whichever way the causality goes, the implications for the nature and impact of public opinion remain the same. Moreover, as I will show presently, most electoral cycles are three to five years long. This makes them relatively close to the constitutional limits. At a minimum we can say that elections are not being called dramatically early in this dataset. I will return to these arguments in Chapter 6.

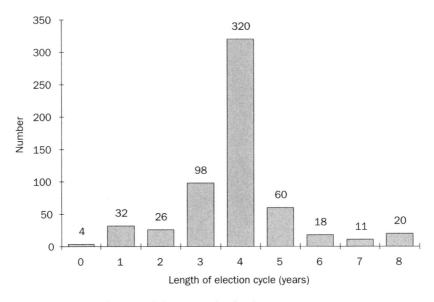

Figure 5. Distribution of election cycles for dispute cases

There are 589 dispute cases involving democracies for which electoral cycle data is available. The distribution of election cycle lengths for those disputes is shown in Figure 5. There are only four disputes within election cycles shorter than one year. The mean election cycle for the 589 dispute cases is 50 months. The median is 48 months.

My argument has focused on the dynamics of foreign policy in the period leading up to an election. Thus, an obvious starting point for this statistical analysis is to look at the distribution of disputes in the years leading up to elections in the democratic states. Figure 6 shows the militarized disputes that democratic states have been involved in, grouped by the number of years from the start of the dispute until the next election. The bar on the far right shows that there have been 159, out of a total of 571, democratic disputes entered in the last twelve months before an election. Democratic states have gotten into increasing numbers of disputes as elections draw closer. This certainly casts some doubt on the pacifying effect of increasing the public influence on foreign policy.

This result cannot, however, be counted as a robust confirmation of the realist view of an irrelevant public, nor of the views of the public as passionate

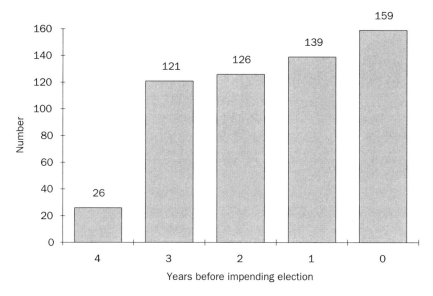

Figure 6. Democratic disputes by years before election

or protean. The moderately increasing number of disputes as elections approach in Figure 6 is to some degree an artifact of using absolute time to measure the electoral effect. Consider what would happen if a state had annual elections: any dispute would start within one year of an impending election. Likewise a very long election cycle would make even random events tend to be far from elections in absolute terms. In Figure 6, for example, the small number of disputes that start four to five years before an impending election is obviously a result of there being relatively few election cycles that last longer than five years. The United States, for example, with a rigid four-year election cycle, could never enter a dispute five years before an upcoming election.

Another angle on this problem can be gained by looking at the distribution of dispute starting dates relative to elections just past, as in Figure 7. This distribution suggests that the further the state gets from the previous election—and hence the closer to the next election—the less likely a dispute entry is. But, for all the same reasons, this can no more serve as confirmation of the populist view than Figure 6 could serve to support the other three views.

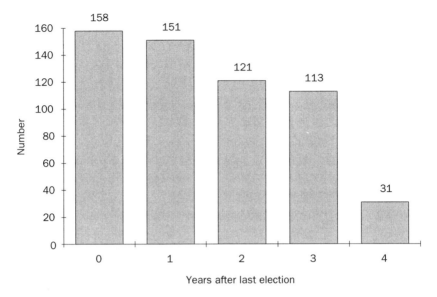

Figure 7. Democratic disputes by years after election

There are two ways to assess the significance of this time bias. The first is to look at the subset of disputes that occurred in more "normal" length election cycles. If we look, for example, at disputes in election cycles of between 36 and 60 months, we find a very even distribution across all the years as indicated in Figures 8 and 9.

A second way to compensate for this problem is to look at relative election cycles. The measure of relative election cycles is based on the percentage of the time between elections that has passed when a democratic state enters a militarized dispute. The use of relative election cycles has the added benefit of establishing a clear expectation about the distribution of disputes under the null hypothesis that there is no relationship between elections and disputes. If election cycles and dispute entries are independent, then there should be a uniform distribution of entries across the election cycle.

Figure 10 shows the distribution of dispute entries for all democratic states between 1816 and 1976, across quintiles of the election cycle. Although there is a slight drop in the number of disputes entered in the fifth quintile, this clearly does not reflect a systematic relationship between dispute entry and the electoral cycle at this level of analysis.

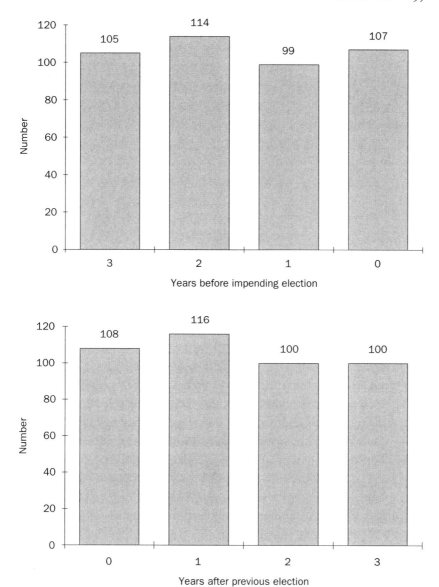

Figure 8. Disputes by years before election (election cycles between 36 and 60 months)

Figure 9. Disputes by years after election (election cycles between 36 and 60 months)

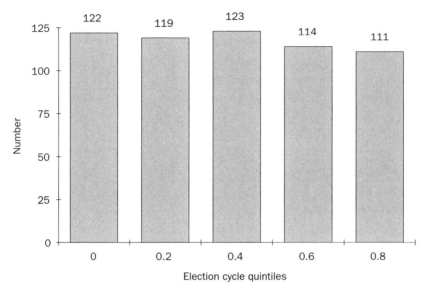

Figure 10. Disputes by election cycle quintile

This relationship, or rather the lack thereof, holds up for all five levels of disputes as coded in the Gochman-Maoz dataset. Figures 11 and 12 show the distribution of disputes across the quintiles for each level of violence. Figure 11 shows the number of disputes at each level in each electoral cycle quintile, while Figure 12 shows the percent of each level in each quintile. In Figure 12, a distribution of disputes that was independent of election cycles would be level at 20 percent all the way across. There is a slight drop in the number of fifth quintile disputes, but it is not nearly enough of a drop to be considered statistically significant. Eliminating the level-one disputes—militarized disputes without a codable military action—causes the fifth quintile to approach the very minimal .1 level of significance, but it hardly serves as evidence of a robust electoral cycle effect.[23]

The distribution of dispute entries across election cycles suggests that if there is an electoral cycle effect, it is not strong enough to overwhelm the other pressures in these simple tests. Over the entire period, the last quintile before an election looks only marginally different than the other quintiles. At first glance, this result would accord most strongly with the realist position that international conflict will be largely independent of internal electoral dynamics.

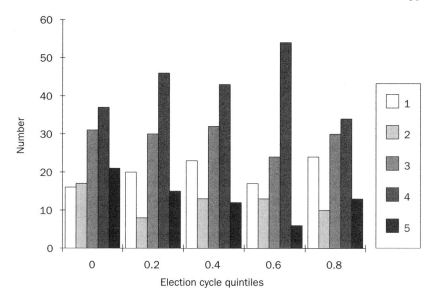

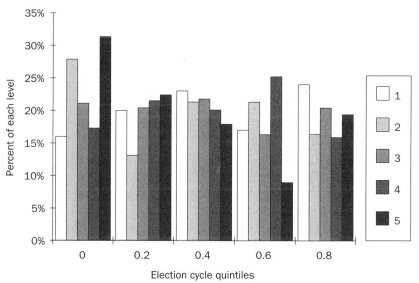

Figure 11. Disputes by level and election cycle quintile

Figure 12. Disputes by percent of each level and election cycle quintile

However, my argument has been that the belligerent or conciliatory nature of foreign policy will be at least partially contingent on public moods. This is a more difficult assertion to test, as moods might well vary over time and across different countries. A more belligerent foreign policy for some countries, or in one period of time, might be canceled out by more conciliatory policies in other countries or in other periods of time. The tests across the entire period do show that—contra the views of both those who see the public as consistently pacifist or consistently belligerent—there is not a consistent electoral effect. But testing across the entire period without some control for public mood is insufficient for distinguishing between the view that the electoral effect is contingent on public mood, and the realist view that there is no electoral effect at all.

There is no effective measure of public moods for this entire period, and it is unlikely that one could be efficiently constructed, given the difficulty of assessing public opinion in many of these countries during much of this period. One alternative is to look at a smaller period of time when public mood was consistent across the majority of the democracies. As I argued in Chapter 3, one such period is the years between the two world wars, when the public mood in all of the major democracies was consistently opposed to getting into foreign conflicts.

ELECTION CYCLES AND DISPUTES IN THE INTERWAR PERIOD: 1920–38

The public reaction to the slaughters of World War I was strong and uniform across the major democracies. As I suggested in the discussions of the previous chapters, isolationist, antiwar, and antimilitarist movements were particularly strong in Britain, France, the United States, and Canada. There are several angles from which to look at the interwar period. First, it is useful to consider the total number of disputes in this period. Figure 4 shows the total number of militarized disputes in which the democratic states were involved in each year. In looking at this chart, it is important to remember that the number of democracies has increased significantly over this period.[24] The small number of disputes at the beginning of the nineteenth century is obviously related to the small number of democracies. The large increases in disputes leading up to World War I and during the Cold War are also clear. The interwar period does

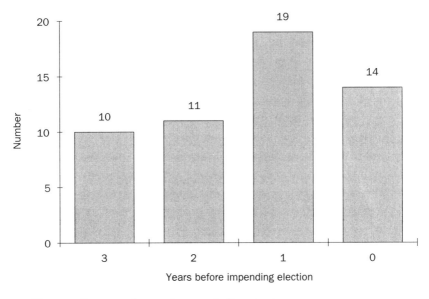

Figure 13. Interwar disputes by years before election

appear to be a time of generally reduced disputes, despite the international pressures associated with the increased militarism of Germany, Japan, and Italy, and the conflicts with the new Communist regime in the Soviet Union.

The reduced number of interwar disputes suggests a general effect of mood. It does not, however, adequately distinguish the role of democratic publics in the policy process. Independent of the public's views, democratic leaders also preferred avoiding disputes in this period. A return to the logic of electoral cycles provides a window into the relative influence of the public voice on interwar democratic foreign policies.[25]

Starting, again, with absolute time, the picture looks cloudy. Figure 13 shows the interwar dispute cases according to the number of years before an impending election.[26] There appears to be little to distinguish the interwar years from the rest of recent democratic experience. Democratic states were involved in a total of 56 disputes between 1920 and 1938, 54 of which occurred within four year of an upcoming election.[27] Fourteen of those disputes came within one year of an impending election. Unlike the pattern for the entire 1816–1976 period (Figures 6 and 8), there is a significant drop from nineteen disputes in the second to last year before an election to fourteen disputes in the last year be-

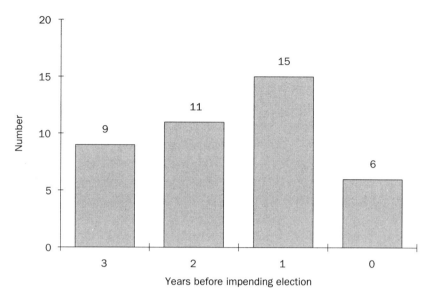

Figure 14. Interwar disputes by years before election (election cycles between 36 and 60 months)

fore an election. But, just looking at the fourteen disputes in the last year, this result is rather undistinguished. This is exactly how many would be expected (one quarter of the total) if elections and disputes were independent and all electoral cycles were exactly four years long.[28]

However, there are some important irregularities in the interwar electoral patterns. The median electoral cycle length during the interwar years is 47 months. This compares with a median electoral cycle length of just 28 months for the fourteen cases of dispute entry within one year of an impending election.[29] Indeed, six of these cases are from what the *Nation* called "a plague of annual elections,"[30] as Britain sorted out the shift from a Liberal to a Labour opposition between 1922 and 1924.

Looking at only the cases in which the election cycle was between 36 and 60 months (inclusive) reveals a much more distinctive pattern for the disputes that started within a year of an impending election. This result, just six disputes in the last year before an election, is significant at the .1 level.[31]

The rising number of disputes across the first three bars of Figure 14 is due to the larger number of possible cases in each subsequent bar, given the large

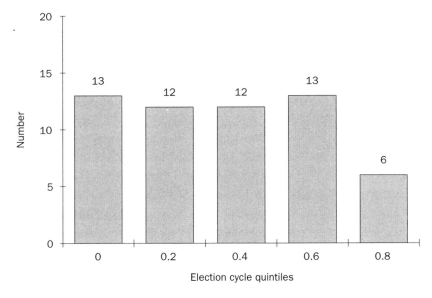

Figure 15. Interwar disputes by election cycle quintile

number of short election cycles in the interwar period. A turn to relative elec-toral cycles evens out the disputes further away from an impending election, but retains the same six cases in the final quintile. Figure 15 shows the distrib-ution of the interwar disputes across the election cycle quintiles. The six dis-putes between 1920 and 1938 that came in the last quintile before an election are roughly half of the number expected under the null hypothesis that elec-tion cycles and disputes should be independent.[32] It is also interesting to con-sider the breakdown of those disputes by level. Gochman and Maoz code no level-five disputes at all during this period, and none of the 24 level-four dis-putes started in the fifth quintile during the interwar years.

Conclusion

Looking at the entire 1816 to 1976 period proved inadequate for assessing the impact of public moods and elections on the conflict behavior of democratic states. However, I drew the strong conclusion from this whole period that the perspectives that view public influence as consistently pacific or belligerent

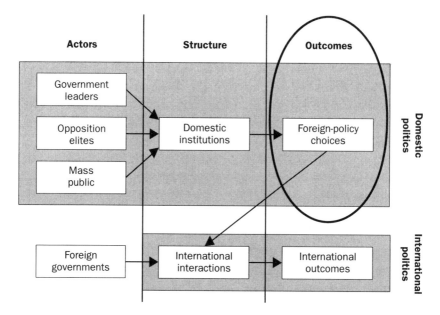

Figure 16. Foreign-policy choices in the two-level model

across time and countries are clearly inadequate. Restricting the analysis to the interwar period, when antiwar moods were common in all of the major democracies, did provide some evidence that public moods would be registered in the conflict behavior of democratic states in the electoral period. In this period an isolationist public mood can have a visible effect on democratic foreign policy that is magnified as elections approach.

Of course, there is another lesson of the interwar years. Goaded on by isolationist publics, and the still vivid memories of the Great War, democratic leaders avoided disputes throughout this period in general, and in the preelection periods in particular. But the bigger picture was the disastrous complacence in the face of fascist aggression.

I will return to the longer-run implications of the electoral cycle effect in the concluding chapter. Before turning to that issue, it is important to focus again on the two-level model of international relations repeated here as Figure 16. I began in Chapter 2 with the nature and preferences of the relevant domestic actors. In Chapter 3, I turned to the interaction of those actors through electoral institutions. In this chapter, I have completed my review of the domestic politics half of the model by turning to the effects of electoral politics on the foreign-policy choices of democratic states. The next step in the process is to move to the international level. This requires a consideration of some of the ways in which democratic electoral politics might interact with the foreign-policy preferences of opposing states. It is to that task that I now turn.

FIVE

Elections and War: The International Connection

[The Athenians] have a wide sea to cross with all their armament, which could with difficulty keep its order through so long a voyage, and would be easy for us to attack as it came on slowly and in small detachments. . . . confounded by so unexpected a circumstance, [the Athenians] would break up the expedition, especially as their most experienced general has, as I hear, taken the command against his will, and would grasp at the first excuse offered by any serious demonstration of ours.

—Hermocrates urging the citizens of Syracuse to take an aggressive stand
in resisting the Athenian attempt to conquer Sicily

In 415 BCE the Athenians set off from the safety of their harbors in Greece to attack Sicily. Word reached Sicily of the expedition, and Hermocrates counseled the Syracusan Assembly that a show of force by Syracuse would send the Athenians back across the Ionian Sea without a real war. Meanwhile, Thucydides tells us, Alcibiades had encouraged the Athenians to undertake the expedition with the argument that an overwhelming show of force could awe the Syracusans into surrender without any war at all.[1] Each side chose to attack because they doubted the resolve of the other. These strategies proved misguided for both sides. The war over Sicily occurred not because of the strategy of Athens alone, or of Syracuse, but because of the interaction of their two strategies. The Syracusans preferred a fight to subjugation. The Athenians preferred a fight to returning home empty-handed. If either side had decided otherwise, the Sicilian expedition would have been recorded in history as a one-sided Athenian intervention in Sicily or as a minor naval skirmish between the two powers.

In this chapter, I turn to the interaction of the foreign-policy effects of electoral politics in one state with the foreign-policy choices of other states. In this regard, the speech of Hermocrates before the Syracusan Assembly is interesting for two reasons. First, it highlights the critical point that international outcomes are the result of the foreign-policy choices of two or more states. But second, the speech of Hermocrates is notable because it suggests the interesting role that the basic transparency of democratic decision-making processes can have on international interactions. Despite the primitive communications of the fifth century BCE, Hermocrates was aware of Nicias's reluctance to lead the Sicilian expedition. The Syracusans developed their strategy based not only on the observed behavior of Athens, but also on their observations of the domestic politics behind that behavior.

Domestic Politics and International Outcomes

Individual states choose policies, but it is the interaction of those policies that leads to outcomes at the international level.[2] The failure to consider strategic interaction is a common error of both the critics and defenders of democratic foreign policies. As I argued in Chapter 1, those who fall to this error are rightly considered naïve. There is no automatic connection, for instance, between the belligerence of a state's foreign policy and the likelihood of war as the international outcome. The prominent examples of World War I and World War II suggest cases in which belligerence and appeasement, respectively, are widely viewed as having led to war.

A common interpretation of World War I attributes its outbreak to a spiral of bluster and mobilization.[3] The lessons learned in World War I, however, led to confusion about whether belligerence or appeasement was the appropriate strategy in the interwar years. An alternative interpretation holds that the Germans wanted a continental war as long as the British stayed out. In this interpretation it was the failure of the British to adequately signal their willingness to intervene on the Continent that contributed significantly to the outbreak of the war.[4]

World War II is often attributed to the inability of the democratic states to take a firm line vis-à-vis the expansionary aims of Hitler and the Nazis. Nonetheless, even after the outbreak of war, and even after Pearl Harbor, many isolationists continued to believe that it was Roosevelt's aggressive policies, and the failure to follow their more conciliatory approach, that led to the war. One senator described the mood of the isolationists in Congress in the weeks after Pearl Harbor in these terms: "So far as this writer has noticed, no isolationist leader has publicly, or even privately, admitted he or she was in error, and plenty of them privately argue that the interventionist policy was responsible for Japan's attack."[5]

A. J. P. Taylor agrees with the more popular perspective that a more resolute response to Hitler's early actions would have stemmed his expansionist ambitions. But Taylor clouds the coercion/conciliation issue even further by arguing that it was the vacillation between the two approaches that brought on the war. In the introduction to his famous explication of the causes of the Second World War, he ties this problem to the very nature of democratic states: "The general moral of this book, so far as it has one, is that Great Britain and France dithered between resistance and appeasement, and so helped to make war more likely. American policy did much the same. . . . It is very hard for a democracy to make up its mind; and when it does so, it often makes it up wrong."[6]

The lack of a theoretical consensus on the causes of conflict affects our thinking about the relationship between elections and wars. Most directly, it serves to reemphasize the importance of analyzing the interaction of different states' foreign policies in thinking through the effects of democratic electoral politics on international outcomes.

As was shown by the Peloponnesian War, democratic electoral politics have two paths of influence on the foreign policy preferences of other states. These are illustrated in Figure 17.

In the first path, electoral dynamics change the external behavior of the democratic state, which in turn changes the interests and incentives of the opponent state. International dynamics may lead a state to act in a more belligerent or more conciliatory manner, and this behavior will, in turn, affect the behaviors of other states. The decision of the Athenian Assembly to send an expedition to Sicily changed the international environment for Syracuse, and thus required a behavioral response on their part. The causal weight in this path is one step removed from electoral dynamics, since the system can be described simply in terms of the external behaviors of the two states. The information that is added to the system by looking inside the democratic state contributes to an understanding of the sources of foreign policy.

The second path is for other states to look *inside* the democratic state and

Path 1:

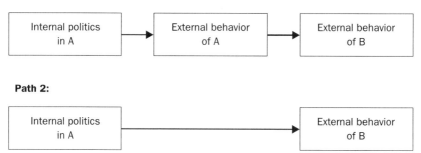

Path 2:

Figure 17. Two paths of influence for domestic politics

to change their behaviors based directly on the electoral developments within the democratic state. The observation of Hermocrates that the Athenians might be easily deterred because of Nicias's reservations is an example of this kind of influence. This path is particularly interesting for this study because it suggests a more direct relationship between electoral dynamics and international outcomes.

THE TRANSPARENT NATURE OF DEMOCRATIC POLITICS

The key to understanding the relationship between the internal politics of democratic states and the behaviors of other states is to appreciate the transparent nature of democratic states.[7] A basic characteristic of democratic states is a high degree of internal communication. Open political competition requires a relatively free flow of political information within the state. This flow of information is necessary for the activity of politicians and voters; but it also creates a situation in which other states can expropriate this information for relatively little cost. Unlike much of the normal foreign-policy decision-making process, electoral procedures are easily and directly observable from the outside. It does not take great networks of spies and analysts to observe the basic nature of democratic campaigns. Any foreign consular officer can provide interpretations of the electoral dynamics simply by reading the newspapers. Of course, these foreign observers may be no more accurate in interpreting the electoral dynamics than the legions of domestic pundits who so often flounder in their attempts to read the implications of polls and popularity indices. But they still will be likely to draw conclusions about the implications of electoral outcomes for their own interests.

One stark form of evidence of the attention that foreign governments pay to democratic politics in other states can be found in their attempts to shape that process. This is most clear in the case of the subtle and not-so-subtle efforts of the Germans to influence the American election of 1940 and to undermine Churchill in the British election of 1935. But even the Filipino insurgents in 1900 recognized the potential benefits of influencing the electoral process in the United States.[8] When the stakes are high, foreign leaders pay attention to democratic electoral dynamics. They demonstrate preferences for, or aversions to, specific candidates or parties.

For the purposes of the present discussion, there are three key effects to consider regarding this democratic electoral transparency, each of which works to reduce the likelihood of war in the electoral period. First, there is the ability of outside states to discount the bluster of democratic leaders, based on the observation of the internal political role of such rhetoric. Second, there are the effects of observed constraints within democratic states on the dynamics of international negotiations and interactions. Third, there are distinctive effects of democratic electoral politics on the ability of democratic states to make clear policy commitments. Each of these deserves more careful discussion.

THE MITIGATION OF THREATS

The internal incentives for belligerent threats that I have discussed in the preceding chapters may be observed by the targets of those threats. Some percentage of campaign trail threats will be seen as intended for a domestic audience in the light of imminent electoral pressures. Thus, the impact of those threats will be less than would be expected in the absence of such discounting. This is not to say that belligerent electoral rhetoric will not increase international mistrust of the democratic state, but other states will expect some degree of return to the status quo ante after the electoral period ends.[9] In his 1988 primary battle against the right wing of the Republican Party, George Bush felt compelled to take a more belligerent foreign-policy line than he would have preferred. He tried to mitigate the effects of this rhetoric outside of the domestic arena by telling Soviet president Mikhail Gorbachev that President

Reagan was surrounded by "marginal intellectual thugs" who would try to portray Bush as a closet liberal. He assured Gorbachev that once he was elected he would work to improve U.S.-Soviet relations. In the meantime, he urged Gorbachev to ignore the many things he might have to do and say to get elected. Gorbachev later recalled this discussion as the most important talk he ever had with George Bush.[10]

THE NEGOTIATING ENVIRONMENT

A more complex phenomenon that results from outside observation of the electoral process within democratic states is a systematic change in the dynamics of international negotiation. Democratic regimes are distinctive because of the relative strength of domestic audiences in the policy process. Democratic leaders must negotiate both in the international arena with other states and in the domestic arena with various internal interests.

Of course all states face some level of internal constraints, but democratic constraints are particularly visible from the outside. The visible domestic constraints of the electoral process may give democratic leaders a distinct advantage in international negotiations. Schelling sets out the basic logic for this situation in his argument that a constrained actor—one whose options are visibly limited—has a negotiating advantage.[11] When other states in the international arena know that a state is constrained by domestic factors, their level of aspirations for the resolution of a given situation may be lowered. Lower aspirations could lead to a greater willingness to make concessions.[12] This dynamic is addressed in the work of Robert Putnam, who identifies it as a basic characteristic of two-level games. States with visibly constraining domestic politics can give less away at the negotiating table.[13] Because of the transparency of democratic states and the starkly political nature of electoral contests, elections may constrain democratic states in a way that is particularly effective at the international level.[14]

Democratic leaders facing an international issue of low electoral salience can try to make the issue more salient, and hope for a rally effect combined with the risky negotiating advantages of a high-salience issue, as discussed previously. Or they can opt to keep the issue's salience low by making greater concessions and thus avoid a high-visibility escalation. A democratic leader running on an "I-kept-the-peace" platform might be willing to make a wider range of concessions to keep the lid on potential international conflicts. Again, as I suggested in Chapter 3, the danger in this approach is that of making too many concessions and being labeled a peace-at-any-price candidate.

ELECTIONS AND COMMITMENT

A third effect of electoral dynamics in the international/national nexus involves the ability of democratic leaders to make credible commitments in the preelection period. Commitment is a critical concept in international relations. It means much more than just the ability of a state to enter into an effective agreement. Commitment is the basic ability of states to stake out a course of action and then stick to it. As Schelling and others have argued, significant gains can be made by states that are able credibly to commit to a course of action.[15] The basic intuition for this is the fact that there are some actions that, taken by themselves, would appear irrational, but may be useful for inducing other actors to take beneficial actions. The American attempt to extend nuclear deterrence to Western Europe is a good example of this phenomenon. The Soviet Union could be deterred from an attack on Europe if the United States could credibly convince the Soviets that it would retaliate with nuclear weapons for such an attack. Many Europeans worried, however, that it would be irrational for the United States to risk a nuclear attack for the sake of Europe. The problem for the United States, then, was sending a strong enough signal that it would take this seemingly irrational action to deter the other side from testing the commitment. The solution in this case was for the United States to station trip wire troops in Germany that would ensure that a significant number of Americans would be killed in any Soviet attack on Western Europe.

The ability of democratic states to make effective commitments is a matter of some controversy, not unlike the basic controversy surrounding the relationship between democracy and peace.[16] The traditional dictate of structural realism is that internal organization is largely irrelevant to the external behavior of states.[17] How states make commitments, in this view, is based on the demands of the distribution of power in the anarchic international system. In this vision, there is little room for different behaviors to arise systematically from variations in domestic regimes. All states will have trouble making commitments because the system is anarchic, but the incentives for keeping or breaking commitments will be no different for democratic or nondemocratic regimes.

On the other hand, there is a very long tradition of skepticism about the ability of democracies to pick a course of action and stick with it. Thucydides writes of the "inconstant commons" and suggests a belief among the Athenian oligarchs that unreliability was a basic hallmark of democratic government. Machiavelli attributes this view to "all writers" and "all historians."[18] Tocqueville's oft-quoted observation that "In the control of society's foreign affairs democratic governments do appear decidedly inferior to others," is bolstered with his claim that a democratic government tends "to obey its feelings rather than its calculations and to abandon a long-matured plan to satisfy a momentary passion."[19]

Recent work in economics has shed new light on the relationship between social organization and the ability of states to make commitments to domestic audiences. Two particularly interesting examples of this literature are North and Weingast's interpretation of the Glorious Revolution as an exercise in recasting a constitution in order to increase the ability of the state to make commitments, and Sargent and Velde's similar interpretation of the French Revolution.[20] These authors argue that democratic institutions can increase the ability of the state to make commitments to large numbers of domestic actors.

The increased ability to make commitments domestically may have a significant effect on the ability of democratic states to make international commitments. Outsiders can observe linkages between commitments made to them and to the domestic audience. When a democratic leader makes a public commitment to a specific course of action, deviation from that course might bring domestic as well as international repercussions. When President Bush vowed that the Iraqi invasion of Kuwait would not stand, the Iraqis should have known that that vow would bear on the president's domestic standing as well as on the international situation.

This linkage is represented formally in James Fearon's work on the role of costly signals in international interactions.[21] When democratic leaders send signals in the international arena that bear domestic costs at home, those signals will have more credibility than would similar signals that bore no significant domestic costs. All states face some domestic costs for their international actions, but democratic states may be distinctive in the degree of domestic accountability. The critical aspect of democracies in this regard is that these domestic costs can be observed from the outside because of the nature of information institutions in democratic states.

The link between the external and internal commitment processes is strengthened in the electoral period. Of course, this goes against both the logic that Machiavelli attributed to "all writers" regarding democratic instability, and against the common view of campaign rhetoric as a particularly unreliable vessel for communicating the intentions of the state. In fact, at least until the election, highly salient campaign promises are particularly costly signals for state action. An incumbent running for reelection who makes a promise not to raise taxes is extremely unlikely to do so in the period just before the election. Once the election is over, such a promise may not be worth very much, but for the electoral period itself it has very high credibility.[22] So too, a democratic leader can make relatively more effective deterrent threats in the electoral period, because those threats have a domestic audience cost.[23] Implicit and explicit stands taken in the electoral period have high short-run credibility. Opponent states will not want to test whether or not a candidate is bluffing until after the election, since in the electoral period the domestic audience effects tie the candidate's domestic credibility to his or her international credibility. During the electoral period, campaign rhetoric functions as a costly signal.[24]

FOREIGN ATTEMPTS TO INFLUENCE ELECTIONS

A final mechanism for electoral dynamics to change the incentives of foreign states is suggested by the possibility that the behaviors of foreign states may have a direct effect on democratic electoral outcomes. Foreign actors can change their behavior in the hope of influencing the opinion environment within the democratic state and thus of having an impact on the election. This often happens unwittingly, but it can also reflect conscious attempts at manipulation by foreign powers.

John Adams warned in his inaugural address of the danger democracies face from the attempt by outsiders to influence electoral dynamics:

> In the midst of these pleasing ideas, we should be unfaithful to ourselves if we should ever lose sight of the danger to our liberties if anything partial or extraneous should infect the purity of our free, fair, virtuous, and independent elections. . . . If that solitary suffrage can be obtained by foreign nations by flattery or menaces, by fraud or violence, by terror, intrigue, or venality,

the Government may not be the choice of the American people, but of foreign nations.[25]

In an electoral environment, the adversary state that acts in a clearly belligerent or escalatory manner runs a strong risk of aiding the political fortunes of the most belligerent political forces in the democratic state. Astute adversaries will recognize the advantages of adopting a more conciliatory policy that may help the less belligerent political party take power. In those cases where escalation would aid the more belligerent domestic forces and where there is no significant advantage to early escalation, there is an incentive for adversary states to avoid escalating disputes during the election season.

The transparency of democratic states allows outside actors to observe electoral dynamics and to form preferences regarding democratic electoral outcomes. In times of high international tension, these preferences will be particularly intense. Moreover, it is during these same times that foreign policy is the most salient in the electoral process, and thus it is at these times that foreign attempts at influence have the greatest impact.

The most dramatic example of all of these effects was the relationship between Germany and the interwar elections in the United States and Britain. Even the relatively small foreign-policy difference between Willkie and Roosevelt was of concern to both Hitler and Churchill. Although he did not have much effect, Hitler tried to slow Mussolini down to avoid exacerbating the role of the European war in the American election of 1940.

The interactive element in international outcomes is demonstrated in two final cases: Britain in the Falklands/Malvinas War and the United States in the Gulf War. Both of these conflicts echo with the dynamics of Athens' Sicilian expedition with the attendant questions raised by Hermocrates about the willingness of states to commit large military forces at great distances. Both of these final cases also demonstrate the continuing relevance of the electoral incentive in the democratic politics of war and peace.

Britain and the Falklands/Malvinas War

Sovereignty over the small group of islands—known as the Falklands in Britain, but as the Malvinas in Argentina—that lie 300 miles east of the southern tip of Argentina has been in dispute since the late eighteenth century. British domination of the seas for most of the nineteenth century had allowed Britain to assert effective sovereignty during most of this period, but Argentina had never dropped its claim to ownership. In the late 1970s, negotiations between Britain and Argentina over the status of the islands were proceeding, but were not moving at a sufficient pace to convince the Argentines that they would regain the islands any time soon.

The islands themselves are of little value, but with changes in the law of the sea that give states much larger zones of littoral control, their economic potential has grown significantly—especially for Argentina, which is close enough to them to exploit them commercially. Indeed, by the early 1970s the British cabinet had largely decided that a withdrawal from the islands was necessary.[26] The difficulties they had implementing that decision point to a more important aspect of the islands, which was their nationalist significance to both states. For the British, they were one of the few vestiges of the naval empire that peaked after World War I. The population of less than 2,000 was rabidly British and reluctant to be disconnected from their homeland. The impasse for British policy came because nationalists and lobbyists for the islands forced the government to accord primacy on the sovereignty issue to the wishes of the islanders. For Argentina, the islands symbolize the country's international weakness; national resentment had been building for many years.

In 1982, the authoritarian regime of General Leopoldo Galtieri was in serious trouble. Dissension in the different branches of the Argentine military and an increasingly restive population led the generals to gamble on an attempt to oust the British.[27] The British garrisoned only a single platoon of Royal Marines on the islands, so the takeover on April 2, 1982, was not militarily difficult. The Argentines did not believe that the British would respond.[28]

In Britain, Margaret Thatcher, the Conservative prime minister, was also facing problems. Thatcher had taken office in May 1979. By May 1980, the British economy had entered the worst recession since the 1930s. Under Conservative government, both inflation and unemployment had doubled.[29] Fortunately for the Conservatives, the Labour Party was in complete disarray due to the internal power of its extreme left wing. In 1981 the Social Democrats broke off from Labour to form a new middle-of-the-road party. By 1982 when the Argentines decided to strike, inflation and economic growth were starting to look a little better, but unemployment was still at peak levels. Dissatisfaction with the Conservative government was running two to one over satisfaction.[30]

Meanwhile, the British had also been scaling back their military forces. The British military was being reoriented with a narrower focus on the central NATO theater and with decreasing capabilities for distant conflicts.[31] The government commitment to an honorable withdrawal from the Falklands was significantly weakened by Thatcher's accession to office. She strongly opposed a transfer of sovereignty, but was unable to propose a feasible alternative and was unwilling to make the large expenditures that would have been required for credible military protection of the islands.[32] With this less than enthusiastic endorsement, Nicholas Ridley, the responsible foreign office minister, reported to Parliament that a lease-back was one of the options being considered. The Parliamentary response was vociferous and ill-informed. The Labour Party called the proposal "shameful," and asked why the Foreign Office could not simply "leave the matter alone?"[33] A senior Conservative Party member opined that "It is almost always a great mistake to get rid of real estate for nothing" and compared the potential loss of the Falklands to the surrender of the Persian Gulf. Although they had no viable alternative, the cabinet was unwilling to make a commitment to the proposal in the face of such Parliamentary hostility. Without leadership, British Falklands policy was adrift.

In a July 1981 memo, Ridley warned that "If Argentina concluded, possibly by early 1982, that the government [was] unable or unwilling to negotiate seriously, retaliatory action must be expected." Lord Carrington, the foreign secretary, rejected Ridley's memo, not on the grounds that it was inaccurate, but because it would be "counter-productive" to attempt to persuade his fellow cabinet members to accept it.[34] The Foreign Office continued to try to develop contingency plans and alternative approaches to the Falklands situation, but from January 1981 on was unable to motivate a formal cabinet meeting on the issue.[35] The only significant cabinet level discussion concerned the removal of the ice-patrol ship HMS *Endurance* from its regular deployments to the South Atlantic. The Ministry of Defense decided to end the *Endurance* patrols as an economy measure in their 1981 Defense Review. The foreign secretary objected, given the clear evidence that the Argentines viewed this as a withdrawal of the British commitment to protect the islands, but Thatcher sided with Defense.

In February 1982, the Argentine Junta demanded a new round of talks with a clear deadline for resolving the issue. At the same time, the tempo of the dispute increased with repeated controversies about various Argentine overflights and incursions onto the island of South Georgia. By late March, the situation finally provoked the cabinet to action, and on March 25, a meeting of the Defense and Overseas Policy Committee was set for the following week. Thus, there was no coordinated cabinet response, even as clear evidence arrived that an Argentine invasion force was at sea.[36] On April 1, 1982, Argentine forces landed on the islands and quickly established control.

Contrary to Argentine expectations, Britain immediately decided to send almost all of its available naval and marine forces to regain the islands. In the emergency Parliamentary session on April 3, Thatcher publicly committed the British to reversing the Argentine action: "It is the Government's objective to see that the Islands are freed from occupation and are returned to British administration at the earliest possible moment."[37] Since so little effective planning for this contingency had taken place in the months leading up to the crisis, the decision to send military force was taken with little appreciation for either its likely financial or human costs. The month it would take to assemble the force and have it sail to the South Atlantic would allow time both for invasion planning and for last-minute negotiations.[38] But the approach of the Antarctic winter and the operational difficulties of maintaining a large force 3,500 miles from the nearest available port also meant that there was no alternative to full-scale use of force when the ships arrived in mid-May. The inability to maintain military forces on station without complete control of the islands also meant that once the fighting began there could be no cease-fire without a complete Argentine withdrawal.[39]

A solid majority in the public rallied to the government, with 60 percent indicating their satisfaction with the way the crisis was being handled, and only 30 percent dissatisfied in an April 14 poll. But the fragility of this support was indicated by the fact that only 44 percent thought that regaining British sovereignty over the Falklands was worth the death of British soldiers. Forty-nine percent were explicitly opposed to sacrificing British lives for the Falklands. At the other end of the spectrum, 28 percent of the respondents favored extending the conflict with direct attacks on the Argentine mainland.[40]

As predicted by the rally theory, public support did increase further as hostilities opened. In a May 5 poll, 72 percent of respondents favored landing troops in the Falklands, although only 53 percent were willing to accept casualties. After British forces landed on May 21, the percentage of respondents favoring this action increased to 89 percent, with 62 percent willing to accept some loss of life.

The Falklands actions also enjoyed broad support in Parliament from both

sides of the aisle. The Labour Party officially supported the government's policy. Opposition leader Michael Foot expressed strong support for military action: "The rights and circumstances of the people of the Falkland Islands must
be uppermost in our minds. . . . It is a question of people who wish to be associated with this country and who have built their whole lives on [that] basis. We have a moral duty, a political duty, and every other duty to ensure that
that is sustained."[41]

But here again the depth of that support had to be considered. Just as the
public opinion polls suggest, there was serious danger of a loss of support in the
event that military operations went awry. Thatcher herself worried about how
long she could hold the pro-war consensus together.[42] An effort by several important Labour members to disassociate the Labour Party from the government
policy only narrowly failed in the Party's National Executive Committee. Tony
Benn, a left-wing Labour leader, called the military policy "an ill-thought-out
enterprise" and advised "that the task force should be withdrawn."[43] The Labour Party's support for the government was made explicitly contingent on "the
maximum use of the United Nations, the exercise of military restraint, and a
genuine search for a peaceful agreement."[44] It was well understood that the
government's electoral fortunes depended on restoring British sovereignty over
the Falklands without a military disaster.[45]

The sagging political fortunes of Margaret Thatcher and the Conservative
Party were dramatically reversed by the Falklands success. Thatcher's approval
rating went from 31 percent before the war to 51 percent at the end of the war.[46]
Buoyed by her newfound popularity and image of resolute strength, Thatcher
called for new elections the following June. This was less than a year after the
Falklands war and a year before elections would have been constitutionally
mandated. Had the election been held in March of 1982, before the conflict,
Gallup polls indicate that the Conservatives would have finished third behind
the Social Democrat/Liberal Alliance and the Labour Party. By the end of the
war they were well ahead of both of those parties.[47] In the 1983 election, the
Conservatives enjoyed the largest majority of both votes and seats since their
defeat of Labour in the 1935 election.[48] The Conservatives did not make the
Falklands an explicit part of the campaign, but their messages about Thatcher's
leadership and the restoration of British self-respect were not subtle.[49]

Although a military and political success, the Falklands War was a policy
failure. Once Argentina attacked, British prestige and national honor, as well

as international principles concerning the use of force, were at stake. Prior to April 1, 1983, however, Britain's material interests in the Falkland Islands were minimal. I doubt any British politician would have assessed them as worth the 236 British servicemen killed or the 2 billion pounds spent.[50] The Thatcher government allowed an obvious foreign-policy problem to languish in a leadership vacuum because it could not see a politically palatable way to deal with the problem. Domestic political concerns in Britain created the environment that gave the Argentine generals an opportunity to pursue the Malvinas strategy in an effort to bolster their own domestic support.

Of course, the Argentine military's attempt to exploit this situation proved an even more consequential miscalculation. Like Hermocrates in Syracuse, they hoped the enemy would not have the will to fight so far from home. This mistake brought about their fall and accelerated Argentina's return to democracy.

For Margaret Thatcher and the British government, the political and material risks of war were clearly present in the Falklands crisis. The Argentines in the South Atlantic and the Labour Party at home were both prepared to step in and take advantage if the policies of the British government faltered. Given these risks, British decision making probably was not dominated by electoral concerns, although the outcome of the conflict significantly changed the political fortunes of Thatcher and the Conservative Party.

Eight years after the Falklands returned to British control, a case with many similar dynamics played out for the United States and President George Bush in the Iraqi invasion of Kuwait. The electoral outcomes in the two cases, however, are quite distinct.

The United States and the Gulf War

In the early morning of August 2, 1990, Iraq sent 120,000 troops into Kuwait. Within 24 hours, Kuwait, taken completely by surprise and with just 16,000 soldiers to defend it, was overwhelmed.

President George Bush had been elected in 1988 with a solid majority of 54 percent of the popular vote. He was a president with substantial foreign-policy experience. In addition to his two terms as vice president, he had served as the director of the CIA, as the top American diplomat in China, and as ambassador to the United Nations. He had also been a decorated aviator in World War II. Nonetheless, in the early days of his administration he was dogged by accusations of being a "wimp" who was unwilling to stand up for American interests abroad.[51] Bush's political freedom of action was further limited by the Congress, which had Democratic Party majorities in both houses.

Concerns about Bush's leadership were matched by worries about the state of the American public. After the trauma of the Vietnam War, the public mood in America was clearly wary about the use of military force abroad. The essence of what came to be called "the Vietnam Syndrome" was well reflected in the statement of President Ronald Reagan's secretary of defense, Caspar Weinberger, that the use of force abroad would require "clearly definable objectives" that would have "the support of the American people and their elected representatives in Congress."[52] From 1975, when the United States withdrew from Vietnam, until 1990, the United States assiduously avoided prolonged military conflict. Nonetheless, on August 5, President George Bush stood on the White House Lawn and said of Iraq's invasion: "This will not stand."[53]

While the Bush administration was quick to determine that the Iraqi invasion of Kuwait had to be reversed, it took a little longer to come up with a rationale that would work with the American public. In an August 15 speech at the Defense Department, Bush said that "our jobs, our way of life, our own freedom, and the freedom of friendly countries around the world would all suffer if control of the world's great oil reserves fell into the hands of that one man, Saddam Hussein."[54] Bob Dole, the senate minority leader, echoed this theme saying that America was in the Gulf for only one reason—"O-I-L."[55] Although unwilling to cut back on their use of it, the American public was noticeably reserved about sending American troops into harm's way for the sake of oil. "No Blood for Oil" was a popular slogan of the antiwar forces.[56] By the middle of October, Bush had moved to a concern about Iraqi nuclear and chemical weapons programs and to the theme of stopping aggression: "The fight isn't about oil; the fight is about naked aggression."[57] Bush made almost daily comparisons between Saddam Hussein and Adolf Hitler.[58] This theme proved more popular with the public.[59]

The immediate reaction to the Iraqi invasion of Kuwait had been to send 200,000 troops to deter any further Iraqi moves toward Saudi Arabia. On November 8, the Bush administration announced that it would add another 200,000 soldiers to the forces in the Gulf in order to be sure that there was an

offensive option. As in the British decision to send the task force to the South
Atlantic, the massive American deployment to the Gulf had the effect of nar-
rowing the policy options and setting the time frame for conflict. General
Schwartzkopf stated that if the alternative was fighting a war, the troops could
sit in the desert for a long time; however, it would again prove difficult to
maintain operational readiness with a long wait in the desert.

Sam Nunn, the respected Democratic chair of the Senate Armed Services
Committee, announced that the Senate would hold hearings on Gulf policy.
The hearings featured a line-up of former senior military officers who urged
giving sanctions more time to work.

While generally supportive of the Bush policy, the public was still not entirely convinced. Public opinion currents were complex and shifting, with significant differences in responses to relatively small changes in the kinds of
questions that were asked.[60] Moreover, support for war in the Gulf was highly
contingent on expected casualty rates. In public opinion polls shortly before the
war, a hypothetical figure of 1,000 casualties could cut support for the war in
half. With 10,000 casualties only a third would still support the use of force.[61]

Once again, democratic transparency enters into this story. Both the Iraqis
and the Kuwaitis paid attention to American domestic politics. Kuwaiti money
paid for a public relations firm to burnish the image of this small, undemocra-
tic oil state run largely for the benefit of a few large, super-rich families. Hill
and Knowlton, a prominent public relations firm, provided media advice to
"Citizens for a Free Kuwait," which was financed by Kuwait's exiled emir.
Craig Fuller, the head of Hill and Knowlton's Washington office, had been
chief of staff to then Vice President George Bush and had organized the Republican Convention at which Bush had been nominated for the presidency.
At one point, Fuller described the connection between the Kuwaiti needs and
the goals of the White House: "Getting [the Kuwaitis'] message across was
completely in line with the goals of the Bush administration. By helping the
Kuwaiti citizens, it was clear we would be helping the Bush administration."[62]
Hill and Knowlton hired the Wirthlin Group—which also had strong White
House connections from the Reagan days—to take daily polls to keep both
the Kuwaitis and the White House abreast of American attitudes toward the
Gulf crisis.[63]

Saddam Hussein also paid attention to the American home front. His
plans were based on expectations of a lack of American resolve. This was not

an expectation that Bush himself was personally irresolute, but that the American public and political system could not sustain a distant and costly conflict. "Yours is a society that cannot accept 10,000 dead in one battle," he explained to the American ambassador, April Glaspie, shortly before his attack on Kuwait.[64]

The Iraqis made several largely clumsy attempts to control American images of the conflict. After the air war started, several Allied prisoners of war were paraded before television cameras and gave leaden testimony about the evil of the war.[65] A purported baby formula factory that had been bombed was provided with a "Baby Formula Factory" sign in English for the benefit of CNN's many viewers who did not read Arabic.[66] Ultimately, Saddam Hussein and the Iraqis proved inept at either influencing or reading American opinion.

The Kuwait crisis came to a head at the midpoint of the American presidential election cycle. The policy issue was framed as a choice between going to war immediately or waiting to see if trade sanctions would work before choosing war. There were, no doubt, many strategic considerations behind the administration's desire to go to war in late 1990, rather than wait for sanctions to work. In particular, there were concerns that with time Kuwait would be completely absorbed into Iraq and that Iraq would be able to continue making effective preparations for war despite the harsh sanctions.[67] Nonetheless, it is plausible that electoral concerns played an important role in the timing of that conflict. American policy makers expected the war to be very expensive. The cost was certain to be in the tens of billions of dollars, and it was anticipated that American casualties could run as high as 20,000.[68] The administration had to be aware of the potential electoral costs of giving sanctions twelve to eighteen months to work—as the former chairman of the Joint Chiefs of Staff, Admiral Crowe, recommended in his testimony before Nunn's Foreign Affairs Committee.[69] Indeed, there was concern among some Republicans that a long period of sanctions, with American troops sweltering in the desert, would allow popular resentment of the policy to grow and would give the Democrats a long period in which to snipe at administration policy.[70] Moreover, if sanctions failed to work after that time, President Bush would have been faced with the unpalatable choice of starting a war in the height of the electoral season or of running for reelection with the substantive issue of the Iraqi occupation of Kuwait still unresolved despite his pledge that Iraqi aggression would not be allowed to stand. The administration's choice to enter the war sooner rather than later was a gamble on gaining a strong policy success to outweigh the potentially very high costs of the war.

Somewhat reluctantly, the Bush administration went to Congress to get approval for the use of force just days before the air war was to begin. Congressional support was obtained, but the vote—largely along party lines—was hardly overwhelming. In the Senate the resolution passed with a slim 52 to 47 margin, while it received a 250 to 183 vote in the House. The votes of members in the House were closely aligned with public opinion in their districts.[71]

Of course, in hindsight, the war was considerably less costly in terms of American lives than most analysts had predicted. The land war ended after just 100 hours, with remarkably few American casualties. Like Thatcher's after the Falklands War, the president's approval ratings shot up dramatically on the basis of this success. And like Thatcher in the Falklands, Bush had faced substantial political risks if the war had gone poorly. Most of the Democrats in Congress were on record as voting against the war. A large antiwar movement was mobilized among college students and peace groups. The press was largely supportive of American policy,[72] but several significant decisions were made not to run stories that were critical of American policy or of the military.[73] It is easy to imagine that if the war had dragged on these kinds of stories would have made their way to the front pages.

Unfortunately for George Bush, by the time the 1992 election rolled around, his exceptional postwar approval ratings had already waned. Although he tried to make foreign policy a central facet of the campaign, by November of 1992 the president's significant foreign-policy accomplishments—managing the end of the Cold War and the Gulf War—were no longer foremost in the minds of most voters. Ironically, the timing of actions that may have been taken early in the election cycle to avoid the electoral risks of a potentially costly war reduced the opportunity for the president to take advantage of the electoral benefits of a successful war. Bush lost an election in which the dour economy dominated the agenda.

Conclusions

Analysis of the relationship between domestic and international affairs requires moving beyond the internal examination of foreign-policy choices. State poli-

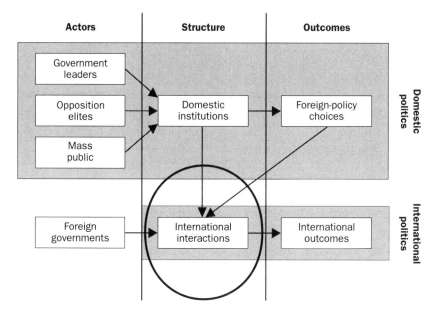

Figure 18. Domestic politics and international interactions in the two-level model

cies interact with the choices of other states in the international system. Whether belligerent or conciliatory foreign policies will lead to war depends on the international environment in which such policies are pursued. Even more directly, the transparency of democratic states can lead to a connection between democratic politics within the state and the policy choices of other states. The electoral dynamics within the democratic state may send signals that affect the policy choices of other states. The two-level model with which I have been working needs to be modified, then, to take into consideration this additional direct link between international and domestic political processes. This linkage is illustrated in Figure 18, which more generally shows the progress of this analysis into the realm of international politics.

Hermocrates was right about Nicias's reluctance to lead the Athenian conquest of Sicily. At the first sign of resistance to the Athenian plans, Nicias urged a hasty retreat back to Athens.[74] But Hermocrates had not followed the debates closely enough to see that Alcibiades and another aggressive general, Lamachus, also had an important say in the tactical decision making. Both states pressed forward with their plans, and the result was war. With more careful attention to the public debates on both sides, this conflict might have been avoided.

In ancient Athens, elections were often about war. In the modern era, elections are about leadership. Because of this, leaders can send strong signals during the electoral period. The result of this dynamic is evident in a broader empirical consideration of the experience of democratic states over the past two centuries. It is to such a consideration that I now turn.

International Outcomes

[The Athenians] were beaten at all points and altogether; all that they suffered was great; they were destroyed, as the saying is, with a total destruction, their fleet, their army—everything was destroyed, and few out of many returned home.

When the news was brought to Athens, for a long while they disbelieved even the most respectable of the soldiers who had themselves escaped from the scene of action and clearly reported the matter, a destruction so complete not being thought credible. When the conviction was forced upon them, they were angry with the orators who had joined in promoting the expedition, just as if they had not themselves voted it, and were enraged also with the reciters of oracles and soothsayers, and all other omenmongers of the time who had encouraged them to hope that they should conquer Sicily.

—Thucydides' description of the result of the Sicilian Expedition

and the reaction in Athens

The Athenian expedition to conquer Sicily did not go according to plan. The outcome of the decision making by Athens and the Sicilian city of Syracuse was a war that proved thoroughly disastrous for Athens. By 413 BCE the Athenian military was in a shambles. The reluctant general Nicias—whose whole life, according to Thucydides, "had been regulated with strict attention to virtue"[1]—had been captured and executed. Meanwhile, the Athenians had arrested Alcibiades on a morals charge. He escaped to Sparta, where, in the Spartan style, he took cold baths, cut his hair, became devoted to athletic exercise,[2] and turned his rhetorical talents to convincing the Spartans to attack Athens.[3]

Nicias had been right in his assessment that the peace between Athens and Sparta was too fragile to support a massive expedition to Sicily that would

TABLE 4

Empirical Predictions for Wars in the Electoral Period

Viewpoint	Causal mechanism	Foreign-policy prediction	Disputes prediction	View of international environment	Wars prediction
Realism	System level incentives dominate domestic incentives	Determined by demands of the international system	No effect	Sophisticated	No effect
Naïve patrician	Popular jingoism	Belligerent	Increase in disputes	Naïve	Increase in wars
Sophisticated patrician	Domestic inducements to deviate from optimal policy	Contingent on mood	Contingent on mood	Sophisticated	Increase in wars
Naïve liberalism (populism)	Popular pacifism	Conciliatory	Decrease in disputes	Naïve	Decrease in wars
Sophisticated liberalism	Temptations to pander, but limited by elite opposition	Contingent on mood	Contingent on mood	Sophisticated	Decrease in wars

leave Athens vulnerable at home. Spurred on by Alcibiades, the Spartans took advantage of the Athenian decision to send their forces abroad. The result was a crushing defeat of Athens both at the hands of the Syracusans in Sicily and the Spartans at home.

As I have argued, the institutions and preferences that have characterized more contemporary democracies should make them less vulnerable to the seductions of electorally motivated demagogues. This dynamic is matched by incentives for foreign states also to avoid war with democratic states in the electoral period. In this chapter, I turn to a more rigorous effort to assess the evidence for these dynamics. I present the essential facts of the relationship between the timing of war entries and the timing of elections in the experience of all the democratic states in the past two centuries.

In Table 2, I presented a summary of five basic viewpoints on the relationship between electoral dynamics and international conflict behavior. I repeat that chart here as Table 4, with the addition of the results on militarized disputes as discussed in Chapter 4.

In Chapter 2, I demonstrated the weakness of the populist view that democratic publics would always be a constraint on belligerent foreign policy. The pre–World War II cases in Chapter 3 showed the weakness of the naïve patrician view that democratic publics would be easily swept up into international military adventures. The examination of militarized disputes in Chapter 4 demonstrated that the increased influence of the public in the preelectoral period did not make states consistently more or less belligerent. Electoral foreign policy is contingent on the public mood, as demonstrated by the interwar period. The final two perspectives to be evaluated are the sophisticated patrician and the sophisticated liberal views.

Both of these perspectives take into account the interaction of democratic foreign-policy behaviors with the policy choices of other states. They differ in their expectations about the ultimate effects of that interaction. For the sophisticated patrician, electorally motivated deviations from optimal policies should lead to more wars. In the sophisticated liberal view, the transparency of democratic processes, and the ability of democratic leaders to make firm commitments should help insulate democratic states from the excesses of electoral politics. Democratic states should enter fewer wars as elections approach. The purpose of this chapter is to test these assertions. Before turning to a more detailed explication of the empirical results, a few words need to be said about the data I use for these tests.

THE DATA

As in Chapter 4, this analysis is based on Doyle's coding of democracy,[4] and on my own collection of electoral data. For data on international wars and their various participants and degrees of severity, I have relied on the Wages of War dataset from the Inter-University Consortium on Political and Social Research (ICPSR).[5] While this dataset is not completely free from controversy, its basic acceptance is widespread.[6] For each participant, disputes are coded for entry and exit dates, for the number of battle deaths, and for several other measures of involvement and severity. Where the exact day of war entry is missing, I have used the fifteenth of the month.

One difficulty in the elections dataset arises from interrupted election cycles. Most prominent in this regard are the European democracies overrun by Germany in World War II. For the tests that examine the whole election cycle, and thus require a beginning election and an ending election, I have had to remove these cases. I have included them in the tests that require only a previous election.

As with the disputes, there are also problems in the variation of election cycle lengths. The length of election cycles in the cases examined has varied from seven months for France between the 1945 and 1946 elections bracketing entry into their Indochinese imbroglio, to nine years and nine months for the Italian election cycle from 1861 to 1870 in which the Seven Weeks War was imbedded.[7] I have compensated for this problem again by looking at relative as well as absolute election cycles.

To summarize, the Wages of War dataset includes 76 instances of democracies being militarily involved in wars between 1815 and 1980.[8] I have been able to collect adequate election data for 74 of these.[9] In the tests that require a beginning and ending election, five cases are omitted because they involve states that were overrun by the Germans in World War II, and thus had their election cycles truncated.[10]

The remaining 69 cases cover the involvement of seventeen different democratic states in 45 wars from the first British-Afghan War in 1838 until the Yom Kippur War in 1973. Of these cases 23 involved fewer than 1,000 battle deaths for the democratic state, while 46 involved more. Twenty-six cases involved participation in a war that lasted for less than one year, while 43 lasted for longer than one year. Thirteen of the cases are coded as losses for the democracy, while there are 45 wins and eleven ties. (Ten of the ties represent the various U.N. participants in the Korean war; the other tie is the Israeli-Egyptian war of attrition in 1969–70.) In 52 of the cases the nondemocracy is coded as the initiator, while there are seventeen cases in which the democratic side is coded as having initiated the war. Twenty-two of the cases begin in the nineteenth century, while the remainder are twentieth-century conflicts.

ELECTIONS AND DEMOCRATIC WAR INITIATION

The appropriate place to begin this analysis is with a consideration of the
seventeen cases in which war is coded as having been initiated by a democratic state. Presumably, these are the cases in which the democratic states
would have had more freedom to directly choose the starting date of a war.
Seventeen is an insufficient number of cases for much statistical analysis.
Nonetheless, there are several interesting descriptive aspects of these cases.
Table 5 lists the democratic initiation cases in terms of the relative election
cycles. Each grouping represents one quintile of the election cycle. Thus,
there are three cases in the first quintile, four in the second, four in the third,
three in the fourth, and three in the fifth. Clearly, the distribution of war initiation dates relative to the election cycle gives us no basis for rejecting the
null hypothesis that war initiation is independent of the election cycle. But
it is notable that the only initiations in the final quintile are the British initiation of the Anglo-Persian War, at a cost of 500 battle deaths, and the British
and American participation in the suppression of the Boxer Rebellion, at 21
and 34 battle deaths, respectively. There have been no serious wars initiated
by a democratic state in the final year before an election. There is a substantial difference between the mean of 185 battle deaths for wars entered in the
last quintile and the mean of 6,766 battle deaths for wars in the first four
quintiles.[11]

A more detailed analysis of the war entry patterns of democratic states relative to their election cycles will require an increase in the number of cases to
be analyzed. There are three good reasons to expand the data to include *all*
cases of war entry, rather than just the cases of war initiation.

First, in most wars, the identification of the initiator has proven a difficult
feat.[12] Singer and Small, in coding for initiators in the Wages of War dataset,
have made a judgment about the state that initiated military action. But in
many cases there is plenty of blame to apportion among all the participants. Israel, for example, is coded as the initiator of the 1967 War, although it is widely
agreed that Israel's attack on June 5, 1967, was a preemptive action in the face
of an imminent attack from Egypt, Jordan, Syria, and Iraq. Similarly, the
Boers are coded as the initiators of the Boer War, yet that initiation came on
the heels of a significant British troop buildup on the border of the Cape
Colony, and a British move to cut off all discussions with the Boers. Many

TABLE 5

Wars with Democratic States Coded as Initiators

Country	War	War Type[a]	Mo	Year	Deaths	Cycle[b]	Entry Ratio
France	Roman Republic	S	6	1849	300	34	.02
U.S.	Vietnamese	S	2	1965	56,000	47	.07
India	Bangladesh	S	12	1971	8,000	71	.12
Lebanon	Palestine	S	5	1948	500	46	.25
Israel	Sinai	S	10	1956	200	47	.32
U.S.	Spanish-American	S	4	1898	5,000	47	.37
U.S.	Mexican-American	S	5	1846	11,000	47	.38
Israel	Six Day	S	6	1967	1,000	47	.40
Greece	Greco-Turkish	S	2	1897	600	45	.48
France	Boxer Rebellion	S	6	1900	24	47	.52
Italy	Italo-Turkish	S	9	1911	6,000	55	.55
India	Hyderabad	I	9	1948	1,000	49	.67
India	Second Kashmir	S	8	1965	3,000	60	.68
France	Sino-French	S	8	1884	2,100	49	.72
U.K.	Anglo-Persian	S	10	1856	500	56	.90
U.S.	Boxer Rebellion	S	6	1900	21	47	.90
U.K.	Boxer Rebellion	S	6	1900	34	62	.94

SOURCE: Michael Doyle, Correlates of War Project; see Appendixes A and B

[a] War Type: S=interstate war, I=imperial war

[b] Length of the election cycle bracketing war entry, in months

states will choose the advantages of a preemptive attack when they believe there is a high probability of attack by the opponent.[13]

A second reason for expanding this analysis to include *all* the cases of democratic war entry comes from the argument about strategic interaction in Chapter 5. Wars occur only when *both* sides decide that war is preferable to the available alternatives.[14] Sometimes, of course, the available alternatives are sufficiently horrible that this does not look like much of a choice. Still, for most cases there are policy choices at any point in time that make war more or less likely. Thus, it is not at all implausible that if, for example, democratic leaders wanted to avoid starting a war in the face of an impending election, they would also be eager to avoid becoming the *target* of an attack in such a period. The more a democratic state wants to avoid a war that an adversary wishes to start, the more effort it may expend in seeking out other alternatives. If these efforts result in a decrease in the relative merits of war for the adversary, then the probability of an ensuing war will decrease.

This logic may be easier to see in thinking about the reverse situation: behaviors that *increase* the relative merits of war for an adversary. Consider the extreme case of Iran after the overthrow of the shah. It is not hard to imagine that the probability of war would increase if, like the leadership of revolutionary Iran, state leaders embarked on a course of making belligerent speeches encouraging revolution in neighboring countries, nationalizing foreign-owned properties, and detaining foreign nationals, while simultaneously dismantling their own military forces and denouncing their allies. Since vulnerability to attack is a continuum, there will almost always be policies available to states that, consciously or unconsciously, either increase or decrease the probability of war.

The Wages of War initiation coding is based on which side fired the first shots. But the timing of those shots will often be determined by the sequence of actions taken by both sides. It is obviously reasonable to code Japan as an initiator of World War II in the attack on Pearl Harbor. It is not, however, unreasonable to think that American actions contributed significantly to the fact that that attack came in December 1941.[15] Similarly, we might view it as suspicious that no democratic state is ever coded as the initiator of a colonial war. It is not farfetched to presume that the administrative policies of the colonial power—the pace of negotiations over independence, the imposition of particularly odious rules, crackdowns on nationalist forces, and the like—may have much to do with the start of those conflicts, even if it has always been the subject peoples who have fired the first shot.

Finally, it is reasonable to expand the data to all cases of war entry because of my argument that there may be a direct link between the internal politics of democratic states and the behavior of other states. The transparency of democratic states allows other states to observe the workings of the electoral process and to form preferences for action based on those observations. The timing of war initiations by the nondemocratic states may, therefore, be directly influenced by democratic electoral politics.

Thus, for both empirical and theoretical reasons, I propose to expand the analysis from a description of the cases of democratic war initiation to a broader analysis of all the cases of democratic war entry. The use of the larger universe of about 70 cases will make possible the employment of more rigorous statistical analysis. The introduction of some cases in which the actions of the democratic state could have little or no influence on the timing of the nondemocratic initiator will weaken the analysis, but strengthen the conclusions. Any results that stand out above the noise of the high-compulsion cases will be all the more noteworthy.

WARS AND IMPENDING ELECTIONS

The starting point for an examination of the relationship between elections and all democratic war entries is a consideration of the distribution of wars entered relative to impending election dates. Figure 19 offers an initial picture of this relationship. On the horizontal axis are the number of years prior to an election that a war was entered. The vertical axis is simply the number of wars that have been entered by the democracies in each period. The distribution is well behaved, but hardly overwhelming. As with the disputes data, the smaller number of war entries more than four years before an election should be discounted to the degree that it is a function of the decrease in the number of electoral cycles that are sufficiently long to allow five- and six-year lags between war entry and an election. For example, the United States, with a rigid four-year election cycle, could never have a five-year gap between war entry and an election.

Figure 19 shows that the democracies have entered fewer wars in the last year before an election than in the second, third, or fourth years before an election. This is consistent with a view that elections and the cycle of state-social power makes a difference in the behavior of democratic states. But statistically, this distribution is not sufficiently skewed to allow the rejection of the hypothesis that the amount of time until an election is irrelevant to war entry patterns.[16]

The picture becomes clearer when considering election cycles in terms of relative rather than absolute time, as in Figure 20. Here, again, the cases are grouped according to the percentage of the electoral cycle that has passed at the time of the war entry. In this picture, the last quintile of the election cycle

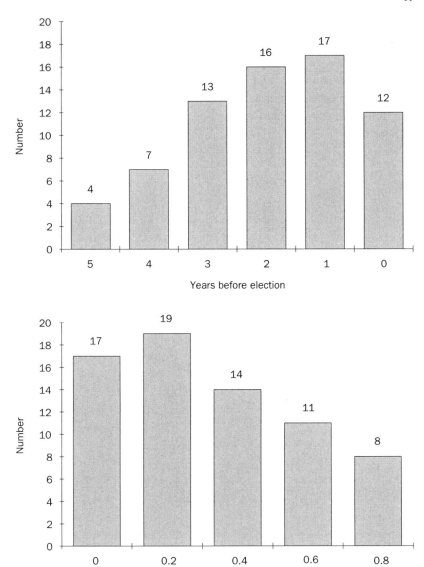

Figure 19. War entries in years before an election

Figure 20. War entries in election cycle quintiles

(the last vertical bar in the figure) begins to gain some statistical as well as visual distinction from the rest of the election cycle. A random distribution of war entries relative to the election cycle should put about fourteen of the 69 wars in the last quintile with the remaining 55 in the first four quintiles. Instead, the numbers are eight and 61 respectively. There is less than a 5 percent probability that this observed distribution would have occurred by chance if war entry and election cycles were statistically independent.[17]

As with the initiation cases, the relationship between war entry and impending elections becomes even more focused when the more serious conflicts are isolated. Figures 21 and 22 show the distribution of war entries for wars in which the democratic state suffered 1,000 battle deaths or more. The distribution of war entries over both the absolute and the relative election cycles becomes significantly more skewed, with decreased war entries in the period immediately preceding elections. Between 1815 and 1980, there were only four serious wars that were entered by any democratic state in the year immediately preceding an election. These four cases were Israel in the Yom Kippur War, Britain in the Boer War, Canada in World War II, and France beginning the struggle against Vietnamese independence following World War II. In Figure 21, these four cases of war entry in the last year prior to an election are represented in the vertical bar on the far right. This period was statistically indiscernible from the other periods when all the cases were included, but it becomes significantly different from the rest of the election cycle when considering only the more serious wars.[18]

The effect is similar when the relative election cycle picture is restricted to the more serious wars. Three of the four cases show up in the final quintile of the election cycle. French entry into the Indochina struggle after World War II drops out because it occurred in the first quintile of the very short seven-month cycle between the postwar election of December 1945, and the subsequent election in June 1946. In Figure 22, the vertical bar on the far right represents the last quintile of the election cycle. When relative election cycles are used, the difference between the last quintile before an election and the other four quintiles increases its statistical significance from the 95 percent level for all wars to the 99 percent level for the serious wars.[19]

One thousand battle deaths is a somewhat arbitrary measure of the seriousness of a war. For example, given the differences in populations, 1,000 battle deaths obviously means a lot more for Israel than it does for the United

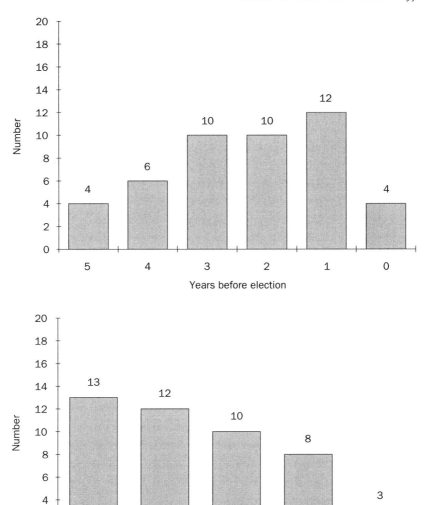

Figure 21. Serious war entries in years before an election

Figure 22. Serious war entries in election cycle quintiles

TABLE 6

Battle Deaths in Wars Entered in
the Last Quintile of the Election Cycle

Country	War	Battle Deaths
U.S.	Boxer Rebellion	21
U.K.	Boxer Rebellion	34
France	Korean War	290
Israel	Israeli-Egyptian	368
U.K.	Anglo-Persian	500
Israel	Yom Kippur War	3,000
U.K.	Boer War	22,000
Canada	World War II	39,300

SOURCE: Michael Doyle, Correlates of War Project;
see Appendixes A and B

States.[20] But, the results presented here are relatively insensitive to the number of battle deaths used as a measure of seriousness. In the total data set there are eight cases of war in the last quintile of the election cycle. The number of battle deaths for these eight cases are presented in Table 6.

As can be seen in Table 6, the basic result—the paucity of serious wars in the final quintile before an election—would change by only one case, for any threshold for a serious war between 500 and 22,000 battle deaths—though surely no one would argue that the 1973 Yom Kippur war was not a very serious war for the Israelis.[21]

Democratic leaders facing imminent elections appear to have been more careful about entering wars that have subsequently involved more battle deaths than in entering wars that have subsequently involved fewer battle deaths. This is, of course, a post hoc measure and can be considered only a secondary indicator of leaders' perceptions of the probable seriousness of the war prior to war entry. It is much more common to err on the side of expecting a war to be small, than to mistakenly predict it will be large.[22] This would make it reasonable to assume that wars that turn out to be small were expected to be small.

More particularly, it seems unlikely that any of the eight wars entered in the last quintile (Table 6) were entered with the expectation that they would be on a different side of the seriousness salient.

One potential difficulty in the data for impending elections is that the majority of observations are for parliamentary systems that do not have fixed election dates. It is plausible that the relationships observed here are an artifact of democracies avoiding elections after the outbreak of war, rather than of avoiding wars in the face of impending elections. Of course, there is a limited degree to which elections can be put off given statutory limits on how long states can go between elections. And, as I discussed with the disputes data, even if avoiding elections were widespread, there would still be something important suggested here about the relationship between domestic politics and international relations for democracies. At a minimum, these findings suggest that getting into wars is not a popular electoral strategy—politicians do not rush to call elections in the flush of popularity and social solidarity that is often assumed to follow war entry.

There are two indicators that gauge the severity of the parliamentary problem. First, are those cases in which election cycles, either through custom or constitution, are highly regularized. The two countries in the dataset that have constitutionally defined cycles are the United States and the Philippines. At least two authors have already noted the propensity of the United States to avoid wars in the second half of the presidential term.[23] In the ten cases involving one of these two countries there is only one observation that falls in the final year before an election: U.S. participation in the suppression of the Boxer Rebellion at the cost of 21 battle deaths.

There are two countries in the dataset that, although parliamentary, have entered wars in periods with highly regularized election cycles. Elections in New Zealand fell quite regularly in a three-year pattern during the period when the National Party enjoyed comfortable electoral margins. The exception to this regularity is the cycle that brackets entry into World War II, which stretched to five years. Still, New Zealand was only one year into its electoral cycle when it entered the war, so even if it had continued the three-year pattern it still would not have been a case of war entry with an impending election. Israel, which had a quite regular four-year cycle during the period of Labor dominance from 1948 until 1974, presents a bigger problem, since two of its four wars have come in the last year before an election. The War of Attrition is coded as having started just seven months before the 1969 election. The Yom Kippur War started with the Egyptian-Syrian surprise attack on October 6, 1973, when elections were already scheduled for October 31 of that year.[24]

A second indicator of the influence of parliamentary systems on these results is to look at the other side of the electoral cycle: the gap between the previous election and war entry. Presumably, elections become more likely as the state gets further from the previous election. War entries that come in the early years of the cycle would be events in which an election was not expected soon. Of the 42 cases in which war entry came more than two years before an election, there is only one case in which war entry came more than four years after a previous election (Italy in the Seven Weeks War), and there are only three cases in which war entry came more than three years after a previous election.[25] Indeed, there are only five cases out of these 42 in which the previous election was more than two years prior to war entry.[26] Thus, it does not look likely that there are many cases in which a democratic state may have entered a war at a time when an election would have been expected soon if it had not been for the war.

WAR AND ELECTIONS JUST PAST

In general, it should be useful to consider more carefully the other end of the electoral cycle: the relationship between war entry and elections just past. Just as there are fewer wars entered in the final periods of the electoral cycle, there are more wars entered in the first periods of the cycle. Figure 23 shows the number of wars entered in one-year periods after elections in democratic states between 1815 and 1980. It is important to remember, again, that in looking at absolute time there is a problem of a decaying number of cases as the number of years increase. Still, if the number of wars entered in the first two years is compared with the number entered in the third and fourth years, as against the null hypothesis that there should be an equal number in both two-year periods, there is a difference that is statistically significant at well above the 99 percent level.[27] In Figure 23 this can be seen by comparing the two leftmost

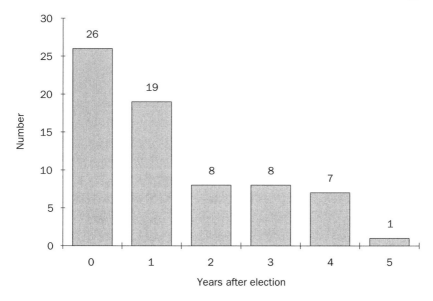

Figure 23. War entries by years after election

vertical bars—the two years right after an election—with the next two vertical bars—the third and fourth year after an election.

The same phenomenon remains clear when the problem of different electoral cycle lengths is controlled by looking at relative election cycles. In this case, the difference between the first two quintiles and the last three quintiles of the election cycle remains statistically significant at above the 99 percent level.[28] Graphically, Figure 20 provides this picture since the relative election cycles include both the preelection and postelection periods. In Figure 20, the postelection effect is observable in the comparison between the first two vertical bars—the postelection period—and the last three bars.

As with the preelection phenomenon, the distribution is more skewed for the more serious wars than for the less serious wars. The dates of entry for the seventeen wars that resulted in fewer than 500 battle deaths for the democratic state are only slightly skewed in favor of the postelection period. Figure 24 again uses 1,000 battle deaths for the democratic state as the threshold of serious war. It shows the number of serious wars entered by the democratic states in each year after an election. Again, comparing the first two vertical bars with the second two shows a substantial difference in the number of serious wars

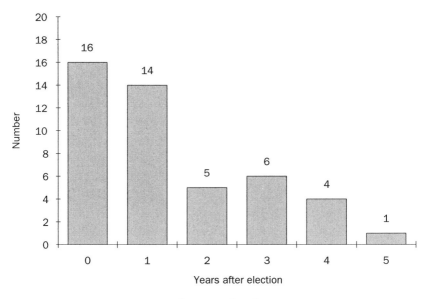

Figure 24. Serious war entries by years after election

entered.[29] The effect in terms of relative cycles can be seen in Figure 22 by comparing the first two vertical bars with the last three vertical bars. As with the preelection effect, the results are quite robust relative to different definitions of seriousness. The entry pattern for "more serious" wars is more skewed than the entry pattern for "less serious wars" for any threshold of seriousness below 20,000 battle deaths.

THE NONINITIATION CASES

I began this analysis with a descriptive consideration of the seventeen democratic initiation cases. Now that I have shown the more general results for all the cases, it is appropriate to finish with a closer look at the 52 noninitiation cases. The initiation measure is problematic, as I have argued. But to the degree that the initiation measure is legitimate, the noninitiation cases lend support to the proposition that democratic electoral politics have a direct effect on the behavior of opponent states.

For the 52 noninitiation cases, both the postelection and preelection effects

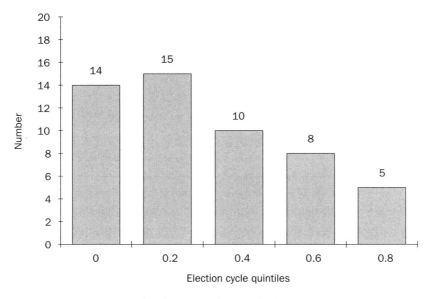

Figure 25. War entries by election cycle quintile (noninitiation cases)

hold strong. Figure 25 shows the distribution of war entries against relative election cycles for the democratic states when they have not been coded as the initiators of violence. The relative paucity of wars in the period preceding an election can again be seen by comparing the last vertical bar—the last quintile of the election cycle—with the other four bars. This comparison yields a difference that is statistically significant at the 95 percent level.[30] The relatively higher number of wars that start in the period shortly after an election can be seen by comparing the first two vertical bars—the first two quintiles of the election cycle—with the last three bars. There is less than one chance in 100 that this difference would occur if electoral cycles and war entries were statistically independent.[31]

Figure 26 shows the noninitiation cases for the wars in which the democratic side suffered 1,000 battle deaths or more. The preelection effect, in the last vertical bar, and the postelection effect, in the first two vertical bars, both remain clear, although the statistical significance of the results declines slightly.[32]

In the postelection period, democracies not only are more likely to start wars, but are more likely to be the targets of others' aggressive aims. Even more

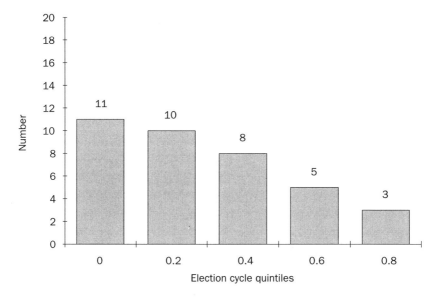

Figure 26. Serious war entries by election cycle quintile (noninitiation cases)

surprising, in the preelection period, democratic states seem not only to resist the international pressures to start wars, but also somehow defuse the international pressures that would lead others to start wars against them.

Conclusions

All states face the problem of dealing simultaneously with internal and external pressures. The possibility considered in these pages is that electoral cycle variations in the relative power of internal and external pressures faced by democratic states will be apparent in their international conflict behavior. The empirical findings presented here suggest that there is an electoral cycle effect on the war entry patterns of democratic states. In the past 200 years, democratic states have entered significantly more wars in the early stages of their electoral cycles and significantly fewer wars in the later stages.

To be sure, these findings are based on aggregate statistics over a relatively small number of cases that bring together the theoretical problems of three different kinds of data—data about wars, data about political systems, and data about elections. Still, the fact that there are any interpretable results at all has to be viewed as important. Even a staunch liberal could offer several reasons that the relationship between election cycles and war entry at the aggregate level might not be observed, *even if* democratic electoral politics do discourage entry into wars. From a perspective that incorporates some of the realists' concerns it is even easier. For instance:

These results obtain despite extreme international pressures. The timing of wars is surely often a function of events independent of electoral cycles. A certain number of Hitlers and Napoleons, of great transitions of power, of opportunistic surprise attacks, and even of the historians' "horseshoe nail" events will occur on their own timetables with little reference to the internal events of that minority of states that have democratic forms of government.

These results obtain despite alliance commitments that constrain a state's war entry decisions. It could hardly be the case that in choosing June 25, 1950, to cross the 38th parallel, North Korea consulted the election timetables of the ten democracies that responded to the U.N. call. Indeed, that single event contributes three of the cases of minor war entry within one year of an impending election. Even if bilateral disputes escalate on an electoral calendar, the aggregate cyclical effect will be washed out to the degree that alliance commitments determine the timing of war entries.

These results obtain despite the waves of jingoism and militarism that infect democracies on occasion. There are times when democratic publics have been whipped into a militaristic frenzy. To the degree that there are times of high popularity for embarking on military expeditions, the traditional wisdom would have predicted more wars entered close to elections.

Similarly, these results obtain despite the fact that a third of the cases predate World War I. John Mueller argues that before the slaughters that began in August 1914, war was quite popular in the public imagination.[33] If Mueller is right, and if publics have more power before elections, then politicians would have been more tempted by war opportunities as elections approached in that era. Comparing the nineteenth and twentieth centuries, the distributions of war entries are statistically indistinguishable. In terms of raw numbers, the nineteenth century is actually slightly more skewed than the twentieth with two out of 22 war entries in the last quintile before an election, compared to six out of 47 in the last quintile for the twentieth century.

Finally, these results obtain despite a weak definition of democracy. Italy's

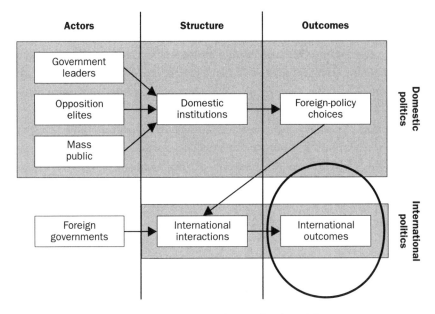

Figure 27. International outcomes in the two-level model

2 percent franchise in the 1860s can be considered democratic in only a highly context-dependent sense. Many of the cases occur in domestic situations where public influence on foreign policy appears minimal at best. In the mid-nineteenth century, John Bright complained that in England, "When you come to our foreign policy, you are no longer Englishmen, you are no longer free; you are recommended not to inquire. If you do you are told you cannot understand it; you are snubbed, you are hustled aside. We are told that the matter is too deep for common understandings like ours."[34] Indeed, in Britain between 1835 and 1874—a period that accounts for seven of the 69 cases examined here—every cabinet that was defeated fell in the House of Commons rather than at the polls.[35] To the degree that the electoral effect reflects social power, the electoral cycle–war entry relationship should be washed out by these cases in which social power is greatly restricted.[36]

There are, then, a great number of factors that should blur the shadow that election cycles cast on the international stage. The persistent results found here suggest that there is indeed some significant force at work. In aggregate, democratic states have been just as prone to fall into militarized disputes in the preelection period as at other times. Nonetheless, they have consistently managed to prevent those disputes from escalating to the level of war at the peak of the electoral season.

I have now concluded the march through the two-level model of international and domestic politics. International level outcomes—the final box emphasized in Figure 27—are clearly connected to domestic-level electoral politics. By way of conclusion, it is time now to pull back and consider the implications of these findings and this model for conceptions of democracy and the efficacy of democratic decision making for the formation and conduct of foreign policy.

SEVEN

Conclusions

Foreign policy does not require the use of any of the good qualities peculiar to democracy but does demand the cultivation of almost all those which it lacks. . . . A democracy finds it difficult to coordinate the details of a great undertaking and to fix on some plan and carry it through with determination in spite of obstacles. It has little capacity for combining measures in secret and waiting patiently for the results.

—Tocqueville

Democracy is a concept of enormous power. As an idea, its pull on the course of world events is undeniable. It is the stuff of reverence and revolutions. It is afforded such universal acceptance on the stage of human ideas that today even those who most embody its antithesis must hide behind convoluted interpretations of its precepts or elaborate excuses for its subversion. That facade has been stripped only recently from the German Democratic Republic and the other East European "People's Democracies." One can hope it is only a matter of time before the concepts of "democratic centralism," "directed democracy," and "one-party" democracy will also be relegated to the dustbin of history.[1]

In the midst of this revolution, it is useful to remember that it was not long ago that democracy was widely perceived to be a crippling form of government for the conduct of foreign policy. Democracy has two faces, one pointed inward toward the governance of a political community, and the other pointed outward, to represent the political community in the international arena. The internal face of democracy is widely praised and valued, but the external face has been subject to considerable criticism. As Tocqueville suggested, the limitations of democracy are often seen as particularly pernicious when it comes to the formation and conduct of foreign policy.

It is said that democratic mechanisms for making foreign-policy choices are prone to stalemate, vacillation, and vast errors of judgment. Even those who clearly side with liberal principles have been highly critical. A. J. P. Taylor was concerned about the defense of democracy against the encroachments of fascism, but still concluded that in foreign policy "It is very hard for a democracy to make up its mind; and when it does so, often makes it up wrong."[2] Theodore Lowi argued that in order "to make democracy safe for the world" it is necessary to minimize the impact of "domestic processes, practices, and values" on foreign-policy decisions.[3] Gordon Craig and Alexander George warn that "The forces of public opinion, of Congress, of the mass media, and of powerful interest groups often make themselves felt in ways that seriously complicate and hamper presidential ability to pursue long-range foreign policy objectives in a coherent and consistent manner."[4]

The realist perspective stands cold against this swirl of reactions to democracy. The bottom line in the realist accounting is that democracy should not make much of a difference one way or the other in international behavior. In the words of Waltz, "International politics consists of like units duplicating one another's activities."[5] In this view, state leaders are both socialized and constrained by the demands of an anarchic and dangerous international system. The realist expectation holds particularly strongly for the basic decisions about war and peace.

In this study I have argued that—contrary to the realist expectation—democracy does make a difference. Democracy is a method for social choice that institutionalizes a balance between internal and external concerns. At regular intervals democratic foreign policies must be subjected to the electoral test. In the period leading up to an election, internal concerns should exert their maximum pressure. In the period after an election, the relative importance of internal pressures should appear to recede.

Using the electoral calendar as a window on the relative power of state and society, I have shown that the domestic requirements of a democratic state do condition its relations with other countries. What is more, I have shown this to be the case within the realm of high politics—in questions of war and peace—where realists would argue such effects are least expected. When elections are approaching, democratic states have avoided wars. After elections, they have tended to enter more wars. Interestingly, this finding holds regardless of who initiates the war. The dynamics of electoral politics change the incentives for war for both the democratic state and the opponent state.

Within democratic states in the past two centuries, there has been considerable variation in attitudes toward war. The public has not been immune either to a reckless enthusiasm for war or a dangerous complacence in the face of international exigencies. It is noteworthy, therefore, that war enthusiasm has not more often infected the electoral process. Democratic leaders and their rivals have generally avoided the temptation to exploit martial fervor for electoral gain.

The empirical results presented here are particularly robust given the many political forces and historical contingencies that might mask the electoral effect. This is a phenomenon of tendencies and not of absolutes. Electoral dynamics work to influence rather than to determine behavior. There are a number of other forces that also influence the desire of states to go to war and the timing of when those wars begin. Because the electoral cycle effect is just a tendency, situations still arise in which other inducements to go to war or to avoid war should overwhelm the election effect. During the past two centuries, these other forces have not been sufficient to mask the role of election cycles in determining the timing of war entries for democratic states. The lexicographic view, in which all external pressures must be addressed before internal pressures can be considered, is inadequate for explaining the behavior of democratic states. Internal and external factors both play a critical role.

THE DIFFERENCE DEMOCRACY MAKES

If democracy does make a difference, the next challenge is to ask whether an assessment can be made of the quality of that difference: does the democratic difference make democratic decision making better or worse than the foreign-policy decision making of other types of states? The traditional argument has been that domestic concerns represent a deviation from international concerns, and thus a divergence from the national interest. Allowing domestic concerns to impact foreign-policy decision making will therefore degrade the quality of that process.[6] I am no longer content that this answer is adequate. Of course, this is a normative question that is fraught with highly subjective elements. To begin a more careful consideration of this question, it will be useful to review the causal argument that I have presented in this book.

The movement from describing a statistical relationship to defending a causal story is a difficult one. The logical and evidential hurdles that stand in the way of a scientific understanding of this issue are formidable. Political actors tend to be disingenuous in describing the relative importance of electoral concerns in shaping their actions. Analytically, careful discrimination between competing causal hypotheses is made difficult by a limited number of cases and by a relative lack of variance across cases in the most relevant variables.

With these cautions in mind, it has still been possible to make a general causal argument about the effect of election cycles on the conflict behavior of democratic states in the modern era. In some cases there has been enough evidence from the principal actors to discern the impact of electoral concerns by tracing the decision-making process. Even in those cases where the evidence is indirect or circumstantial, it has been possible to submit some of the most important causal elements to at least a test of basic plausibility.

As a starting point, I have shown that the naïve populist and patrician perspectives are inadequate for thinking about the nature of democratic regimes and their distinctive behavior in the international arena. One significant variation is the degree of popular pressure for war. As seen in the period leading up to World War II, there have been times when the public has been exceptionally difficult to rouse to action. Orators and politicians as skilled as Winston Churchill and Franklin Roosevelt were unable to provoke public passions for a strong stand toward Hitler until war was literally at the doorstep. At the same time, there is little in the historical record to support the argument that democratic masses are inherently pacific. The fact that citizens may pay for war with their lives or property does not seem a sufficient brake on militaristic passions. Once a war is underway, these sacrifices may prove sobering. But, in the period before war breaks out, there have been occasions when vicarious military adventure has struck a responsive chord in the public mind. This enthusiasm has extended to a personal willingness to risk life and limb on the part of individuals in democratic societies. This willingness has not been limited to conflicts involving immediate and overwhelming threats to the national defense.

If not in the pacifism of the electorate, where is the source of the electoral cycle effect? I have focused on two primary explanations, one domestic and the other international. At the domestic level, a picture of democratic distinctiveness can be garnered from a focus on the institutional makeup of democratic states and the specific distribution of preferences that has characterized the public debate about war entry. It is important to think about democracy in a larger sense than just popular rule. Liberal democracy requires freedom of speech, freedom of association, and freedom of assembly. A by-product of these freedoms is an enhanced role for minority voices. These freedoms allow even relatively small groups of antiwar elites to constrain the behavior of the state. War is an undertaking of enormous consequence, and thus it is rarely entered into lightly. The prospect of fighting a war without a high level of societal cohesion must be viewed with trepidation by any leader who contemplates war for the satisfaction of the oft clamorous, but fickle, masses rather than for the underlying necessities of national interest.

The decision to go to war poses very high risks for democratic leaders. These risks are imposed by the capacity for independent action of both the opponent state and the democratic public itself. In this regard, social choices about war are distinct from other social choices in two important ways. In other areas, the increased role for mass views as elections approach stifles the influence of minority voices that cannot find suitable coalition partners. But the decision to go to war is akin to a vote that requires a sizable rather than a simple majority to pass: a rather small minority may be able to wield veto power. The veto power of this group is also enhanced by the second important characteristic of war decisions: the need for sustained support over time. For most issues, winning a vote today is sufficient to commit the state tomorrow. But in deciding to go to war, the danger that a vote of confidence may be lost at some point in the near future has a direct bearing on the desirability of going to war today. A decision for war requires both breadth and depth in public support. The ability to manufacture a momentary coalition is insufficient for sustaining a longer-term war effort.[7]

Politicians face a difficult set of incentives when the public is clamoring for war. Small-scale military adventures can increase their popularity and silence critics, at least in the short run. But the political risks attendant to genuine war provide a strong disincentive for escalation. This disincentive is particularly potent in electoral periods, when antiwar elites have the greatest potential to fracture the social cohesion required for as expensive an undertaking as war.

Some empirical leverage on this issue is provided by the difference between the effect of electoral cycles on disputes and their effect on wars. Disputes are a more direct representation of the belligerence of a state's foreign-policy choices. Aggregation over the entire period I have examined suggests little reason to believe that domestic electoral politics have a consistent effect on the belligerence of foreign policy. This result presents a problem for the views that democratic influences should lead to a foreign policy that is consistently less belligerent, as in the naïve populist view, or consistently more belligerent as in the naïve patrician view. But, a distinct period of identifiable foreign-policy mood such as the interwar years demonstrates a much clearer effect of public influence on foreign policy. In that period, strongly isolationist publics pushed democratic leaders to avoid foreign-policy disputes as elections approached.

This phenomenon leads sophisticated patricians to ask how democratic leaders have managed to conduct foreign policy under this domestic constraint without more often blundering into war in the preelection period. The answer to this question lies in the international arena and in the interaction of electoral dynamics in the democratic state with the incentives of opponent states. In the first place, the electoral process gives democratic states a mechanism for demonstrating commitment and resolve, even when the underlying calculations suggest that the democratic state strongly wants to avoid war. Elections are public affairs that are easily visible to other states. By taking some degree of control over foreign policy away from democratic leaders, they may actually enhance control over foreign crises.

The visibility of democratic elections also gives foreign actors a clear stake in the outcome. To the degree that aggressive policies on the part of foreign actors are likely to help the more belligerent party in an election, those foreign actors will have an incentive to wait until after an election to take provocative actions. In both of these ways—the increased ability of democratic states to make clear commitments and the incentives of other states to influence the electoral outcome—electoral politics can decrease the motivations for war on both sides of a conflict.

There is an element in the nature of democratic states that has made their behavior less likely to lead to war when public accountability is at its highest. A broad view of democratic society that includes a focus on the role of elites in these states, rather than an undifferentiated view of mass pressures, reveals a pacific element in democratic organization. The pacific nature of democracies is to be found in the combination of the specific preferences that have been extant during the past two centuries and the institutional structures that have allowed the antiwar perspective a sort of veto power in this issue area. In deciding to go to war, democratic leaders feel constrained by the need for public cohesion, rather than feeling the need to go to war in order to increase public cohesion.

The historical record, then, supports the sophisticated liberal perspective. Democracy has not consistently undermined effective foreign policy. The increase in public influence that comes with the electoral season has helped democratic states stay out of wars, at least in the short run. That said, there are three factors that must temper this positive evaluation of democratic foreign policy-making.

First, democratic leaders are still willing to flirt with dangerous conflicts in the interest of gaining public support. Whether from a belief in deterrence, or simply out of a desire for vicarious adventure and national aggrandizement, democratic leaders are not immune to the appeal of acting tough. To the degree that these belligerent posturings are induced by the demands of popular politics rather than by perceptions of the demands of national interest, they must be accounted in the debit column for democratic foreign policy-making.

Second, the electoral suppression of the war incentive is only a short-term result. Sooner or later the election passes and the dynamics of international tension can come to a head. Indeed, there may be a significant reversal as the high-commitment force of rhetoric during the campaign melts into the low expectations for fulfillment of campaign promises after the ballots are counted. The heightened tension of electoral-period belligerence combined with the decreased expectation of commitment once the election is past could combine to increase the probability of war in the postelection period. The behaviors induced by electoral incentives may lead to both more, and more severe, conflicts. While democratic leaders may derive an electoral benefit from irresponsible behaviors in the short run, in the longer run the nation as a whole may have to pay heavily for these kinds of electoral indiscretions. The bills for preelection behaviors may come due in the postelection period.

Finally, there is the realist assertion that deviation from the dictates of national interest in either the belligerent or conciliatory direction will have a negative fallout. Win or lose, war is a bad outcome, per se. There is, therefore, a temptation to think only in terms of the benefits of slowing the war decision. This temptation is not new. When Admiral McGowan suggested a war referendum with the requirement that those who voted "yes" should be sent to the front lines, he did so with the expectation that this would make a war declaration virtually impossible.[8] In the discussion of war powers at the Philadelphia constitutional debates of 1787, George Mason of Virginia argued for giving that power to the legislative branch because "he was for clogging rather than facilitating war."[9] But, as should be apparent from many of the cases that I have discussed in these pages, it is also important to remember that the irresponsible behavior of leaders will not always be in the direction of trying to assuage or distract the jingoism of the masses with acts of bluster and belligerence. Even in our technological age, there will be crises in which war is not necessarily the *worst* outcome. To the degree that there are worse outcomes, it is necessary to acknowledge that the ability to go to war is an important state capability. Sometimes war itself may be deemed necessary. In an anarchic international order, the ability to go to war will be important to avoid exploitation by other states that are less constrained by internal pressures.[10] There is reason to share Lippmann's concern, expressed in the aftermath of World War II, that the dynamics of democratic decision making may sometimes work against taking more decisive action when a belligerent line is desperately warranted.

ASSESSING THE PATHOLOGIES OF DECISION MAKING

What is to be made of these limitations on democratic decision making? I suggest several responses, addressing the limitations in reverse order.

First, considering the danger that democratic states are constrained in their ability to make credible threats, it is important to remember that the need for broad public support for engaging in external conflicts is both the weakness and the strength of democratic states. Internal politics are important for the waging of war, and if on occasion democracies go to war a little later or earlier than seems optimal from an international standpoint, it may well be that this change in timing provides a net benefit in terms of democratic resolve in the longer run. That World War II could have been a less costly conflict with earlier American intervention seems true. But the nature of American participation in that war might have looked quite different if Roosevelt had used his considerable political skills to maneuver the United States into the war before Pearl Harbor, rather than after.[11] The reserve of antiwar sentiments that had been built up throughout the isolationist 1930s makes it likely that early entry into the war would have been undertaken with much less public support. The difficulties Canada faced with the conscription problem suggest some of the ways this might have changed the ability of the United States to successfully prosecute the war.

Even if electoral politics cause some distortions in the choice of belligerence or conciliation, it is important to remember that discerning when to be belligerent and when to be conciliatory is no mean feat. That democracies do not always do so perfectly, or occasionally vacillate between the two, is hardly grounds for excess pessimism about the prospects of democracy in the longer run. Attempts to demonstrate that democratic states have been involved in fewer wars than the nondemocratic states during the past two centuries have proven inconclusive.[12] But, if there are problems in the foreign-policy decision making of democratic states, these at least have not led them into *more* frequent wars than the nondemocratic states.

This same point can be made from the opposite direction: the greater foreign policy wisdom that is often attributed to the nondemocratic states has not gotten them into any *fewer* wars than the democracies. It is important to remember that this has not been a comparative study. In his evaluation of the American and British foreign-policy process, Kenneth Waltz warns that:

> The question of democracy's capacities in the realm of foreign policy requires comparison with the political characteristics and performance of nondemocratic political systems. . . . It is sufficient to say that in the foreign policy of every country disappointments abound, and after the event errors are easy to identify. Criticism of British and American policies and evaluation of the democratic political systems that produce them can be made without any necessary implication that authoritarian governments can be expected to do better.[13]

I have looked only at some decision pathologies of democratic states. Nondemocratic states may also be prone to internal influences that shift the timing of wars or degrade the quality of foreign-policy decisions. A dictator contemplating the possibility of losing power is likely to be even more willing than a democratic leader to sacrifice external goals for the internal necessities of maintaining domestic control. Failed dictators often face serious threats to their personal wealth and safety. Failed democratic leaders become "elder statesmen" and have more time for golf. The shifting fashions of isolation and intervention in democratic publics may pale in comparison to the sea changes in policy that can accompany the rough transitions of power in nondemocratic countries. Consider the changes in foreign policy from the shah to Khomeini, from Mao to Deng, or from Brezhnev to Gorbachev.

A comparative consideration of the behavior of the Western powers and the Soviet Union at the onset of World War II speaks to both the stability and wisdom of democratic states. While the Western powers vacillated in their response to Nazi aggressions, the dictators in both Germany and the Soviet Union were experimenting with diametric swings in their policies toward each other. Despite Churchill's warning that Hitler's views were spelled out in his book, *Mein Kampf,* the West took too long to discern Hitler's expansionist aims and to recognize that the values of the Nazi regime were inimical to Western ideals. Stalin, on the other hand, refused to see the immediacy of the German threat despite Hitler's views, set out explicitly in *Mein Kampf,* that the Soviet leadership were "the scum of humanity" and that in the quest for more living space Germany should not look to the south and west, but that it should "have in mind only *Russia* and her vassal border states."[14]

The Spanish-American War provides another example. If public opinion was the driving force for American belligerence, so too concerns about domestic legitimacy pushed the Spanish into that conflict.[15] Fifty thousand Spanish soldiers had died in Cuba between 1895 and 1898.[16] Another 100,000 had died between 1868 and 1878.[17] Military elites do not always follow the economists' edict to ignore sunk costs in thinking about future policies. The Spanish military was not prepared to walk away from those sacrifices.[18] But the Spanish military was also unprepared to fight a war with the United States. At the end of the nineteenth century, the Spanish Empire was close to bankruptcy. Their fleet was short of coal and ammunition, and several of their important naval vessels were desperately in need of repairs.[19] A number of important Spanish military leaders warned that there was little hope that they could defeat the Americans in battles so far from Spain. On February 26, 1898—a scant two months before the outbreak of the war—Admiral Cervera wrote to Sigismund Bermejo, the Spanish Minister of the Marine:

> I am very uneasy about this. I ask myself if it is right for me to keep silent, make myself an accomplice in adventures which will surely cause the total ruin of Spain. And for what purpose? To defend an island which was ours, but belongs to us no more, because even if we did not lose it by right in the war we have lost it in fact, and with it all our wealth and an enormous num-

ber of young men, victims of the climate and the bullets, in the defense of what is now no more than a romantic idea.[20]

Admiral Cervera's prescient warnings fell on deaf ears. The Spanish government had decided "that a disastrous war was preferable to supine surrender: a noble defeat would at least *preserve the established order at home.*"[21] Domestic opinion goaded the United States into a war that was probably tangential to American national interest. Domestic opinion goaded Spain into a war that was foreseeably disastrous for Spanish national interest.

In considering the *relative* wisdom of democratic states, it might also be instructive to consider the win/loss column in the list of democratic wars.[22] It takes two sides to make a war. Even if all these wars pointed to some kind of decision-making failure on the democratic side, the fact that the democracies were the initiators for only one-third of the wars considered here and were the winners for two-thirds of them, strongly suggests that there may also be some serious limitations in the way that nondemocratic states are making decisions about going to war. Table 7 shows the cumulative war experience of democratic states according to whether they are identified as the initiator of the war and whether they are seen as the winner or the loser. The democratic states are the initiators in about a quarter of the cases. They are identified as the winners in three-quarters of the wars they have initiated. They have lost in only 20 percent of the wars where they have been attacked first. Overall, democratic states have lost only 20 percent of the wars they have been in. By this measure, democratic foreign-policy decision making does not appear at all inferior to the decision making of their nondemocratic opponents.

The world would probably be a safer place if there were a more widespread and discriminating awareness of the nature of electoral effects on the foreign policy of democratic states.[23] To recognize systematic behavioral patterns is the first important step in trying to mitigate their harmful effects. This means recognizing both that saber-rattling may be as much for internal as external consumption, and that public debate is not necessarily a sign of weakness. Such recognition can be beneficial on both the domestic and the international fronts.

On the international front increased awareness of the pathologies of democratic electoral behavior could help mitigate the negative effects of electoral bluster, as I suggested in Chapter 5. This awareness should help foreign leaders more accurately discount preelection saber-rattling. In the same vein, how-

TABLE 7

Cumulative War Experience of Democratic States

	Win	Loss	Tie	Total
Democratic initiator	13	4	0	17
Nondemocratic initiator	35	11	11*	57
Total	48	15	11	74

SOURCE: Michael Doyle, Correlates of War Project; see Appendixes A and B*
*Ten of these cases are the Korean War.

ever, after the election they should recognize that vocal opposition is a fixture in democratic states that does not necessarily reduce resolve. Democratic states do go to war, and as Saddam Hussein learned in the Gulf War, overreliance on the veto power of domestic oppositions can lead to serious miscalculations.

On the domestic front, politicians walk a fine line between taking advantage of policy manipulations for improved electoral performance, and blatant vote-mongering that in itself provides fuel for an opponent's critique.[24] Elections are an institutional mechanism for giving voice to opposition views. The more the effects of elections on behavior are understood, the more potential there is for opposition voices to point to those effects in criticizing overblown claims of threats to the national interest. Thus, a more widespread awareness of the distortions that electoral politics can wreak on foreign policy could help decrease the attractiveness of foreign-policy manipulation as an electoral strategy.

As so often, this leads to yet another plea for more responsible leaders and for a more educated and sophisticated citizenry. The old saw that people get the leaders they deserve is worth repeating here. Until the public becomes more discerning about international relations—rather than just blowing hot or cold for isolationism or interventionism—democratic societies will get the foreign policies they deserve. I have argued here that, although erratic, the adjustments of other states may make those foreign policies less dangerous than some have suggested. Still, a wiser public dialogue on foreign policy will contribute to wiser democratic politics both internally and externally. This is not to say that an informed democratic foreign policy will be able to avoid significant mistakes—"the best and the brightest" have made their share of foreign-policy errors despite much education and focused attention on international relations. But when people pay more discerning attention to international events, politicians may prove less prone to playing on international crises to bolster their domestic popularity.

This, I am afraid, will be viewed as a rather pessimistic prescription, since there are so many proposals that have ended with this same plea for a more informed electorate. Improving the capabilities of voters has always been a difficult task. Voters who pay more attention without being more informed may actually increase the temptation for politicians to pander to public emotions.[25] A few words should be said in conclusion, then, about the final implications of this research for our general assessment of democracy as a system of social organization.

Democracy and the Problem of War

In the various discussions of the democratic peace hypothesis, it has sometimes been forgotten that democracy does not necessarily stand or fall on its pacifism, nor even on the basic wisdom of its foreign-policy decisions. There are many goals for our political systems, of which keeping out of unnecessary wars is just one. Granted it is an important one, particularly in the nuclear age. As with the Hobbesian Leviathan, legitimacy for democracies is tied to an ability to offer some minimal protection of life and limb. But, unlike the Leviathan, the legitimacy of democracy rests on something more. It might well be worth exchanging a few extra wars or foolish foreign-policy decisions for the benefit of the greater freedoms that liberal democracy has provided internally to its citizens. It is a grim calculus, but it would be wise to remember that in the past century war has wrought significantly less death than have the internal slaughters of the brutal nondemocratic regimes of the modern era. By Rudolph Rummel's estimates, some 119 million people have died at the hands of their own governments compared to 36 million who have died in all the wars of this century.[26]

I can conclude only that *both* of the perspectives on democracy that I set out at the beginning of this chapter are correct. Democracy is rightly revered: its justification comes from a belief in the intrinsic value of individual human beings and a recognition of the intrinsic frailties of human leaders. At the same time, democracy is a system prone to corruption, stalemate, vacillation, and vast errors of judgment. These problems might be expected to be most apparent in the electoral period. In fact, I have shown here that they have not led directly to more involvement in wars at that time. In the end we are left with the aphorism of Churchill, a wartime democratic leader who knew firsthand the limitations and strengths of the democratic states:

> Democracy is the worst form of government, except for all those other forms that have been tried from time to time.[27]

Appendixes

Liberal Regimes, 1700–1982

This appendix contains Michael Doyle's list of liberal regimes existing between 1700 and 1982. Doyle, "Liberalism and World Politics," 1164. Doyle excludes states with a population less than 1 million. Doyle considers the United States and Switzerland to be only partly democratic in the earliest period: Switzerland being democratic in only some cantons, and the United States being democratic only north of the Mason-Dixon line before the Civil War.

Doyle provides the following explanation with this list:

> I have drawn up this approximate list of "Liberal Regimes" according to the four institutions Kant described as essential: market and private property economies; polities that are externally sovereign; citizens who possess juridical rights; and "republican" (whether republican or parliamentary monarchy), representative government. This latter includes the requirement that the legislative branch have an effective role in public policy and be formally and competitively (either inter- or intra-party) elected. Furthermore, I have taken into account whether male suffrage is wide (i.e., 30%) or, as Kant would have had it, open by "achievement" to inhabitants of the national or metropolitan territory (e.g., to poll-tax payers or householders). This list of liberal regimes is thus more inclusive than a list of democratic regimes, or polyarchies (Powell, 5). Other conditions taken into account here are that female suffrage is granted within a generation of its being demanded by an extensive female suffrage movement and that representative government is internally sovereign (e.g., including, and especially over military and foreign affairs) as well as stable (in existence for at least three years). . . . Finally, these lists exclude ancient and medieval "republics," since none appears to fit Kant's commitment to liberal individualism.

pre–1800

Swiss Cantons	
French Republic	1790–95
United States	1776–

1800–50

Swiss Confederation		Great Britain	1832–
United States		Netherlands	1848–
France	1830–49	Piedmont	1848–
Belgium	1830–	Denmark	1849–

1850–1900

Switzerland		Denmark	–1866
United States		Sweden	1864–
Belgium		Greece	1864–
Great Britain		Canada	1867–
Netherlands		France	1871–
Piedmont	–1861	Argentina	1880–
Italy	1861–	Chile	1891–

1900–45

Switzerland		New Zealand	1907–
United States		Colombia	1910–49
Great Britain		Denmark	1914–40
Sweden		Poland	1917–35
Canada		Latvia	1922–34
Greece	–1911	Germany	1918–32
	1928–36	Austria	1918–34
Italy	–1922	Estonia	1919–34
Belgium	–1940	Finland	1919–
Netherlands	–1940	Uruguay	1919–
Argentina	–1944	Costa Rica	1919–

France	−1940	Czechoslovakia	1920–39
Chile	−1924	Ireland	1920–
	1932–	Mexico	1928–
Australia	1901	Lebanon	1944–
Norway	1905–40		

1945–

Switzerland		Ecuador	1948–1963
United States			1979–
Great Britain		Israel	1949–
Sweden		W. Germany	1949–
Canada		Greece	1950–67
Australia			1975–
New Zealand		Peru	1950–62
Finland			1963–68
Ireland			1980–
Mexico		El Salvador	1950–61
Uruguay	−1973	Turkey	1950–60
Chile	−1973		1966–71
Lebanon	−1975	Japan	1951–
Costa Rica	−1948	Bolivia	1956–69
	1953–		1982–
Iceland	1944–	Colombia	1958–
France	1945–	Venezuela	1959–
Denmark	1945–	Nigeria	1961–64
Norway	1945–		1979–1984
Austria	1945–	Jamaica	1962–
Brazil	1945–54	Trinidad/Tobago	1962–
	1955–64	Senegal	1963–
Belgium	1946–	Malaysia	1963–
Luxembourg	1946–	Botswana	1966–
Netherlands	1946–	Singapore	1965–

Italy	1946–	Portugal	1976–
Philippines	1946–72	Spain	1978–
India	1947–75	Dominican Rep.	1978–
	1977–	Honduras	1981–
Sri Lanka	1948–61	Papua New Guinea	1982–
	1963–71		
	1978–		

Wars Involving Democratic States, 1816–1980

The following is a list of cases in the Wages of War dataset for countries that are coded as democratic by Doyle.

T = War Type:
> S = Interstate War
> C = Colonial War
> I = Imperial War

Mo: Month in which war was entered.

Year: Year in which war was entered.

W = Win:
> W = Democratic state was on the winning side.
> L = Democratic state was on the losing side.
> T = The war is coded as a tie.

I = Init:
> Y = Democratic state initiated military conflict.
> N = Democratic state did not initiate military conflict.

C = Cycle:
> Length of election cycle bracketing war entry in months.

E.R. = Entry Ratio:
> Proportion of electoral cycle already passed at time of war entry.

Country	War	T	Mo	Year	W	Battle deaths	I	C	E.R.
U.K.	First Afghan	I	10	1838	W	20,000	N	46	.29
France	Franco-Algerian	I	11	1839	W	15,000	N	39	.19
U.K.	Second Syrian	C	9	1840	W	10	N	46	.78
U.K.	1st British-Sikh	I	12	1845	W	1,500	N	73	.72
U.S.	Mexican-American	S	5	1846	W	11,000	Y	47	.38
U.K.	2nd British-Sikh	I	10	1848	W	1,500	N	58	.23
France	Roman Republic	S	6	1849	W	300	Y	34	.02
U.K.	Crimean	S	3	1854	W	22,000	N	56	.35
U.K.	Anglo-Persian	S	10	1856	W	500	Y	56	.90
U.K.	Sepoy	C	5	1857	W	3,500	N	24	.01
Italy	Seven Weeks	S	6	1866	W	4,000	N	117	.55
U.K.	Second Afghan	I	11	1878	W	4,000	N	74	.77
U.K.	British-Zulu	I	1	1879	W	3,500	N	74	.79
France	Franco-Indochina	I	4	1882	W	4,500	N	49	.15
U.K.	Mahdist	C	9	1882	L	20,000	N	67	.42
France	Sino-French	S	8	1884	W	2,100	Y	49	.72
France	Madagascan	I	12	1894	W	6,000	N	56	.27
Italy	Italo-Ethiopian	I	12	1895	L	9,000	N	21	.28
Greece	Greco-Turkish	S	2	1897	L	600	Y	45	.48
U.S.	Spanish-American	S	4	1898	W	5,000	Y	47	.37
U.S.	2nd Philippine	C	2	1899	W	4,500	N	47	.56
U.K.	Boer	C	10	1899	W	22,000	N	62	.81
U.S.	Boxer Rebellion	S	6	1900	W	21	Y	47	.90
U.K.	Boxer Rebellion	S	6	1900	W	34	Y	62	.94
France	Boxer Rebellion	S	6	1900	W	24	Y	47	.52
Italy	Italo-Turkish	S	9	1911	W	6,000	Y	55	.55
U.K.	World War I	S	8	1914	W	908,000	N	95	.45
Belgium	World War I	S	8	1914	W	87,500	N	65	.04
France	World War I	S	8	1914	W	1,350,000	N	66	.05

Country	War	T	Mo	Year	W	Battle deaths	I	C	E.R.
Italy	World War I	S	5	1915	W	650,000	N	72	.26
U.S.	World War I	S	4	1917	W	126,000	N	47	.11
Poland	Russo-Polish	S	2	1919	L	40,000	N	45	.01
France	Riffian	C	4	1925	W	4,000	N	47	.23
France	Druze	C	7	1925	W	4,000	N	47	.30
Canada	World War II	S	9	1939	W	39,300	N	53	.88
U.K.	World War II	S	9	1939	W	270,000	N	114	.40
France	World War II	S	9	1939	W	210,000	N	—	—
Australia	World War II	S	9	1939	W	33,826	N	34	.64
New Zealand	World War II	S	9	1939	W	17,300	N	59	.18
Finland	Russo-Finnish	S	11	1939	L	40,000	N	—	—
Norway	World War II	S	4	1940	W	2,000	N	—	—
Netherlands	World War II	S	5	1940	W	6,200	N	—	—
Belgium	World War II	S	5	1940	W	9,600	N	—	—
U.S.	World War II	S	12	1941	W	408,300	N	47	.27
U.K.	Indonesian	C	11	1945	L	1,000	N	56	.09
France	Indochinese	C	12	1945	L	95,000	N	7	.18
France	Madagascan	C	3	1947	W	1,800	N	54	.08
India	1st Kashmir	I	10	1947	W	1,500	N	49	.45
Lebanon	Palestine	S	5	1948	L	500	Y	46	.25
India	Hyderabad	I	9	1948	W	1,000	Y	49	.67
U.S.	Korean	S	6	1950	T	54,000	N	47	.41
U.K.	Korean	S	8	1950	T	670	N	19	.31
Philippines	Korean	S	9	1950	T	90	N	48	.21
Turkey	Korean	S	10	1950	T	720	N	47	.11
Canada	Korean	S	12	1950	T	310	N	49	.36
Australia	Korean	S	12	1950	T	281	N	16	.72
Netherlands	Korean	S	1	1951	T	110	N	47	.64
Belgium	Korean	S	1	1951	T	100	N	46	.16

Country	War	T	Mo	Year	W	Battle deaths	I	C	E.R.
France	Korean	S	1	1951	T	290	N	54	.90
Greece	Korean	S	1	1951	T	170	N	18	.58
France	Algerian	C	11	1954	L	18,000	N	54	.74
U.K.	Sinai	S	10	1956	W	20	N	52	.33
France	Sinai	S	10	1956	W	10	N	34	.29
Israel	Sinai	S	10	1956	W	200	Y	47	.32
India	Sino-Indian	S	10	1962	L	500	N	60	.13
U.S.	Vietnamese	S	2	1965	L	56,000	Y	47	.07
Australia	Vietnamese	S	2	1965	L	492	N	35	.40
South Korea	Vietnamese	S	5	1965	L	5,000	N	42	.44
India	2nd Kashmir	S	8	1965	L	3,000	Y	60	.68
Philippines	Vietnamese	S	10	1966	L	1,000	N	47	.22
Israel	Six Day	S	6	1967	W	1,000	Y	47	.40
Israel	Israeli-Egyptian	S	3	1969	T	368	N	47	.84
India	Bangladesh	S	12	1971	W	8,000	Y	71	.12
Israel	Yom Kippur	S	10	1973	W	3,000	N	48	.98

Reference Material

Notes

1. *Freedom Review*, January 1996, 1. Of these formal democracies, Freedom House rates 76 as states in which the citizens enjoy a broad range of political rights and civil liberties. In the other 41 of these states there are some constraints on political rights and civil liberties. There is a total of 191 states in the Freedom House survey.

2. On these trends, see Gaubatz, "Kant, Democracy, and History"; Diamond; Huntington.

3. There is some variance in realist analysis on this point. The position is held most strongly by "structural realism," represented in the work of Kenneth Waltz. "Classical realists" are somewhat mixed. Quincy Wright, for example, concludes that states with widely different constitutions "have tended to react similarly under similar external pressures" (824). Hans Morgenthau, on the other hand, considers the internal democratization of states to have had a major, and largely negative, impact on international relations (239–41).

4. See Waltz, *Theory of International Politics*, especially 93–99.

5. Small and Singer, "War-proneness"; Chan; Weede; Maoz and Abdolali, "Regime Types." A dissenting voice on this issue is Rummel, "Libertarianism."

6. These numbers come from the war experience codings of the Correlates of War Project. See Singer and Small, *Wages of War*.

7. Babst.

8. In addition to the citations given in note 5, see Doyle, "Liberal Legacies" parts I and II; Doyle, "Liberalism"; Russett, *Controlling the Sword* and *Grasping the Democratic Peace*; Bueno de Mesquita and Lalman, *War and Reason*; Russett and Maoz, "Normative and Structural Causes"; and Owen. Recent dissenting views can be found in Spiro; Layne; and Mearsheimer.

9. The absence of war between democracies—the dyadic effect—has proven a relatively robust finding. The overall war-proneness of democratic states—the monadic effect—remains more hotly contested. See Rousseau, Gelpi, and Huth.

10. On the difference between the approaches of the historians and the political scientists to domestic politics and war, see Levy, "Domestic Politics and War." An important exception to the tendency to exclude war from the analysis of domestic/international interactions is Jack Snyder's argument that imperial overextension and the wars that go with it are a result of domestic coalition building. Snyder, *Myths of Empire*.

11. Brams and Kilgour, *Game Theory*, 2.

12. See, for example, Almond; Rosenau; Cohen; and Hughes.

13. Ironically, one of the most sustained discussions of elections and foreign policy is by the preeminent realist, Kenneth Waltz. See Waltz, *Foreign Policy and Democratic Politics*, chap. 10.

14. There are two oblique references to elections on pp. 55 and 85 of Rosenau, but no direct discussion of their importance.

15. Cohen, 185.

16. See Craig and George, *Force and Statecraft*, chap. 5; Waltz, *Foreign Policy and Democratic Politics*. Waltz deals with Britain in general, but his most sustained discussion of the role of public opinion concerns public opinion and American involvement in the Korean and Vietnamese Wars.

17. See Wolfers, intro.; George, *Presidential Decisionmaking*, chap. 14; and Waltz, *Theory of International Politics*.

18. Waltz, *Theory of International Politics*.

19. Gilpin, chap. 1.

20. Grieco.

21. Keohane.

22. Waltz, *Theory of International Politics*, 121.

23. Ibid.

24. Krasner, 12.

25. See Nettl, "The State as a Conceptual Variable"; Krasner; Evans, Rueschemeyer, and Skocpol. Mastanduno, Lake, and Ikenberry present a state-based model but label it a realist theory in line with the traditional realists like Morgenthau and Carr in "Toward a Realist Theory."

26. Krasner.

27. See Wolfers, chap. 6; Morgenthau, chap 2.

28. Morgenthau, 548. See also 141–44.

29. Krasner, 15.

30. Wright, 819.

31. Thucydides, 533.

32. Putnam.

33. Krasner.

34. Hume, 346–47.

35. Kant, 438.

36. See Bolt.

37. Ibid., 141.

38. Ibid., 136.

39. See Richards, 24–30.

40. Kissinger, 40–42.

41. *New York Times*, November 11, 1992, A8.

42. See Lippmann; Hermens; and Kennan.

43. Kennan, 61–62.

44. See Mueller, *War, Presidents, and Public Opinion*; Lee; Kernell; Sigelman and Conover; Brody and Shapiro; and Brody.

45. Polsby, 25; Lee, 253.

46. Brody, 58.

47. Hartz.

48. Klingberg; Holmes.

49. Almond.

50. Ibid., 67.

51. Page and Shapiro. See also Holsti, who argues that public opinion has been stable, though not necessarily well informed in this period.

52. Mueller, *Retreat from Doomsday* and "Changing Attitudes Toward War."

53. Campbell, et al. See also McClosky and Zaller; and Zaller, *The Nature and Origins of Mass Opinion*.

54. Riker.

55. See also Arrow. For an application to public opinion on foreign policy issues, see Gaubatz, "Intervention and Intransitivity."

56. Of course, each of these actors could exhibit varying degrees of support or opposition to war. The combination of positions would, therefore, be most accurately reflected in a three-dimensional space. For the purposes of this discussion, however, a set of three dichotomous variables illustrates the critical combinations of attitudes.

57. Most democratic states have been at peace in 60 to 90 percent of the years between 1816 and 1980. This permutation might be more interesting if the international environment were pushing strongly for war. It seems rather unlikely, however, that this would be the case without some vocal opposition group taking up the call for war.

58. See Zaller, *The Nature and Origins of Mass Opinion*.

59. Kennan, 62.

60. Vasquez, 221–23.

61. As I will argue in Chapter 2, the Boer War, World War I, and the Spanish-American War are three good examples of this phenomenon. The Crimean War may be an exception, as there was some expectation that it would be a quite serious war, although it is difficult to gauge to what degree this was an elite versus a mass perception. On this point, see Andersen, 1–5. There is some potential that this dynamic would not hold if there were a widespread belief that war would somehow be "redemptive." While this view has proponents, I do not know of a case where it has had a very widespread following. See Mueller, *Retreat from Doomsday*, chap. 2.

62. Bueno de Mesquita, Siverson, and Woller argue that political leaders have systematically faced punishment for doing badly in wars.

63. Tocqueville, 1:135.

64. See George, "Domestic Constraints."

65. On the vulnerability of public opinion to shifts, see Gaubatz, "Intervention and Intransitivity."

66. Mayhew; Downs.

67. Dallek, 201.

68. Russett, *Controlling the Sword*, 48; Cotton; and Bueno de Mesquita, Siverson, and Woller.

69. Bueno de Mesquita, Siverson, and Woller.

70. The prospect theory literature provides some important insights into the evaluation of risks. Particularly relevant is the generally greater willingness of people to gamble with potential losses than to gamble for gains. See Levy, "Introduction to Prospect Theory" and "Prospect Theory and International Relations."

71. See Downs and Rocke, *Optimal Imperfection?*, chap. 3. For a discussion of prospect theory and attitudes toward risk in international relations see Levy, "Prospect Theory and International Relations," 299–306.

72. Lalman.

73. See Jervis; Bueno de Mesquita and Lalman, "Reason and War"; and Patchen.

74. Carr.

75. See Fearon, "Domestic Political Audiences" and "Signaling"; Putnam.

76. Morgenthau, 238–39.

77. I use *liberalism* as a convenient label to describe this outlook. It is not supposed to serve as a philosophical description of liberalism—a subject on which many books have been written. The working definition of liberal democracy that informs the empirical parts of this study is drawn from Michael Doyle and is provided in Appendix A.

78. Eckstein.

79. For a review of some of the interpretive variety possible with Thucydides' *History of the Peloponnesian War*, see Gaubatz, "Teaching Thucydides."

CHAPTER TWO: ATTITUDES TOWARD WAR IN DEMOCRATIC STATES

1. There is some speculation that Alcibiades was one of Thucydides' prime sources for his history, and thus his role in these events may have been somewhat exaggerated. See Kagan, 256–59.

2. Plutarch describes Alcibiades this way: "For he had, as it was observed, this peculiar talent and artifice for gaining men's affections, that he could at once comply with and really embrace and enter into their habits and ways of life, and change faster than the chameleon." Plutarch, "Alcibiades," 165.

3. Kagan, 62.   4. Kennan; Lippmann.

5. Kant, 438.   6. Lippmann, 26.

7. See Gaddis, 119–25.   8. Martin, 21.

9. See Rich, 19, 22–26. The Ottomans had previously given similar rights to the French to protect Latin Catholics. But Latin Catholics were only a small mi-

nority. The czar also may have observed the success of the Austrians in wresting concessions from the Turks in the Montenegro crisis of January 1853.

10. At this point in time, Palmerston was nominally a Liberal, but his allegiance to the Liberal Party was weak after being ousted as foreign secretary by Russell in 1851.

11. Snyder argues that the incoherence of the mid-nineteenth-century party system contributed directly to the outbreak of the war by creating a situation in which imperial interests could create a coalition around intervention in order to avoid the more divisive domestic issues. Snyder, *Myths of Empire*, chap. 5.

12. The Russians had secured the right to control the Danube delta, as well as certain rights to interfere in the principalities in the treaty of Adrianople after the Russo-Turkish War of 1828.

13. Lord Russell, for example, opined that "If we do not stop the Russians on the Danube, we shall have to stop them on the Indus." Quoted in Conacher, 182.

14. Martin, 45.

15. Smoke, 47; Martin, 183.

16. Andersen, 20; Martin, 236–42.

17. Conacher, 155.

18. Quoted in Martin, 116.

19. Conacher, 118.

20. Ibid., 173, 184. Aberdeen expressed a desire to retire, but referring to the Eastern Question said he did not want to "give the appearance of running away from an unfinished question."

21. Conacher, 190–91.

22. Rich, 61.

23. Martin, 116–17.

24. Conacher, 159.

25. Martin, 23. See also, 82–84.

26. Conacher, 172–73.

27. Ibid., 266–67.

28. Ibid., 184–85.

29. Ibid., 187.

30. Ibid., 186.

31. Martin, 87.

32. Conacher, 26.

33. Martin, 149–50.

34. Marx, 12.

35. From August 13, 1853. In Martin, 146. I am indebted to John Owen for pointing out the biblical origin of this phrase which is used to describe foolish behavior in Proverbs 26:11.

36. The *Times* changed its position after the Battle of Sinope, in which the Russians abandoned the mostly defensive posture they had struck to this point, destroyed a Turkish squadron, and then bombarded the Turkish city of Sinope.

37. Andersen, 31–32; Martin, 185.

38. Martin, 185.

39. Ibid., 156.

40. Conacher, 199, 203–4.

41. Ibid., 199–200.

42. Editorial, the *Morning Herald*, October 1853, quoted in Martin, 189.

43. Martin, 203–14.

44. Editorial, the *Morning Advertiser*, January 18, 1854, quoted in Martin, 208.

45. Martin, 221–22.

46. Conacher, 157.

47. Martin, 224.

48. Conacher, 279–80.

49. Ibid., 283.

50. Briggs, 216.

51. Ibid., 219.

52. Ibid., 216, 219.

53. Ibid., 216–17, 219.

54. Quoted in Conacher, 282.

55. Palmerston had deftly resigned from Parliament over issues of domestic political reforms just as some of the most important war decisions were being made. Aberdeen and the Peelites took the blame for the war from a public that believed that Palmerston's more militant stand might have prevented the war in the first place. See Parry, 176.

56. Martin, 243.

57. See, for example, Barker, 286; Albrecht-Carrié, 85; Rich, 4; Conacher, 137, 261; Martin, 24; Smoke, "The Crimean War," 36.

58. Rich, 4.

59. Martin, 24. In traditional just-war thought, necessity is an absolute prerequisite for a just war.

60. Ibid., 226. The Quakers maintained their opposition, but they did so at a considerable social cost.

61. To go even one step further from the liberal prediction, the royal family may well have been the most pacific of all.

62. See Wisan; Wilkerson.

63. Editorial, *New York Sun*, March 14, 1895, 6, cited in Wilkerson, 18.

64. O'Toole, 73.

65. Dobson, 63; Trask, 41; O'Toole, 148.

66. Quoted in Trask, 42.

67. Doyle, "Liberal Legacies, and Foreign Affairs," part II.

68. Quoted in O'Toole, 146–47. Proctor's speech was particularly important in the business community. Two days later, the *Wall Street Journal* noted that "Senator Proctor's speech converted a great many people in Wall Street who had heretofore taken the ground that the United States had no business to interfere in a revolution on Spanish soil."

69. O'Toole, 195–96.

70. Trask, 157.

71. Swanberg, 146–47.

72. O'Toole, 235; Hobson, 43, 74, 82–83; Trask, chap. 11; Shaw. At this time, monthly pay for enlistees in the Army was thirteen dollars. To finish the story, the *Merrimac* was quickly spotted by the Spanish. The firing from the Spanish ships and shore batteries was so intense that the Spanish were convinced that the *Merrimac* was armed—indeed Spain suffered 34 casualties in the strange one-sided battle. In the barrage, the *Merrimac* lost its steering gear and the lifeboat, and several of the ignition mechanisms for the charges that were to sink the boat were damaged. Nonetheless, the Spanish obliged in sinking the drifting *Merrimac*, and though it did not seal off the harbor entirely, it narrowed the channel significantly. When the Spanish fleet finally tried to escape from Santiago Bay on July 3, 1898, it had to do so in daylight and in single file. It was completely destroyed with a

heavy loss of life. Miraculously, though captured, the entire crew of the *Merrimac* survived with only minor injuries.

73. Doyle, "Liberal Legacies," part II.

74. On the legitimating benefits of democracy in war, see Lake. See also Gaubatz, "The Hobbesian Problem."

75. See Schirmer.

76. Schirmer, 219–20.

77. Richardsen and Van-Helten, 19.

78. The annexation marked the end of the conflict between regular military forces. It took the British two more years and the use of brutal and highly controversial methods to subdue a tenacious force of Boer guerrillas.

79. B. Porter, 239.

80. See Blanch, 210; and B. Porter, 239.

81. Wilson, 327.

82. MacKenzie and MacKenzie, 269. Of course, it should be remembered that mob action was a fairly routine mode of public participation in Victorian politics: "Victorian elections were expected as a matter of course to be punctuated by excessive drinking, mob action ranging from exuberance to intimidation, an exchange of cash and a judicious application of the 'screw.'" (Pugh, 9.)

83. The *Economist*, October 7, 1899, 57:1418.

84. Quoted in Matthew, 39.   85. Ibid., 43.

86. Pugh, 102.   87. Wilson, 314.

88. Ibid., 308.   89. Quoted in Wilson, 317–18.

90. The Rand is the principal gold mining area, which would almost certainly have been politically dominated by enfranchised Uitlanders. The Raad is the South African parliament.

91. See Pakenham, 64.

92. Quoted in A. Porter, 224. By mid-August 1899, Kruger had agreed to a five-year retrospective franchise. See Pakenham, 81.

93. Quoted in Wilson, 300.   94. Ibid., 301.

95. Quoted in Pakenham, 81.   96. Lowe, 1:223.

97. Quoted in Pakenham, 93.   98. Ibid., 56.

99. Matthew, 40–41.

100. Mueller, *Retreat from Doomsday*.

101. Quoted in Martin, 17. Bentham's views in this area are also well explicated by E. H. Carr in *The Twenty Years' Crisis*.

102. See Spitz. Morgenthau draws the opposite conclusion from Mueller, arguing that democratization and nationalism have made international relations more dangerous in the twentieth century. (Morgenthau, 238–39).

103. For a recent summary of the lack of foreign affairs knowledge in the American public, see Graham.

104. Lippmann.

CHAPTER THREE: ELECTORAL INSTITUTIONS AND THE DEMOCRATIC
POLITICS OF WAR AND PEACE

1. Thucydides, 2:65, 127–28.

2. See Boller. The 1812 election campaign is ambiguous, since the war of 1812 broke out in the middle of the campaign. (Madison was nominated to stand for reelection in late May, the war started in June, and the election was held at the end of the year.)

3. See Rakestraw.

4. See Johnson, *National Party Platforms*.

5. Fiorina.

6. Bueno de Mesquita, Siverson, and Woller.

7. See Aldrich, Sullivan, and Borgida; Page and Shapiro.

8. See Gaubatz, "None Dare Call it Reason."

9. In this case, of course, the conclusion was that action could not be put off. The important thing in this story is that the electoral concern was high in Kennedy's thinking. George, Hall, and Simons, 89.

10. Tocqueville, 1:135.

11. Pomper, 37.

12. Kernell, *Going Public*, 188.

13. Discussion of the nature of policy cycles can be found in the literature on political business cycles. For a review of this literature, see Alt and Chrystal, chap. 5.

14. Hibbs.

15. Brody.

16. Levy, "Misperception and the Causes of War."

17. Key, chap. 11.

18. Bueno de Mesquita, Siverson, and Woller argue that political leaders have systematically faced punishment for doing badly in wars.

19. Brody and Shapiro.

20. Levy, "The Diversionary Theory of War."

21. Stein.

22. Lowe, 20.

23. Ibid., 28.

24. Pugh, 29–30. For a general discussion of the differences in incentives faced by opposition politicians and politicians in power, see Gaubatz, "None Dare Call it Reason."

25. Taylor, 98.

26. Labour had briefly formed a minority government in 1924. The 1929 election was the first time Labour had received a majority of votes at the polls.

27. Blake, 192.

28. Overy and Wheatcroft, 67.

29. Ibid., 68. While Churchill did not see the speed with which Germany would rebuild, he was already concerned about the inevitability of that event. See Gilbert, 16.

30. Overy and Wheatcroft, 76.

31. Ibid., 318. In that same three years, German military spending went from 720 million Marks to 5,480 million Marks and then to 10,270 million Marks in 1936. Italian spending went from 4,880 million lire to 12,624 million lire.

32. These choices were not exclusive on the ballot. Eleven million votes in all were cast, so not surprisingly, most people who favored military sanctions also favored economic sanctions. The balloting started in October 1934, but the results were not announced until June 1935. See Blake, 190.

33. Harris, 120.

34. Blake, 192.

35. Taylor, 94.

36. Dominion status would put India on par with Canada, Australia, New Zealand, and South Africa in the Empire.

37. Gilbert, 139–40.

38. Quoted in Manchester, 150.

39. Manchester, 150.

40. Gilbert, 140–41; Manchester, 151.

41. Gilbert, 141.

42. Six Independent Labour and four Lloyd George Liberals joined the Labour Party in opposition.

43. Harris, 117–18.

44. Burridge, 102.

45. Ibid., 103.

46. Attlee and Churchill both favored reorganizing the services to create a co-ordinated command structure. This point should not be pushed too far, however, as Churchill's perspective was decidedly national, while Attlee hoped to see the discussion in a more internationalized frame. Burridge, 105.

47. Harris, 116–17.

48. Quoted in Harris, 117.

49. Quoted in Harris, 117.

50. Harris, 117.

51. Ibid., 118.

52. Burridge, 109–10.

53. The Labour proposal was, again, set in a thoroughly internationalized context, with a call for the development of international political and economic unity and the abolishment of national armies.

54. Overy and Wheatcroft, 76–78.

55. Gilbert, 141.

56. Manchester, 150.

57. Burridge, 112.

58. Taylor, 93.

59. Overy and Wheatcroft, 76–78.

60. Taylor, 127.

61. Laybourn, 160.

62. Ibid., 162.

63. Burridge, 115.

64. King served as Prime Minister 1921–30, and then 1935–48.

65. Perras, xi.

66. Nolan, 15. King kept an extensive private diary from 1893 until his death in 1950. He indicated in his will that the diaries were to be destroyed except for the parts he had marked. As he had neglected to mark any parts, the executors made the controversial decision to save all the diaries. See Stacey, *A Very Double Life*.

67. Nolan, 17.

68. Ibid., 19.

69. Perras, 16. To be fair, it should be noted that American military exercises in this period were often based on the premise of a British invasion through Canada. Overy and Wheatcroft, 279.

70. Ibid., 15.

71. Ibid., 17.

72. Nolan, 114.

73. Ibid., 92. For comparison: Britain entered the war with a navy of 274 ships with 15 battleships and 145 destroyers. Italy had 255 ships with 2 battleships and 126 destroyers. France had 178 ships with 7 battleships and 72 destroyers.

74. Nolan, 19. King regularly conducted séances. The degree to which they affected his public life is a matter of debate. See Stacey, *A Very Double Life*.

75. In September 1939, Duplessis still had a year and a half before an election would have been required.

76. Nolan, 30.

77. The price also proved high as Duplessis and the Union Nationale returned to power immediately after the war, throwing out the Liberals who were seen as puppets of King and the federal government. The Union Nationale retained power in Quebec until 1960.

78. Neatby, 140–41.

79. Stacey, *Arms, Men, and Governments*, 5–6.

80. Nolan, 50–51.

81. Stacey, *Arms, Men and Governments*, 400.

82. Nolan, 119. The war hero was Connie Smythe, who had earned the Military Cross in World War I, and was the founder of the Toronto Maple Leafs hockey team. He then distinguished himself and was seriously wounded as an artillery officer in World War II.

83. Stacey, *Arms, Men and Governments*, 443.

84. Ibid., 446.

85. Nolan, 151.

86. Stacey, *Arms, Men and Governments*, 476.

87. Ibid., 483.

88. Quoted in Douglas and Greenhous, 227.

89. Overy and Wheatcroft, 266.

90. Ibid., 269.

91. Quoted in Overy and Wheatcroft, 271.

92. Overy and Wheatcroft, 318. U.S. fiscal years run from July to June.

93. Ibid., 276.

94. Dallek, 152.

95. Gallup polls, reported in Overy and Wheatcroft, 283.

96. Dallek, 200.

97. Overy and Wheatcroft, 284.

98. See Divine, vol. 1, chap. 1.

99. Ibid., 26.

100. Leigh, 29–51; Dallek, 247.

101. Divine, 1:28.

102. Ibid., 33.

103. Ibid., 35.

104. Lash, 266.

105. Overy and Wheatcroft, 286.

106. Divine, 1:68.

107. Ibid., 81.

108. Ibid., 82.

109. Ibid.

110. Quoted in Mayer, 459.

111. Divine, 1:54.

112. Ibid., 79.

113. Ibid., 81.

114. Ibid., 50.

115. Ibid., 59.

116. Ibid., 59–60.

117. Ibid., 60.

118. Stout.

119. Ibid..

120. Divine, 1:27.

121. Moscow, 4.

122. Divine, 1:74.

123. Overy and Wheatcroft, 288.

124. Lash, 266.

125. Divine, 1:88.

126. Overy and Wheatcroft, 290.

127. A. J. P. Taylor makes the highly controversial claim that Hitler and Mussolini were also ultimately unwilling to push their belligerence all the way to war. This was clearly not recognized by the Western powers, though Taylor calls it "one of the few well-documented facts of this time." Taylor, 119.

128. See Bobbio; Manning.

CHAPTER FOUR: ELECTORAL INCENTIVES AND FOREIGN-POLICY CHOICES

1. The Sicilian expedition is also problematic for the democratic peace theory, since Syracuse and Athens were both democratic (at least by the standards of that time). See Russett, *Grasping the Democratic Peace*, chap. 3 for a discussion of conflict between democracies in ancient Greece.

2. Staveley.

3. Doyle, "Liberal Legacies," part II.

4. Quoted in Wilson, 300.

5. Ibid, 301.

6. Ibid., 673, note 8.

7. Consider, in this regard, the most powerful body of theory on American Congressional behavior, which is based on the assumption that reelection is the primary motivation of members of the American Congress. Advocates of this view rarely attempt to find explicit confessions of electoral motivations on the part of individual members of Congress. See, for example, Mayhew.

8. Nathan.

9. Kennedy, 45.

10. Brzezinski, 483.

11. Ibid., 489. The domestic electoral role of the Iranian hostage crisis is also indicated by the considerable attention paid to that crisis by the Reagan electoral strategists. A particularly extreme version of this thesis is advanced by Gary Sick in his book, *October Surprise.*

12. Brzezinski, 490.   13. Patchen, 135.

14. Woodward, 309.   15. Patchen.

16. Fearon, "Signaling."

17. Waltz, *Theory of International Politics,* 72.

18. Doyle, "Liberal Legacies" and "Liberalism." Doyle's list of democracies is included in Appendix A.

19. The identification of stable democratic regimes is a subjective and context-dependent undertaking. Doyle includes the Commonwealth countries, for example, before many consider them to have gained independent control of their foreign policy (and thus, before being coded as countries by the Singer and Small standards). Many states are included before the franchise was extended to women or to non-property holders. For example, Italy is included in the middle of the nineteenth century when the franchise extended to less than 2 percent of the population. Doyle's criteria for these choices are outlined in Doyle, "Liberal Legacies," part I, 212.

20. The major sources of election data were: Mackie and Rose; *The Statesman's Yearbook*; Rokkan and Meyriat.

21. Singer and Small.

22. Ibid.

23. Throughout this study the tests of statistical significance are based on cumulative binomial probabilities. This simple test compares the number of observations found in a given period to the number that would be expected under the null hypothesis that the distribution of events is independent of the periodization. In Figure 11, there is a total of 489 disputes, excluding the level-one disputes. If the distribution of disputes were independent of the periodization, 20 percent would be expected, or about 98 disputes in each period. The actual distribution is 106, 99, 100, and 97 disputes in each of the first four periods, with just 87 disputes in the last period leading up to an election. The probability of getting 87 or fewer disputes in the last period under the null hypothesis of no periodization effect is .12. This makes it seem likely that the last period is different from the first four, but does not meet the traditional thresholds of statistical significance.

24. For a discussion of the patterns of democratization, see Huntington.

25. It could be argued on the basis of the lower number of disputes in general in this period that public mood was so strong that dispute involvement was depressed throughout the period, and therefore election cycle effects appear minimal.

26. This data is limited to the European democracies and the United States, as none of the other non-European democracies were involved in militarized disputes during this period.

27. Because I show only four years on the chart, Figure 14 drops the two disputes that came more than four years before the next election.

28. The statistical significance of any difference in frequency for absolute electoral cycle lengths is dependent on what length of electoral cycle is used as a baseline. If a four-year cycle is the baseline, for example, there is a .25 probability of any case falling in the last year before an election, and 14 is precisely the number expected in the last year.

29. The role of the baseline cycle length is again apparent. If the baseline is 28 months then 14/56 is significant at the .005 level. It remains statistically significant at the .1 percent level at any baseline up to 36 months. There is no similar difference in the 1816–1976 dataset. The median cycle length is the same, at 48 months, for both the disputes in the last year before an election and for all the disputes in the period.

30. Quoted in Pugh, 241.

31. In this test I have eliminated the two cases of wars starting between four and five years before an election, and then used the null hypothesis that there is an even .25 probability of a dispute falling in any of the four remaining periods.

32. The probability of getting this result under the null hypothesis of no relationship is .05.

CHAPTER FIVE: ELECTIONS AND WAR: THE INTERNATIONAL CONNECTION

1. Thucydides, 6.17, 371; Kagan, 213.

2. Lalman.

3. See, for example, Snyder, "Civil-Military Relations."

4. See, for example, Levy, "Preferences, Constraints, and Choices."

5. Quoted in Darilek, 26.   6. Taylor, xi.

7. Kahler, 3.   8. Schirmer, 219–20.

9. Some of these dynamics are discussed in Nincic.

10. Beschloss and Talbott, 3–4.   11. Schelling.

12. Pruitt, chap. 1.   13. Putnam.

14. In order for these constraints to increase the willingness of opponents to make concessions, the perceived costs of a failure to come to an accommodation must be greater than the costs of making those concessions. If the costs of failure to reach agreement are insufficient, then the narrowed options of the democratic state will be outside the range of acceptable outcomes for the adversary state, and negotiations will be *more* likely to break down.

15. Schelling.

16. Gaubatz, "Democratic States and Commitment."

17. On some of the limitations of the realist approach in this area, see Barnett and Levy.

18. Machiavelli, bk. 1, discourse 59, 259.

19. Tocqueville, part II, chap. 5, section 13, 228–29.

20. North and Weingast; Velde and Sargent.

21. Fearon, "Signaling."

22. George Bush's promise not to raise taxes during the 1988 election did not prevent him from doing so during his first term. Nonetheless, reneging on his dramatic "read-my-lips" promise did prove very costly during his 1992 reelection bid.

23. Fearon suggests that democratic states may prevail more often in deterrence crises in general because of their ability to take advantage of their high audience costs. "Domestic Political Audiences."

24. Fearon, "Domestic Political Audiences."

25. Adams, 10.   26. Dillon, 1.

27. Levy and Vakili.   28. Freedman, 34;. Dillon, 95.

29. Freedman, 5.   30. Dillon, 127–28.

31. Freedman, 7–10. By 1976, the British military had already determined that retaking the Falklands after an Argentine assault was militarily impracticable. Dillon, 11–12.

32. Dillon, 25.   33. Ibid.

34. Ibid., 32.   35. Ibid.

36. Ibid., 52.   37. Quoted in Dillon, 131.

38. Dillon, 102–3.   39. Ibid., 106, 163.

40. Reported in Dillon, 116–17.   41. Quoted in Little, 71.

42. Thatcher, 184.   43. Quoted in Little, 72.

44. Dillon, 122. The government did succeed in gaining a U.N. Security Council resolution (UN 502) on April 3, demanding an immediate withdrawal of Argentine forces from the islands. There was a "genuine search" for peaceful agreement, as long as it was on British terms. Evidence of military restraint is a little harder to identify. The secretary of defense admitted to the House that "When we say that we wish to pursue minimum force that does not mean in any way that we are asking our forces to hold back on the pursuit of their objectives". Quoted in Dillon, 183.

45. Little, 72; Dillon, 136–37. The military success of the campaign to retake the Falklands was in no way assured. Argentina had significant naval and air capabilities, including an aircraft carrier and attack submarines. The loss of either of the British aircraft carriers would have doomed the operation. Even with both carriers, the British task force had too few airplanes (22 Harriers) to assure air superiority for the amphibious landing. There was little potential for strategic surprise. With the approaching Antarctic winter, the weather could easily have turned against the British.

46. Crewe, 158–59. The 31 percent figure is Thatcher's average approval rating in 1981. She registered 51 percent in June 1982.

47. Dillon, 129.

48. Crewe, 155.

49. Ibid., 161. While Thatcher's popularity clearly increased with the war, the long-term effect on the election is a matter of debate. Thatcher's popularity would have been expected to rise with the improving economy. While the "Falklands Factor" was perceived as quite significant at the time, later, more sophisticated analyses have suggested that the long-term rally effects were relatively modest. See Sanders, et. al.; Norpoth.

50. Two billion pounds covers the direct cost of the war (800 million pounds) and the cost of replacing lost capital equipment (1,200 million pounds). Dillon estimates the total cost of the Falklands war at more than 5 billion pounds. Dillon, 237–42.

51. Zaller, "Strategic Politicians," 253.   52. Quoted in Donaldson, 139.

53. Quoted in Sciolino, 205.   54. Quoted in Sciolino, 234.

55. Sciolino, 234.   56. Donaldson, 170.

57. Quoted in Sciolino, 234.   58. Dorman and Livingston.

59. Mueller, "Public Opinion and the Gulf War," 203.

60. Mueller, "Public Opinion and the Gulf War." See also Gaubatz, "Intervention and Intransitivity."

61. Mueller, "Public Opinion and the Gulf War," 210.

62. Manheim, "Strategic Public Diplomacy," 144.

63. Ibid., 141.

64. Mueller, "Public Opinion and the Gulf War," 199.

65. Donaldson, 171.

66. Manheim, "Strategic Public Diplomacy," 137.

67. Woodward, 282.

68. Broder.

69. Woodward, 318.

70. Zaller, "Strategic Politicians," 257–58.

71. Ibid., 260.

72. See Bennett, ed., *Taken by Storm*.

73. Mueller, "Public Opinion and the Gulf War," 211–12.

74. Thucydides, 6.47, 387.

CHAPTER SIX: INTERNATIONAL OUTCOMES

1. Thucydides, 7.86.5, 478.

2. Plutarch, 165.

3. Thucydides, 6.88–93, 410–16. It is impossible to do justice in this venue to the twists and turns of Alcibiades' life after the disastrous Sicilian expedition. A thumbnail sketch would include the following: Alcibiades was forced to leave Sparta, after being indiscreet in an affair with the Queen. He proceeded to Persia,

where he encouraged an attack on Sparta, and ultimately worked for the oligarchic coup of the Four Hundred in Athens. The Four Hundred slighted him, however, so he went to work for the restoration of democracy. He was in and out of favor with the Athenian democracy, leading various military expeditions during its waning years, but remained mostly in exile in Thrace, where in 404 BCE he was assassinated either by political opponents or by the brothers of a young noblewoman he had debauched. Plutarch, 174.

4. Doyle, "Liberal Legacies," part I, 210–12. See Appendix A for a complete list of Doyle's codings.

5. Singer and Small.

6. Maoz suggests that to a large measure the Singer-Small data has become the standard dataset on international conflict. For a discussion of the state of international conflict data development, see Maoz.

7. Forty-four of the cases fall between 45 and 60 months. The median election cycle for these cases is 48 months, the mean is 51 months, and the standard deviation is 18 months.

8. See Appendix B for a list of these cases.

9. The two missing cases are Denmark in the Second-Schleswig War of 1864 and the Netherlands in the Dutch-Achinese War of 1873.

10. These states are Belgium, Netherlands, Norway, Finland, and France. In none of these cases was the truncated election cycle sufficiently advanced to suggest that an election was imminent.

11. If the extreme case of Vietnam is dropped, the mean number of battle deaths for the first four quintiles drops to 2,979, but remains quite different from 185.

12. See Singer and Small; Blainey, chap. 11.

13. Levy, "The Preventive Motivation for War."

14. See Bueno de Mesquita and Lalman, "Reason and War"; Lalman.

15. As late as September 1941, Emperor Hirohito was urging his government to emphasize diplomatic efforts. Prange, 208.

16. The probability of the observed distribution occurring if war entries and election cycles are statistically independent can be calculated with the cumulative binomial formula. If the fifth- and sixth-year cases are dropped, then there is about a 14 percent probability of twelve or fewer war entries in the last year before an election when there are 58 total war entries and the probability of a war entry falling within any one of the four years is .25. This probability is not small enough to allow the rejection of the null hypothesis that elections and war entries are statistically independent.

17. There is a 4.9 percent probability of eight or fewer war entries out of a total of 69 occurring in the last quintile of the election cycle if the probability of a war entry falling in any quintile is .2—that is, if there is no relationship between election cycles and war entries. The use of quintiles is a somewhat arbitrary definition of the prewar period. The statistical significance of the results tends to get

better as the relative size of the prewar period is increased, and gets worse if the prewar period size is reduced. As in Chapter 4, tests of statistical significance are based on the cumulative binomial probabilities (see Note 23, Chapter 4).

18. Again, years five and six are dropped, so the comparison is made between the last year before an election in which one quarter of the cases is expected to fall under the null hypothesis, and the previous three years, in which three quarters of the cases are expected to fall. There is less than a 5 percent probability of four or fewer wars out of a total of 36 in the last year before an election if the probability of any given war entry falling in the last year is 25 percent.

19. The probability of three or fewer war entries in the last quintile of the election cycle is 1 percent, when the total number of war entries is 69, and when there is a 20 percent probability of any war entry occurring in the last quintile.

20. In evaluating the number of battle deaths, it should also be remembered that in the Wages of War dataset the number of battle deaths includes deaths of native troops from a state's colonies, if they fought on the same side as that state. See Singer and Small, 11.

21. While no more cases could show up close to an impending election in this range of battle deaths, the statistical significance of the result could vary as the number of cases in the other four quintiles varied with the different definitions of seriousness. More specifically, as the battle death threshold goes higher, the total number of observations and the number of wars entered in the first four quintiles both decrease, and thus statistical significance declines. Because of this decrease in the total number of cases, definitions of serious war above 5,000 battle deaths produce distributions that, while still quite skewed, are no longer statistically significant at the 95 percent level.

22. Levy, "Misperception"; U.S. expectations in the Persian Gulf War are an obvious exception to this tendency.

23. Small, 308; Beer.

24. The election was then delayed until December 1973. Notably, the Labor government fell the following April after considerable recriminations concerning the surprise attack.

25. These are the United Kingdom in W.W.I and W.W.II and Italy in the Seven Weeks War.

26. To the three cases above, add the United Kingdom in the Mahdist War (1882) and Italy in the Italo-Turkish War of 1911.

27. The probability of sixteen or fewer war entries in the third and fourth year after an election when there are 61 entries in the first through fourth year is .0001 if the timing of war entries and elections are statistically independent.

28. There is a .4 percent probability of getting 39 war entries in the first two quintiles and 30 war entries in the last three quintiles, if election cycles and war entries are statistically independent.

29. There is a .05 percent probability of getting 32 or more war entries out of

a total of 46 in the first two-year period if there is an equal probability of a war entry occurring in either the first or second two-year period after an election.

30. Under the assumption of statistical independence, the probability of five out of 52 war entries in the last quintile of the election cycle is 3.7 percent.

31. The probability of 29 out of 52 war entries in the first two quintiles of the election cycle is .15 percent, if war entries and election cycles are statistically independent.

32. The probability of the preelection effect (three or fewer cases in the fifth quintile, out of a total 37 cases) is 4.5 percent. The probability of the postelection effect (21 or more of the 37 cases falling in the first two quintiles) is 2.9 percent.

33. Mueller, *Retreat from Doomsday*, 38.

34. Quoted in Richards, 19.

35. Richards, 19.

36. Both Lippmann, and Craig and George combine this point with the previous one to argue that in the nineteenth century public opinion did not count for much in the formation of foreign policy. Lippmann, 16–17. Craig and George, 60–61.

CHAPTER SEVEN: CONCLUSIONS

1. On the patterns of democratic expansion see Huntington; Gaubatz, "Democracy and History."

2. Taylor, xi.

3. Lowi, 302.

4. Craig and George, 102

5. Waltz, *Theory of International Politics*, 97. In this regard, it is interesting to note that Waltz's book that argues for the merits of democratic foreign policymaking, *Foreign Policy and Democratic Politics*, is largely consistent with the realist assertions that domestic organization does not make a significant difference. Against the critics of democratic foreign policy, he argues that democratic states are no worse at foreign policy than authoritarian states (chap. 1; 310–11).

6. Lowi; Wright, chap. 8.

7. Gaubatz, "Intervention and Intransitivity."

8. Bolt, 136.

9. Madison, 476.

10. Bueno de Mesquita and Lalman, "Domestic Opposition."

11. Stein, 97.

12. Small and Singer; Chan; Weede; Maoz and Abdolali. It should be noted that there have been some results that point to fewer wars for systems with competitive elections for executive office (Maoz and Abdolali) and to a reticence to escalate to war for major democratic powers (Morgan and Campbell). Rummel, in

"Libertarianism," argues that libertarianism and pacifism are related, but he examines only the period from 1976 to 1980.

13. Waltz, *Foreign Policy and Democratic Politics*, 17.

14. Hitler, 660, 654.   15. Dobson, 73.

16. Small, 123.   17. Ibid., 116.

18. Ibid, 123.   19. Trask, chap. 3.

20. Quoted in Trask, 63–64.   21. Trask, 67 (emphasis added).

22. See Appendix B.   23. Nincic, 395–96.

24. Russett, *Controlling the Sword*, 11.

25. See Gaubatz, *None Dare Call It Reason*. Snyder argues for this effect in the Crimean War case, when rising literacy combined with the penny press to inflame passions on the Turkish issue. Snyder, *Myths of Empire*, 206.

26. Rummel, *Lethal Politics*, xi.

27. Churchill, Speech in the House of Commons, Nov. 11, 1947.

Bibliography

Adams, John. Inaugural Address, March 4, 1797. In *Inaugural Addresses of the Presidents of the United States: From George Washington, 1789, to George Bush, 1989.* Washington, D.C.: U.S. Government Printing Office, 1989.

Albrecht-Carrié, René. *A Diplomatic History of Europe: Since the Congress of Vienna.* Rev. ed. New York: Harper and Row, 1973.

Aldrich, John, John L. Sullivan, and Eugene Borgida. "Foreign Affairs and Issue Voting: Do Presidential Candidates Waltz Before a Blind Audience?" *American Political Science Review* 83 (March 1989): 123–41.

Almond, Gabriel. *The American People and Foreign Policy.* New York: Praeger, 1950.

Alt, James, and K. Alec Chrystal. *Political Economics.* Berkeley: University of California Press, 1983.

Andersen, Olive. *A Liberal State at War: English Politics and Economics During the Crimean War.* New York: St. Martin's Press, 1967.

Arrow, Kenneth. *Social Choice and Individual Values.* 1951. Reprint, New Haven: Yale University Press, 1963.

Babst, Dean. "A Force for Peace." *Industrial Research* (April 1972): 55–58.

Barker, A. J. *The Vainglorious War: 1854–56.* London: Weidenfeld and Nicolson, 1970.

Barnett, Michael, and Jack Levy. "Domestic Sources of Alliances and Alignments: The Case of Egypt, 1962–73." *International Organization* 45 (summer 1991): 369–95.

Beer, Francis. "American Major Peace, War, and Presidential Elections." *Peace and Change* 10 (spring 1984): 23–39.

Bennett, W. Lance. "The News About Foreign Policy." In *Taken by Storm: The Media, Public Opinion, and U.S. Foreign Policy in the Gulf War,* edited by W. Lance Bennett and David L. Paletz. Chicago: University of Chicago Press, 1994.

Beschloss, Michael, and Strobe Talbott. *At the Highest Levels: The Inside Story of the End of the Cold War.* Boston: Little, Brown, 1993.

Blainey, Geoffrey. *The Causes of War.* London: Macmillan, 1973.

Blake, Robert. *The Decline of Power: 1915–1964*. London: Granada, 1985.

Blanch, M. D. "British Society and the War." In *The South African War: The Anglo-Boer War, 1899–1902*, edited by Peter Warwick and S. B. Spies. London: Longman, 1980.

Bobbio, Norberto. *Liberalism and Democracy*. Translated by Martin Ryle and Kate Soper. London: Verso, 1990.

Boller, Paul F., Jr. *Presidential Campaigns*. New York: Oxford University Press, 1984.

Bolt, Ernest. *Ballots Before Bullets: The War Referendum Approach to Peace in America, 1914–1941*. Charlottesville: University Press of Virginia, 1977.

Brams, Steven J., and D. Marc Kilgour. *Game Theory and National Security*. New York: Basil Blackwell, 1988.

Briggs, Asa. *Victorian People: A Reassessment of Persons and Themes, 1851–67*. Rev. ed. Chicago: University of Chicago Press, 1972.

Broder, John. "U.S. Was Ready for 20,000 Casualties." *Los Angeles Times*. VIIO (June, 13 1991), p. A1, col. 1.

Brody, Richard A. *Assessing the President: The Media, Elite Opinion, and Public Support*. Stanford, Calif.: Stanford University Press, 1991.

Brody, Richard, and Catherine Shapiro. "A Reconsideration of the Rally Phenomenon in Public Opinion." *Political Behavior Annual*, ed. Samuel Long, vol. 2. Boulder, Col.: Westview Press, 1989.

Brzezinski, Zbigniew. *Power and Principle: Memoirs of the National Security Adviser, 1977–1981*. New York: Farrar, Straus, & Giroux, 1983.

Bueno de Mesquita, Bruce, and David Lalman. "Reason and War." *American Political Science Review* 80 (December 1986): 1113–30.

———. "Domestic Opposition and Foreign War." *American Political Science Review* 84 (September 1990): 747–66.

———. *War and Reason: Domestic and International Imperatives*. New Haven: Yale University Press, 1992.

Bueno de Mesquita, Bruce, Randolph Siverson, and Gary Woller. "War and the Fate of Regimes: A Comparative Analysis." *American Political Science Review* 86 (September 1992): 638–46.

Burridge, Trevor D. *Clement Attlee: A Political Biography*. London: Jonathan Cape, 1985.

Campbell, Angus, Philip Converse, Warren Miller, and Donald Stokes. *The American Voter*. New York: Wiley, 1960.

Carr, Edward Hallett. *The Twenty Years' Crisis, 1919–1939: An Introduction to the Study of International Relations*. 1939, 1946. Reprint, New York: Harper and Row, 1964.

Cashman, Sean Dennis. *America, Roosevelt, and World War II*. New York: New York University Press, 1989.

Chan, Steve. "Mirror, Mirror on the Wall: Are the Freer Countries More Pacific?" *Journal of Conflict Resolution* 28 (December 1984): 617–48.

Cohen, Bernard C. *The Public's Impact on Foreign Policy*. Boston: Little, Brown, 1973.

Conacher, J. B. *The Aberdeen Coalition, 1852–1855: A Study in Mid-Nineteenth-Century Party Politics*. Cambridge: Cambridge University Press, 1968.

Cotton, Timothy. "War and American Democracy." *Journal of Conflict Resolution* 30 (December 1986): 616–35.

Craig, Gordon A., and Alexander L. George. *Force and Statecraft: Diplomatic Problems of Our Time*. New York: Oxford University Press, 1983.

Crewe, Ivor. "How to Win a Landslide Without Really Trying: Why the Conservatives Won in 1983." In *Britain at the Polls 1983: A Study of the General Election*, edited by Austin Ranney. Durham, N.C.: Duke University Press, 1985.

Dallek, Robert. *Franklin D. Roosevelt and American Foreign Policy, 1932–1945*. New York: Oxford University Press, 1979.

Darilek, Richard E. *A Loyal Opposition in Time of War: The Republican Party and the Politics of Foreign Policy from Pearl Harbor to Yalta*. Westport, Conn.: Greenwood Press, 1976.

Diamond, Larry. "Is the Third Wave Over?" *Journal of Democracy* 7 (July 1996): 20–37.

Dillon, George. *The Falklands, Politics, and War*. Houndsmill, England: Macmillan, 1989.

Divine, Robert A. *Foreign Policy and U.S. Presidential Elections, 1940–1948*. Vol 1. New York: New Viewpoints, 1974.

Dobson, John. *Reticent Expansionism: The Foreign Policy of William McKinley*. Pittsburgh: Duquesne University Press, 1988.

Donaldson, Gary A. *America at War Since 1945*. Westport, Conn.: Praeger, 1996.

Dorman, William A., and Steven Livingston. "News and Historical Content: The Establishing Phase of the Persian Gulf Policy Debate." In *Taken by Storm: The Media, Public Opinion, and U.S. Foreign Policy in the Gulf War*, edited by W. Lance Bennett and David L. Paletz. Chicago: University of Chicago Press, 1994.

Douglas, William A. B., and Brereton Greenhous. *Out of the Shadows: Canada in the Second World War*. Toronto: Oxford University Press, 1977.

Downs, Anthony. *An Economic Theory of Democracy*. New York: Harper and Row, 1957.

Downs, George, and David Rocke. *Optimal Imperfection? Domestic Uncertainty and Institutions in International Relations*. Princeton: Princeton University Press, 1995.

Doyle, Michael. "Kant, Liberal Legacies, and Foreign Affairs." Parts 1 and 2. *Philosophy and Public Affairs* 12, 80 (summer/fall 1983): 205–35, 323–53.

————. "Liberalism and World Politics." *American Political Science Review* 80 (December 1986):1151–69.

Eckstein, Harry. "Case Study and Theory in Political Science." In *Handbook of Political Science*, edited by Fred Greenstein and Nelson Polsby. Vol. 7. Reading, Mass.: Addison-Wesley, 1975.

Evans, Peter, Dietrich Rueshemeyer, and Theda Skocpol. *Bringing the State Back In.* Cambridge: Cambridge University Press, 1985.

Fearon, James. "Signaling Versus the Balance of Power and Interests: An Empirical Test of a Crisis Bargaining Model." *Journal of Conflict Resolution* 38 (June 1994): 236–69.

————. "Domestic Political Audiences and the Escalation of International Disputes." *American Political Science Review* 88 (September 1994): 577–92.

Fiorina, Morris P. *Retrospective Voting in American National Elections.* New Haven: Yale University Press, 1981.

Freedman, Lawrence. *Britain and the Falklands War.* London: Basil Blackwell, 1988.

Gaddis, John Lewis. *Strategies of Containment: A Critical Appraisal of Postwar American National Security Policy.* Oxford: Oxford University Press, 1982.

Gaubatz, Kurt Taylor. "Election Cycles and War." *Journal of Conflict Resolution* 35 (June 1991):212–44.

————. "The Hobbesian Problem and the Microfoundations of International Relations Theory: or If Politics Stops at the Water's Edge, How Did Everybody Get to Be So Wet?" Paper presented at the Annual Meeting of the American Political Science Association. New York, New York, September 1–4, 1994.

————. "Intervention and Intransitivity: Public Opinion, Social Choice, and the Use of Military Force Abroad." *World Politics* 47 (July 1995): 534–54.

————. "Democratic States and Commitment in International Relations." *International Organization* 50 (January 1996):109–39.

————. "Kant, Democracy, and History." *Journal of Democracy* 7 (October 1996): 136–50.

————. "Teaching Thucydides: Athens, Sparta, and the Politics of History." Paper presented at the Annual Meeting of the American Political Science Association. Washington, D.C., August 28–31, 1997.

————. "None Dare Call It Reason: Domestic Incentives and the Politics of War and Peace." In *Strategic Politicians and Foreign Policy*, edited by Randolph Siverson. Ann Arbor: University of Michigan Press, 1998.

George, Alexander. *Presidential Decisionmaking in Foreign Policy: The Effective Use of Information and Advice.* Boulder, Col.: Westview, 1980.

————. "Domestic Constraints on Regime Change in U.S. Foreign Policy: The Need for Policy Legitimacy." In *Change in the International System*, edited by Ole Holsti, Randolph Siverson, and Alexander George. Boulder, Col.: Westview, 1980.

George, Alexander L., David K. Hall, and William E. Simons. *The Limits of Coercive Diplomacy: Laos, Cuba, Vietnam.* Boston: Little, Brown, 1971.

Gilbert, Martin. *Winston Churchill: The Wilderness Years.* London: Macmillan, 1981.

Gilpin, Robert. *U.S. Power and the Multinational Corporation.* New York: Basic Books, 1975.

Grieco, Joseph. "Anarchy and the Limits of Cooperation." *International Organization* 42 (summer 1988): 485–507.

Graham, Thomas W. "The Pattern and Importance of Public Knowledge in the Nuclear Age." *Journal of Conflict Resolution* 32 (June 1988): 319–34.

Harris, Kenneth. *Attlee.* London: Weidenfeld and Nicolson, 1982.

Hartz, Louis. *The Liberal Tradition in America.* New York: Harcourt, Brace, Jovanovich, 1955.

Hermens, Ferdinand. *The Tyrant's War and the People's Peace.* Chicago: University of Chicago Press, 1944.

Hibbs, Douglas A. *The American Political Economy: Macroeconomics and Electoral Politics.* Cambridge: Harvard University Press, 1987.

Hitler, Adolf. *Mein Kampf.* Translated by Ralph Manheim. 1925. Boston: Houghton Mifflin, 1971.

Hobson, Richmond Pearson. *The Sinking of the Merrimac.* New York: Century, 1899.

Holmes, Jack. *The Mood/Interest Theory of American Foreign Policy.* Lexington: The University Press of Kentucky, 1985.

Holsti, Ole. *Public Opinion and American Foreign Policy.* Ann Arbor: Michigan University Press, 1997.

Hughes, Barry B. *The Domestic Context of American Foreign Policy.* San Francisco: W. H. Freeman, 1978.

Hume, David. "Of the Balance of Power." In *Essays: Moral, Political, and Literary.* 1741. Reprint, Oxford: Oxford University Press, 1963.

Huntington, Samuel P. *The Third Wave: Democratization in the Late Twentieth Century.* Norman: University of Oklahoma Press, 1991.

Jervis, Robert. *Perception and Misperception in International Politics.* Princeton, N.J.: Princeton University Press, 1971.

Johnson, Donald Bruce. *National Party Platforms: 1840–1976.* Urbana: University of Illinois Press, 1978.

———. *National Party Platforms of 1980: Supplement to National Party Platforms, 1840–1976.* Urbana: University of Illinois Press, 1982.

Kagan, Donald. *The Peace of Nicias and the Sicilian Expedition.* Ithaca: Cornell University Press, 1981.

Kahler, Miles. "Liberalization and Foreign Policy." In *Liberalization and Foreign Policy,* edited by Miles Kahler. New York: Columbia University Press, 1997.

Kant, Immanuel. *Perpetual Peace.* In *The Philosophy of Kant: Immanuel Kant's*

Moral and Political Writings, edited by Carl J. Friedrich. New York: Random House, 1949.

Kennan, George. *American Diplomacy: 1900–1950*. Chicago: University of Chicago Press, 1951.

Kennedy, Robert F. *Thirteen Days: A Memoir of the Cuban Missile Crisis*. New York: W. W. Norton, 1969.

Keohane, Robert. "Theory of World Politics: Structural Realism and Beyond." In *Political Science: The State of the Discipline*, edited by Ada Finifter. Washington, D.C.: American Political Science Association, 1983.

Kernell, Samuel. "Explaining Presidential Popularity." *American Political Science Review* 72 (June 1978): 506–22.

———. *Going Public: New Strategies of Presidential Leadership*. Washington, D.C.: CQ Press, 1986.

Key, V. O., Jr. *Public Opinion and American Democracy*. New York: Alfred A. Knopf, 1961.

Kissinger, Henry. *American Foreign Policy: Three Essays*. New York: Norton, 1969.

Klingberg, Frank. "The Historical Alternation of Moods in American Foreign Policy." *World Politics* 4 (January 1952): 239–73.

Krasner, Stephen. *Defending the National Interest: Raw Materials Investments and U.S. Foreign Policy*. Princeton, N.J.: Princeton University Press, 1978.

Lake, David. "Powerful Pacifists: Democratic States and War." *American Political Science Review* 86 (March 1992): 24–37.

Lalman, David. "Conflict Resolution and Peace." *American Journal of Political Science* 32 (August 1988): 590–615.

Lash, Joseph P. *Roosevelt and Churchill, 1939–1941: The Partnership That Saved the West*. New York: Norton, 1976.

Laybourn, Keith. *Britain on the Breadline: A Social and Political History of Britain Between the Wars*. Gloucester: Alan Sutton, 1990.

Layne, Christopher. "Kant or Cant: The Myth of the Democratic Peace." *International Security* 19 (fall 1994): 5–49.

Lee, Jong-Ryool. "Rallying 'Round the Flag." *Presidential Studies Quarterly* 7, 4 (1977): 252–56.

Leigh, Michael. *Mobilizing Consent: Public Opinion and American Foreign Policy, 1937–1947*. Westport, Conn.: Greenwood Press, 1976.

Levy, Jack. "Misperception and the Causes of War." *World Politics* 36 (October 1983): 76–99.

———. "Declining Power and the Preventive Motivation for War." *World Politics* 40 (October 1987): 82–107.

———. "Domestic Politics and War." *Journal of Interdisciplinary History* 18 (spring 1988): 653–73.

———. "The Diversionary Theory of War: A Critique." In *Handbook of War Studies*, edited by Manus I. Midlarsky. 259–88. Boston: Unwin Hyman, 1989.

————. "Preferences, Constraints, and Choices in July 1914." In *Military Strategy and the Origins of the First World War*, edited by Steven Miller, Sean Lynn-Jones, and Stephen Van Evera. Rev. and exp. ed. Princeton: Princeton University Press, 1991.

————. "An Introduction to Prospect Theory." *Political Psychology* 13 (June 1992): 171–86.

————. "Prospect Theory and International Relations: Theoretical Applications and Analytical Problems." *Political Psychology* 13 (June 1992): 283–310.

Levy, Jack, and Lily I. Vakili. "Diversionary Action by Authoritarian Regimes: Argentina in the Falklands/Malvinas Case." In *The Internationalization of Communal Strife*, edited by Manus Midlarsky. 118–46. London: Routledge, 1992.

Lippmann, Walter. *Essays in the Public Philosophy.* Boston: Little, Brown, 1955.

Little, Walter. "Public Opinion in Britain." In *Toward Resolution? The Falklands/Malvinas Dispute*, edited by Wayne Smith. 63–80. Boulder, Col.: Lynne Rienner, 1991.

Lowe, Cedric J. *The Reluctant Imperialists: British Foreign Policy, 1878–1902.* Vol. 1. London: Routledge and Kegan Paul, 1967.

Lowi, Theodore. "Making Democracy Safe for the World: National Politics and Foreign Policy." In *Domestic Sources of Foreign Policy*, edited by James Rosenau. 295–331. New York: Free Press, 1967.

McClosky, Herbert, and John Zaller. *The American Ethos: Public Attitudes Toward Capitalism and Democracy.* Cambridge, Mass.: Harvard University Press, 1984.

Machiavelli, Niccolò. *The Discourses.* Translated by Leslie Walker. Edited by Bernard Crick. 1530. Reprint, Middlesex, England: Penguin, 1970.

MacKenzie, Norman, and Jeanne MacKenzie. *The Fabians.* New York: Touchstone, 1977.

Mackie, Thomas, and Richard Rose. *The International Almanac of Electoral History.* 2d ed. New York: Facts on File, 1982.

Madison, James. *Notes of Debates in the Federal Convention of 1787.* New York: W. W. Norton, 1969.

Manchester, William. *The Caged Lion: Winston Spencer Churchill, 1932–1940.* London: Michael Joseph, 1988.

Manheim, Jarol B. "The War of Images: Strategic Communication in the Gulf Conflict." In *The Political Psychology of the Gulf War: Leaders, Publics, and the Process of Conflict*, edited by Stanley A. Renshon. Pittsburgh: University of Pittsburgh Press, 1993.

————. "Strategic Public Diplomacy: Managing Kuwait's Image During the Gulf Conflict." In *Taken by Storm: The Media, Public Opinion, and U.S. Foreign Policy in the Gulf War*, edited by W. Lance Bennett and David L. Paletz. Chicago: University of Chicago Press, 1994.

Manning, David J. *Liberalism.* New York: St. Martin's Press, 1976.

Maoz, Zeev. "Conflict Datasets: Definitions and Measurement." *International Interactions* 14, no. 2 (1988): 165–72.

Maoz, Zeev, and Nasrin Abdolali. "Regime Types and International Conflict, 1816–1976." *Journal of Conflict Resolution* 33 (March 1989): 3–35.

Martin, B. Kingsley. *The Triumph of Lord Palmerston: A Study of Public Opinion in England Before the Crimean War.* New York: Dial Press, 1924.

Marx, Karl. *The Eastern Question: A Reprint of Letters Written 1853–1856 Dealing with the Events of the Crimean War by Karl Marx,* edited by Eleanor Marx Aveling and Edward Aveling. London: Sonnenschein, 1897.

Mastanduno, Michael, David A. Lake, and G. John Ikenberry. "Toward a Realist Theory of State Action." *International Studies Quarterly* 33 (December 1989): 457–74.

Matthew, Henry C. G. *The Liberal Imperialists: The Ideas and Politics of a Post-Gladstonian Elite.* Oxford: Oxford University Press, 1973.

Mayer, George H. *The Republican Party, 1854–1966.* New York: Oxford University Press, 1967.

Mayhew, David. *Congress: The Electoral Connection.* New Haven: Yale University Press, 1974.

Mearsheimer, John. "Back to the Future: Instability in Europe After the Cold War." *International Security* 15 (summer 1990): 5–56.

Morgan, T. Clifton, and Sally Howard Campbell. "Domestic Structure, Decisional Constraints and War." *Journal of Conflict Resolution* 35 (June 1991): 187–211.

Morgenthau, Hans. *Politics Among Nations: The Struggle for Power and Peace.* 4th ed. New York: Alfred A. Knopf, 1967.

Moscow, Warren. *Roosevelt and Willkie.* Englewood, N.J.: Prentice-Hall, 1968.

Mueller, John. *War, Presidents, and Public Opinion.* New York: John Wiley, 1973.

———. *Retreat from Doomsday: The Obsolescence of Major War.* New York: Basic Books, 1989.

———. "Changing Attitudes Toward War: The Impact of World War I." *British Journal of Political Science* 21 (January 1991) 1–28.

———. "American Public Opinion and the Gulf War." In *The Political Psychology of the Gulf War: Leaders, Publics, and the Process of Conflict,* edited by Stanley A. Renshon. Pittsburgh: University of Pittsburgh Press, 1993.

Nathan, James A. "The Missile Crisis: His Finest Hour Now." *World Politics* 27 (January 1975): 256–81.

Neatby, H. Blair. *The Politics of Chaos: Canada in the Thirties.* Toronto: Macmillan of Canada, 1972.

Nettl, J. P. "The State As a Conceptual Variable." *World Politics* 20 (July 1968): 559–92.

Nincic, Miroslav. "U.S. Soviet Policy and the Electoral Connection." *World Politics* 42 (April 1990).

Nolan, Brian. *King's War: Mackenzie King and the Politics of War, 1939–1945.* Toronto: Random House, 1988.

Norpoth, Helmut. "Guns and Butter and Government Popularity in Britain." *American Political Science Review* 81 (September 1987): 949–59.

North, Douglas, and Barry Weingast. "Constitutions and Commitment: The Evolution of Institutions Governing Public Choice in Seventeenth-Century England." *Journal of Economic History* 49, no. 4 (1989): 803–32.

O'Toole, George J. A. *The Spanish War: An American Epic 1898.* New York: W. W. Norton, 1984.

Overy, Richard, with Andrew Wheatcroft. *The Road to War.* London: MacMillan, 1989.

Owen, John. "How Liberalism Produces Democratic Peace." *International Security* 19 (fall 1994): 87–125.

Page, Benjamin, and Robert Shapiro. *The Rational Public: Fifty Years of Trends in America's Policy Preferences.* Chicago: University of Chicago Press, 1992.

Pakenham, Thomas. *The Boer War.* New York: Random House, 1979.

Parry, Jonathan. *The Rise and Fall of Liberal Government in Victorian Britain.* New Haven: Yale University Press, 1993.

Patchen, Martin. *Resolving Disputes Between Nations: Coercion or Conciliation.* Durham, N.C.: Duke University Press, 1988.

Perras, Galen. *Franklin Roosevelt and the Origins of the Canadian-American Security Alliance, 1933–1945: Necessary: But Not Necessary Enough.* Westport, Conn.: Praeger, 1998.

Plutarch, *The Lives of the Noble Grecians and Romans.* Translated by John Dryden. Circa A.D. 100. Chicago: Encyclopedia Britannica, 1952.

Polsby, Nelson. *Congress and the Presidency.* Englewood Cliffs, N.J.: Prentice-Hall, 1964.

Pomper, Gerald M. *Elections in America: Control and Influence in Democratic Politics.* New York: Dodd Mead, 1970.

Porter, Andrew N. *The Origins of the South African War: Joseph Chamberlain and the Diplomacy of Imperialism, 1895–99.* Manchester: Manchester University Press, 1980.

Porter, Bernard. "The Pro-Boers in Britain." In *The South African War: The Anglo-Boer War 1899–1902*, edited by Peter Warwick and S. B. Spies. London: Longman, 1980.

Powell, G. Bingham. *Contemporary Democracies.* Cambridge, Mass.: Harvard University Press, 1982.

Prange, Gordon. *At Dawn We Slept: The Untold Story of Pearl Harbor.* New York: McGraw-Hill, 1981.

Pruitt, Dean. *Negotiation Behavior.* New York: Academic Press, 1981.

Pugh, Martin. *The Making of Modern British Politics: 1867–1939.* Oxford: Basil Blackwell, 1982.

Putnam, Robert. "Diplomacy and Domestic Politics: The Logic of Two-level Games." *International Organization* 42 (summer 1988): 427–60.

Rakestraw, Donald. *For Honor or Destiny: The Anglo-American Crisis over the Oregon Territory.* New York: Peter Lang, 1995.

Rich, Norman. *Why the Crimean War: A Cautionary Tale.* Hanover and London: University Press of New England, 1985.

Richards, Peter. *Parliament and Foreign Affairs.* Toronto: University of Toronto Press, 1967.

Richardson, Peter, and Jean Jacques Van-Helten. "The Gold Mining Industry in the Transvaal, 1886–99." In *The South African War: The Anglo-Boer War, 1899–1902,* edited by Peter Warwick and S. B. Spies. London: Longman, 1980.

Riker, William. *Liberalism Against Populism.* San Francisco: W. H. Freeman, 1982.

Rokkan, Stein, and Jean Meyriat, eds. *International Guide to Electoral Statistics.* Vol. 1. "National Elections in Western Europe." The Hague: Mouton, 1969.

Rosenau, James N. *Public Opinion and Foreign Policy: An Operational Formulation.* New York: Random House, 1961.

Rousseau, David, Christopher Gelpi, and Paul Huth. "Assessing the Dyadic Nature of the Democratic Peace, 1918–88." *American Political Science Review* 90 (September 1996): 512–33.

Rummel, Rudolph. "Libertarianism and International Violence." *Journal of Conflict Resolution* 27 (March 1983): 27–71.

———. *Lethal Politics: Soviet Genocides and Mass Murders Since 1917.* New Brunswick: Transaction Publishers, 1990.

Russett, Bruce. *Controlling the Sword: The Democratic Governance of National Security.* Cambridge, Mass.: Harvard University Press, 1990.

———. *Grasping the Democratic Peace: Principles for a Post–Cold War World.* Princeton: Princeton University Press, 1993.

Russett, Bruce, and Zeev Maoz. "Normative and Structural Causes of Democratic Peace: 1946–1986." *American Political Science Review* 87 (September 1993): 624–38.

Sanders, David, Hugh Ward, and David Marsh (with Tony Fletcher). "Government Popularity and the Falklands War: A Reassessment." *British Journal of Political Science* 17, no. 3 (1987): 281–313.

Sargent, Thomas, and François Velde. "The Macro-economic Features of the French Revolution." *Journal of Political Economy* 103 (June 1995): 474–518.

Schelling, Thomas. *The Strategy of Conflict.* Cambridge, Mass.: Harvard University Press, 1960.

Schirmer, Daniel B. *Republic or Empire: American Resistance to the Philippine War.* Cambridge, Mass.: Schenkman Publishing, 1972.

Sciolino, Elaine. *The Outlaw State: Saddam Hussein's Quest for Power and the Gulf Crisis.* New York: John Wiley & Sons, 1991.

Shapiro, Robert, and Benjamin Page. "Foreign Policy and the Rational Public." *Journal of Conflict Resolution* 32 (June 1988): 211–47.

Shaw, Barton C. "The Hobson Craze." *Proceedings*. Annapolis, Md.: United States Naval Institute 102 (February 1976): 54–60.

Sick, Gary. *October Surprise: America's Hostages in Iran and the Election of Ronald Reagan*. New York: Times Books, 1991.

Sigelman, Lee, and Pamela Johnston Conover. "The Dynamics of Presidential Support During International Conflict Situations." *Political Behavior* 4 (1981): 303–18.

Singer, J. David, and Melvin Small. *Wages of War, 1816–1980: Augmented with Disputes and Civil War Data*. ICPSR #9044. Ann Arbor, Mich.: ICPSR, Winter, 1984.

Small, Melvin. *Was War Necessary? National Security and U.S. Entry into War*. Beverly Hills, Calif.: Sage, 1980.

Small, Melvin, and J. David Singer. "The War-proneness of Democratic Regimes, 1816–1965." *The Jerusalem Journal of International Relations* 1 (summer 1976): 50–69.

Smoke, Richard. "The Crimean War." In *Avoiding War: Problems of Crisis Management*, edited by Alexander L. George. 36–61. Boulder, Col.: Westview Press, 1991.

Snyder, Jack. *Myths of Empire: Domestic Politics and International Ambition*. Ithaca: Cornell University Press, 1991.

———. "Civil-Military Relations and the Cult of the Offensive, 1914 and 1984." In *Military Strategy and the Origins of the First World War*, edited by Steven Miller, Sean Lynn-Jones, and Stephen Van Evera. Rev. and exp. ed. Princeton: Princeton University Press, 1991.

Spiro, David. "The Insignificance of the Liberal Peace." *International Security* 19 (fall 1994): 50–86.

Spitz, David. *Patterns of Anti-Democratic Thought*. Westport, Conn.: Greenwood Press, 1965.

Stacey, Charles P. *Arms, Men, and Governments: The War Policies of Canada, 1939–1945*. Ottawa: The Queen's Printer, 1970.

———. *A Very Double Life: The Private World of Mackenzie King*. Toronto: Macmillan of Canada, 1976.

Staveley, E. S. *Greek and Roman Voting and Elections*. Ithaca: Cornell University Press, 1972.

Stein, Arthur. *The Nation at War*. Baltimore: Johns Hopkins, 1980.

Stout, David. "How Nazis Tried to Steer U.S. Election." *New York Times*. July 19, 1997, p. A17.

Swanberg, W. A. *Citizen Hearst*. New York: Charles Scribner's Sons, 1961.

Taylor, Alan J. P. *The Origins of the Second World War*. 2d ed. New York: Fawcett, 1961.

Thatcher, Margaret. *The Downing Street Years.* London: Harper Collins, 1993.

Thucydides. *The Peloponnesian War 400 BCE.* In *The Landmark Thucydides: A Comprehensive Guide to the Peloponnesian War,* edited by Robert B. Strassler and translated by Richard Crawley. New York: Random House, 1996.

Tocqueville, Alexis de. *Democracy in America.* Translated by George Lawrence. 1835. Reprint, Garden City, N.Y.: Doubleday & Co., 1969.

Trask, David. *The War with Spain in 1898.* New York: Macmillan, 1981.

Vasquez, John. *The War Puzzle.* Cambridge: Cambridge University Press, 1993.

Waltz, Kenneth. *Man, the State and War: A Theoretical Analysis.* New York: Columbia University Press, 1959.

———. *Foreign Policy and Democratic Politics: The American and British Experience.* Boston: Little, Brown, 1967.

———. *Theory of International Politics.* Reading, Mass.: Addison-Wesley, 1979.

Weede, Erich. "Democracy and War Involvement." *Journal of Conflict Resolution* 28 (December 1984): 649–64.

Wilkerson, Marcus. *Public Opinion and the Spanish-American War: A Study in War Propaganda.* Baton Rouge: Louisiana State University Press, 1932.

Wilson, John. *C.B.: A Life of Sir Henry Campbell-Bannerman.* London: Constable, 1973.

Wisan, Joseph. *The Cuban Crisis as Reflected in the New York Press (1895–1898).* New York: Octagon, 1965.

Wolfers, Arnold. *Discord and Collaboration: Essays on International Politics.* Baltimore: Johns Hopkins Press, 1962.

Woodward, Bob. *The Commanders.* New York: Simon and Schuster/Pocket Books, 1991.

Wright, Quincy. *A Study of War.* 2d ed. Chicago: University of Chicago Press, 1965.

Zaller, John. *The Nature and Origins of Mass Opinion.* Cambridge: Cambridge University Press, 1992.

———. "Strategic Politicians, Public Opinion, and the Gulf Crisis." In *Taken by Storm: The Media, Public Opinion, and U.S. Foreign Policy in the Gulf War,* edited by W. Lance Bennett and David L. Paletz. Chicago: University of Chicago Press, 1994.

Index

In this index an "f" after a number indicates a separate reference on the next page, and an "ff" indicates separate references on the next two pages. A continuous discussion over two or more pages is indicated by a span of page numbers, e.g., "57–59." *Passim* is used for a cluster of references in close but not consecutive sequence.

Library of Congress Cataloging-in-Publication Data

Gaubatz, Kurt Taylor.
    Elections and war : the electoral incentive in the democratic
politics of war and peace / Kurt Taylor Gaubatz.
        p.   cm.
    Includes bibliographical references.
    ISBN 0-8048-3566-2 (cloth : alk paper)
        1. Democracy—History.   2. Elections—History.
3. War—Public opinion—History.   4. War—History.
I. Title.
JC421.G255   1999
324.9—dc21   99-17333

(∞) This book is printed on acid-free, archival-quality paper.

Original printing 1999
Last figure below indicates year of this printing:
08   07   06   05   04   03   02   01   00   99

Designed by Janet Wood
Typeset by James P. Brommer in 10.5/14 Garamond
and Franklin Gothic display